LEADING AMERICAN NOVELISTS

Nathaniel Hawthorne

LEADING AMERICAN NOVELISTS

BY

JOHN ERSKINE, Ph. D.

Adjunct Professor of English in Columbia University

WITH SIX PORTRAITS

Essay Index Reprint Series

BOOKS FOR LIBRARIES PRESS
FREEPORT, NEW YORK

First published 1910
Reprinted 1966, 1968

TO
MY FORMER COLLEAGUES
THE FACULTY OF AMHERST COLLEGE

LIBRARY OF CONGRESS CATALOG CARD NUMBER:
67-22091

MANUFACTURED
BY
HALLMARK LITHOGRAPHERS, INC.
IN THE U.S.A.

PREFACE

IT is always a daring thing to name the leaders among men of genius. No matter how wisely the choice is made, there will be advocates of the rejected and assailants of the elect. The present choice of the leading American novelists is offered with a proper sense of critical frailty, but in the belief that time has already sifted out these names for special remembrance. The death of F. Marion Crawford, for example, is so recent that it has not seemed wise here to attempt either a biographical or a critical account of his work.

In the critical portions of each biography I have attemped to make the novels more intelligible to the general reader, who, I take for granted, will have made himself familiar with the particular book under discussion. In so far as each biography pronounces any final judgment on the writer, I have tried to render the opinion of the best critics of to-day, rather than my own impression.

For biographical matter I have availed myself of the standard sources—William Dunlap's life of Brockden Brown, and Prescott's essay, founded on Dunlap; Professor Thomas R. Lounsbury's life of Cooper in the American Men of Letters Series, and the original prefaces to Cooper's novels; the life of Simms, in the American Men of Letters Series, by Professor W. P. Trent; Professor G. E. Woodberry's life of Hawthorne in the same series, and Mr. Henry James's life of Hawthorne in the English Men of Letters Series; *N. Hawthorne; Sa Vie et Son Œuvre*, par L. Dhaleine; Mr. Julian Hawthorne's *Nathaniel Haw-*

PREFACE

thorne and his Wife; the *Study of Hawthorne* by George Parsons Lathrop, and Mrs. Rose Hawthorne Lathrop's *Memories of Hawthorne;* Horatio Bridge's *Personal Recollections of Nathaniel Hawthorne,* the introductions to the various volumes of the Old Manse Edition of Hawthorne, and J. T. Fields's *Yesterdays with Authors,*—also Lindsay Swift's *Book Farm, its Members, Scholars, and Visitors,* and the account of the Hawthorne Centenary Celebration at the Wayside; the life of Mrs. Stowe by her son, the Rev. Charles Edward Stowe; the life of Bret Harte by T. Edgar Pemberton, and the introductions to the various volumes of the Standard Library Edition of Bret Harte's works. The biography which Henry C. Merwin is preparing for the American Men of Letters Series will doubtless add much to our knowledge of Bret Harte ; I wish I might have availed myself of it. I am indebted to other books and to magazine articles innumerable, but I must name two very different but equally helpful works—Mr. W. C. Brownell's *American Prose Masters,* and Miss Lillie D. Loshe's *Early American Novel,* which contains further bibliographical material.

It is a pleasure to record here my debt to my brother, for assistance in preparing this book for the press. During the writing of it I had a thousand occasions to thank the librarians of Amherst College for unfailing coöperation. And most of all I have reason to be grateful to my teacher, and friend, and colleague, Professor W. P. Trent.

J. E.

Columbia University
February 1, 1910

CONTENTS

PORTRAITS

LEADING AMERICAN NOVELISTS

C. B. Brown

CHARLES BROCKDEN BROWN

I

THE American novel is usually supposed to begin with Charles Brockden Brown. His individual though immature genius connects the new literature with the fashions of thought current in his time abroad, and his obvious inheritance from Godwin, the writers in the Gothic style, and the revolutionary thinkers, accredits him with some importance he might not otherwise have. But in his own right he laid hold on fame through the dignity of his social and artistic ideals; he has in spite of his priggishness and pedantry an air of largeness; his complete devotion to all causes of humanity and his interest in the mystery of the human spirit fit him to introduce the novel of our democracy, in which Cooper and Hawthorne and Mrs. Stowe have dignified with their art man's great experiment in self-knowledge and liberty.

Brockden Brown has one other title to consideration in the influence upon Hawthorne that has been claimed for him. He was essentially a psychologist interested in moral problems, and the total impression of his searchings into the mystery of evil is not unlike the impression Hawthorne makes. But the relation between them will perhaps always seem to the lay mind hard to establish; for not only do they differ widely in the technical equipment of their art and in their acquaintance with life, but they also have little kinship in their imaginative power. Hawthorne is among other things a poet; Brockden Brown belongs as much as he can to the

3

eighteenth century, the age of reason, and his dependence is upon reason rather than upon imagination. Such a generalization may be difficult to prove, but the element of truth in it can be felt in reading almost any of his novels. Hawthorne reminds us of that temper of the eighteenth century we know in Addison and Irving; Brockden Brown even at his best is related to Benjamin Franklin.

Brown's psychological, moral interests are supplemented in his books by unusual realism; he can give the last touch of life to the record of his actual observations or experiences, as in his account of the plague in *Arthur Mervyn*. This faculty also is of a kind with Franklin's clear-headed memory of what he had seen; it has nothing in common with the imaginative portrayal of scenes that never occurred; it is far from the realism of either Hawthorne or Defoe. And in his moral investigations Brockden Brown often illustrates the disadvantages of detached reason as compared with imagination in dealing with life; for him morality is standardized, and all departures from the normal have a kind of pathological interest. For this reason what he observed had a tendency to fall into preconceived relations; his reasoning sometimes prevented him from seeing true. The truest thing in the *Scarlet Letter*, the faith of Hester and Dimmesdale that their love was holy, would no more have appeared true to Brockden Brown than it would to Dr. Johnson. We can hear him pronounce, "But, Sir, they knew it was sin,—and that's an end of it!" Though he was the pupil of Godwin and wrote in the age of Shelley, Brockden Brown had the moral conservatism of the new world.

A very slight glance at his work is enough to show that he is hardly typical of American literature. He would be a solitary figure in it, if he were not so largely a forgotten one. He is known chiefly to scholars. But no account of the American novel can neglect him, and even a passing glance at the development of American thought, if it missed him, would miss much.

II

Brockden Brown has derived more than his portion of oblivion from his authoritative biographer, Dunlap, who passed lightly over the human side of his subject, if he was acquainted with it, and laid stress upon Brown's moral and intellectual virtues, until the author is invested with that special kind of priggishness that the world is most willing to let die. "His parents," says Dunlap, "were virtuous, religious people, and as such held a respectable rank in society; and he could trace back a long line of ancestry holding the same honorable station." More specific is the record that Charles Brockden Brown, of Quaker descent, was born in Philadelphia, January 17, 1771.

The name of Brown is no longer distinctive, as Dunlap wisely remarks, and he gives us no further comment on the author's immediate parentage. The name of Brockden was derived from an ancestor who, in the reign of Charles II, had what is presumably the only adventure the family line could boast; he overheard a plot against the King, and was discovered by the conspirators, but escaped by pretending to have been asleep. His danger was so great, however, that he came to America and settled in the province of Philadelphia.

Somewhat like Hawthorne, Brockden Brown was trained for his life-work by circumstances—almost accidental—of childhood. His home seems to have been full of a kind of silent culture; there were books and maps, and encouragement to use both, but apparently there was little society of the sort a boy needs. Brown was a delicate child, and his physical inactivity combined naturally with the atmosphere of his home to make him what his parents thought, perhaps justly, an infant prodigy. In his earliest childhood, when they wished to leave him at home, they would put him in the charge, not of his nurse, but of a book, knowing that he would still be reading when they returned. Later, when he came home from school, he would be found in the parlor, "where, having slipped off his shoes, he was mounted on a table and deeply engaged in the consultation of a map suspended on the side of the wall." This curiosity as to the boundaries of nations was displayed chiefly at dinner-time. His proud parents encouraged the nervous child in abnormal study; his father would ask him to point out on the map places in all parts of the world, which the boy would do with ease, usually giving his father some account of the city or country. In expression he was no less precocious. When he was ten years old a visitor called him "boy." After the visitor's departure the offended child asked, "Why does he call me boy? Does he not know it is neither size nor age but understanding that makes a man? I could ask him an hundred questions, none of which he could answer."

As for amusement of any sort, the child seems to have had none. When he was eleven years old he entered the school of Robert Proud, then well known for his history of Pennsylvania. This gentleman taught the boy Greek and Latin and had reason to be proud of his pupil's skill. But, as the biographer says, "What a pity it is that the application which assimilates man most to the exalted idea which we form of immortal perfection should so certainly tend to enfeeble his body and shorten his mortal existence, while the brutalizing occupations of continued and thought-expelling labor, give firmness and vigor and duration to the frame of man." In short, the boy's health was ruined, and even the enthusiastic teacher of Latin and Greek advised that he should cease all study for a time. This was in his sixteenth year. By that time he had made versions of portions of the book of Job, the Psalms, and Ossian; he also contemplated three epic poems,—on the discovery of America, on the conquest of Peru, and on Cortez's expedition to Mexico.

Upon the supposed cessation of his studies he was sent to take long walks in the country. His parents were perhaps not convinced of his real need of relaxation; certainly their provision for it was half-hearted. His walks were solitary, for some unexplained reason, and as he was absent-minded, he frequently forgot to come back, so absorbed was he in his thoughts. This vagary, we are told, excited great uneasiness in the different members of his family. He probably convinced his parents, as he convinced his biographer, that a variety of intellectual excitement would be the equivalent of relaxation. Accordingly he added stenography to his other accomplishments, and began to study French.

Perhaps we should credit Brockden Brown with a far more generous boyhood than is recorded of him. His affection for his three older brothers, Joseph, Armit and James implies some early comradeship. He must have been an idealist from the first; he never lost his high dreams of life. Doubtless a man as attractive as he must have had a certain charm as child and youth. The somber picture of his early years is not his fault. If he had ever been visited by a ray of humor, his biographer was not the man to notice it. But it should further be remembered that Brockden Brown grew up in troubled times, and a more than usual seriousness enveloped his boyhood. His premature interest in the parlor map may have been almost a natural thing in the years when the Revolution in America and the war with France and Spain abroad were altering England's holdings and making that map obsolete. When he was protesting against being called a boy by the visitor, Cornwallis was surrendering at Yorktown. If his boyhood gave him no other wholly sane and admirable training, it gave him patriotism and a sense of the dignity of mankind which he never lost.

III

When the time came to choose a profession, Brockden Brown was apprenticed to a Philadelphia lawyer, Alexander Wilcox. Probably his reason for undertaking this profession was the opportunity it afforded for intellectual improvement; it is hard to believe that he ever cared for the practical opportunities it gave him for advancement in public life. His office duties left him sufficient time to cultivate his gifts as he chose; otherwise he perhaps would have taken the necessary time, for his zeal for literary improvement seems to have been insatiable. He corresponded with a few friends, chosen for their sympathies with his own interests, and he kept a journal, wherein he entered his thoughts, exercised himself in composition, and even copied those letters he received which seemed unusually well written. He also attended carefully to his handwriting, a clear hand being, in his opinion, a substantial aid to success in the law. Of one of his correspondents, a youth named Davidson, he inquired what were "the relations, dependence, and connection of the several parts of knowledge," and as Davidson was apparently in no position to reply, he answered himself at some length in his diary. Whatever amusement this ambitious entry will occasion to the casual reader, at least it shows the writer's conscientious groping in regions of thought most often neglected by literary youth; it would indicate, if we had no other means of knowing, that Brockden Brown by nature was a philosopher—perhaps far more that than artist. At the same time the disproportion between the large question and its answer indicates a characteristic lack of thoroughness; the manner of his utterance is stately, but he seems appallingly short of facts. From this cause his curious and energetic mind, in most if not all of his writing, is unconvincing, and the result is more disastrous because he depends, not upon emotion, but upon reason.

His first publication was in the *Columbian Magazine*, in August, 1789, and for some time his contributions were of the newspaper level of those days, interesting chiefly to his friends. The first public attention he received was due to a printer's blunder. He had composed a poetical address to Franklin, and the printer for reasons unknown substituted Washington's name throughout; "Washington," as the author says, "therefore stands arrayed in awkward colours. Philosophy smiles to behold her darling son; she turns in horror and disgust from those who have won the laurel of victory in the field of battle, to this her favourite candidate who had never participated in such bloody glory, and whose fame was derived from the conquest of philosophy alone. The printer by his blundering ingenuity made the subject ridiculous. Every word of this clumsy panegyric was a direct slander upon Washington, and so it was regarded at the time."

Some of Brown's friends formed a debating society, in which legal cases were considered and decisions pronounced. In this club Brown distinguished himself by his powers of expression and by the judicial manner which he learned to assume, but there is no record that he showed special acquaintance with law. In another organization, a Belles-Lettres Club, founded by that friend Davidson who failed to settle the several branches of knowledge, Brockden Brown was a more important figure—apparently the leader. At the first meeting of this literary society he was chosen to read a paper defining its aims. In spite of his stilted style the reader needs only a little sympathy with his seriousness to find solid qualities in the essay. It is worth while to quote the passage in which he suggests the directions from which the study of language may be approached; few young men at any time could display a clearer understanding of the general field. "The student," he says, "may examine the etymology of a language, or review the various periods of its history. He may trace the various changes it has undergone to their respective causes, determine whether they have been produced by the lapse of time, the confusion of events, or by foreign colonization. He may set forth the variety of its dialects, for the specific, as well as generic difference in languages, point out the difference or resemblance between them, and survey them, accompanied with all their appendages of causes, contrast and consequence. Is the language of its poetry distinct from that of its prose, in what do they severally consist? Compare its present state with any period past or future, and thereby discover whether it be yet in its progess towards perfection, or stationary, or in its decline. . . . Besides the local or provincial dialects of a language, another variety must also arise founded upon the difference in manners and education of those who speak it. This distinction can only take place in a living tongue; in such, a certain elegance of phrase, as well as of manner, is the criterion of politeness." The essay proceeds to suggest the inquiries that can be made into comparative grammar and the general history of language.

One wonders what the Philadelphia youths who formed Brockden Brown's audience on this occasion really thought of the frail, untidily dressed author as he declaimed his weighty sentences. From all we can learn they respected him, but very naturally did not like him. He had fostered in his tastes, perhaps unconsciously, a fine contempt for ordinary practical life; human beings were fast becoming to him objects of study, or opponents to reason with. He neglected his law books more and more and devoted his time to letters and the sort of philosophy he was capable of. Perhaps it was less a surprise than a disappointment to his parents and brothers when he announced that the law was too earthly and sordid for his nature; he would devote himself to literature. The fact that he depended for his support entirely upon his parents, somewhat obscures the magnanimity of his decision, but he was sincere in his choice and none of his friends could dissuade him.

IV

It was some time before he began his literary career—such careers not being easy to start; and meanwhile, perhaps to avoid the expostulations of disappointed relatives and friends, he went to New York, where he already had a few acquaintances. His stay in that city was at first an aimless sort of visiting, but gradually he came under positive influences that began to shape his character and his career. His best friend was a Dr. Elihu Hubbard Smith, a Yale graduate who had made his acquaintance while studying medicine in Philadelphia. In many respects his interests were akin to Brown's; they both were literary and disposed to the same sort of studies. Smith's example had the good effect, it is said, of making Brown less untidy in dress and more systematic in his habits. It was through Smith that Brown met William Dunlap, his future biographer; through Smith also he was introduced to the Friendly Club, a literary society that met once a week at the home of some member. Apparently the purpose of this circle was much like that of the Belles-Lettres Club, where Brown had cut something of a figure, but in the New York society he was immediately subjected, as a provincial, to some wholesome discipline. In his journal he wrote: "Last evening spent with the clubists at K.'s. Received from the candour of K. a severe castigation for the crimes of disputatiousness and dogmatism. Hope to profit by the lesson that he taught me."

These days in New York seem to have given Brown the best part of his education—some acquaintance with life. They came too late to remold his character, but they broadened his outlook and interested him in common things. He traveled a little in Connecticut and elsewhere. The first really human document we have from him is the record of a trip to Rockaway with some others of his literary circle. This account, in the form of a letter, was published in a literary magazine, and can therefore hardly be reckoned as a spontaneous composition, but it has vivacity, and it throws a pleasant light on Brown's character. Many of the incidents are obviously true. He began the trip by forgetting to take enough clothes for the stay, and he broke his umbrella on the way down. He tried sea-bathing at sundown, the usual time for it, and the following day went in late in the morning, which he found much more comfortable. Unless some of the details are inserted for effect, he had learned to join in mild forms of conviviality. Toward the end of the paper, however, the unsocial note is heard; the author passes from his gentle glow of good fellowship to the dull gray of his recluse mood,—

"As to myself, I am never at home, never in my element at such a place as this. A thousand nameless restraints incumber my speech and my limbs, and I cannot even listen to others with a gay unembarrassed mind. . . . This jaunt to Rockaway has left few agreeable traces behind it. All I remember with any pleasure, are the appearance of the wide ocean, and the incidents of bathing in its surges. Had I been a botanist, and lighted upon some new plant; a mineralogist, and found an agate or a petrifaction; a naturalist, and caught such a butterfly as I never saw before, I should have reflected upon the journey with no little satisfaction. As it was, I set my foot in the City with no other sentiment, but that of regret, for not having employed these two days in a very different manner."

One other passage in this rather significant account may well serve as unconscious criticism of the novels he was later to write. At the table, he says, there was much good humor and some wit, but he could not remember a single *good thing* deserving of record, and, he goes on, "my powers do not enable me to place the commonplace characters around me in an interesting or amusing point of view." It is not without interest as a paradox that the first American novelist, writing in the first years of conscious American democracy, should have been distinguished by his apathy toward every-day, commonplace humanity.

His own discomfort in society he seems not to have attributed to narrowness of interest or fault in his breeding. For a youth of his temperament it was simpler to find the fault in society. Yet it is mere justice to make plain that this reasoning resulted from better causes than egotism. The generous estimate in which all high-spirited youth then held human nature filled them with dreams of social reform, such as would adapt the world to the needs of the soul. Brown thought too nobly of his literary ideals to blame himself for lack of culture; it was society that was wrong,—that discomforted him with its frivolities.

Social reforms of the Utopian sort began at this time to occupy him, partly because of his reading in Godwin and other Old World revolutionaries, and partly because of the uneasiness of social convention he himself had come to feel. The censorious tone belongs of necessity to reformers. There was no persecution nor misunderstanding in Brockden Brown's life, as there was in Shelley's, to justify it. If he had been unfortunate in the forcing process of his education, he was the last person in the world to realize it, and upon the social system that lay about him time and convention had as yet laid little burden. It is perhaps not ungenerous to ascribe the Utopias he dreamt of in New York, the changes he recommended in the society with which he supposed himself familiar, to certain twinges of conscience. This high but vague career upon which he was entering had for a background a disappointed family and his financial dependence upon them. It was not unnatural he should come to see that the time was out of joint.

In 1797 appeared *Alcuin*, a dialogue upon the social position of women. This dialogue, a natural development of Brown's debating, presented with some thoroughness the problems of the modern institution of marriage, and ended by advocating divorce of that summary kind that Milton and Shelley—more convincingly—pleaded for. Brown's interest in the subject was purely academic. Only a year or so before he had been congratulating himself in a letter to a friend that his eyesight was poor and his health weak; perhaps Providence by that circumstance, he thought, destined him to happy freedom from the temptations and entanglements of life. Certainly his Socratic dialogue—in which the mantle of Diotima falls upon one Mrs. Carter—indicates no depth of experience, nor even of interest in the subject. To this same period, or somewhat later, belong also the fragmentary *Sketches of a History of Carsol* and *Sketches of a History of the Carrils and Ormes*, in which he intended to incorporate historical romance with Utopian proposals.

A peculiar faith in human nature, even when it was in error, and a Utopian vein in his attitude toward society, continued to distinguish Brown's maturer work. Of his faith in the individual something will be said later. His Utopian schemes are ineffectual for the reason just suggested, that they grew out of a literary fashion, not out of the pressure of life's necessities. They are no more insincere than were Shelley's far more splendid dreams in *Queen Mab*, but they take from Brown's writing the impression of reality.

V

Brown's literary career begins in 1798, with his first published novel, *Wieland, or The Transformation*. An earlier novel had indeed been written and prepared for publication, but on account of difficulties following the death of the printer it was abandoned. The material of this novel, *Sky Walk*, was reworked into later stories. This earlier attempt had been preceded by an unfinished romance, in the form of letters between the different characters, after the model furnished by Richardson, but in substance showing a transition from the journalizing and debating that had been Brown's training, to the manner of the story-teller. The fragments are sufficiently complete to indicate at least one character, Colden, who in the mystery of his behavior and his history is a typical Brockden Brown hero. But the fragments are more occupied with life in general than with any particular character or story, and this also remains typical of the author, even at his best.

Wieland gives Brown his place in American literature. Other stories of his, such as *Arthur Mervyn*, have better qualities, but this first book fixed the type of his writing, and his reputation would probably have suffered little had he added nothing more. It was evident at once that he belonged to the so-called Gothic school, then the fashion in Europe. Briefly, the mark of this school was the representation of horror and mystery such as might accumulate in the legends of medieval castles. Supernatural appearances, the expiation of crimes and the working out of curses, were the substance of such tales, of which Horace Walpole's *Castle of Otranto*, 1764, is usually taken as the first English example. The most typical story of this sort, however, is Mrs. Anne Radcliffe's *Mysteries of Udolpho*, 1794, in which the effects of horror are richer and more convincing than in Walpole's amateurish book.

The interest in medieval romance was, of course, but a part of the so-called romantic revival, which turned from classicism to the old ballads and legends, the old buildings and superstitions of the Middle Ages. Walpole's attempt to tell a Gothic legend was but one aspect of that enthusiasm for the past which made him try to turn his house into a Gothic castle. The antiquity of legend or architecture was for him

its charm, and the remoteness of time was also for Mrs. Radcliffe and the romancers generally essential to the effect of
mystery they desired. In dealing with this mystery, however,
two very different methods might be followed. The author
might accept it imaginatively, and make it live convincingly
before the reader, as Scott would do, or Poe; or the mystery
might be explained more or less rationally, and the ghost
would turn out to be but a sleep-walker, or some fugitive with
a knowledge of secret doors. For either method the story
needed an architectural setting,—the gloom of Gothic castles,
to prepare the mind for the supernatural; the house is almost
a character in the tale. This typically German setting was
imitated effectively by Poe, as in *The Fall of the House of
Usher*, and was naturalized on American soil by Hawthorne,
in *The House of The Seven Gables*.

Brockden Brown follows the rationalizing method of Mrs.
Radcliffe; at the end of the tale he explains the mystery.
He places no dependence upon age or architecture for his effects; for it was his ambition to write truly American stories,
and he liked to set the plot in his own state, or in the country
he knew, and in his own time. As a result he could make no
use of the trap-doors, the secret passages and hooting owls
with which the Gothic romance is usually furnished; but this
loss was of no importance, as he depended for his mystery
upon more refined phenomena. In *Wieland* we have the
story of a susceptible mind driven to crime and suicide by
supernatural voices, which turn out to be the work of a ventriloquist. Given the hero's character, with its tragic pro-
pensities, and the inexplicable ventriloquist, there is no need
of a particular setting. The environment in Brown's novels
habitually takes what color it has from the temper of the story;
he had no command whatever of local color, and was as far
from portraying American as Gothic scenery.

The quality of Brown's literary genius has been investigated by comparing his method of explaining the mystery in a supernatural tale, with Scott's method of leaving the reader to digest the mystery according to his imaginative power. A better understanding, however, of Brown's limitations can be reached by a comparison with Hawthorne, who adopted Brown's method of explaining the mystery rationally, yet kept the poetic atmosphere of his romance unharmed. In *The House of The Seven Gables* the Pyncheon curse is rationalized without ceasing to appear a divine judgment. In *The Marble Faun* the rationalizing is of the utmost delicacy; the mystery of the Faun is kept in the realm of superstitious legend, yet explanations are suggested, and no vulgar curiosity interferes with the deep psychological interest in the characters. Brockden Brown, however, tries to increase the mystery by reserving its solution till the end, thereby appealing to an intellectual curiosity rather than to that emotional sympathy Hawthorne rouses; and when the solution does come, it is insufficient. In *Wieland* the reader does not believe that ventriloquism can accomplish the effects he has witnessed. The disclosure of the secret to the miserable Wieland is clearly intended as the tragic climax, wherein the hero realizes the extent of his delusions; but the reader is too preoccupied himself with the surprising disclosure to follow the hero's fortunes.

It is quite evident that if Brown's reputation depended only upon his plots, it would have starved entirely. The story of *Wieland* is of the utmost absurdity, if recounted without sympathy, as plain fact. A youth named Carwin, who has secretly made himself an expert ventriloquist, happens upon a family already predisposed to insanity, and straightway uses his art to ruin what little reason they still have. That is the bare plot. It is incredible that ventriloquism should accomplish all that we are told; it is almost incredible that such a family as the Wielands should exist. They believe everything the voices utter, even when they are comparatively sane.

Their tendency to insanity is attributed not only to inheritance,—natural enough, in view of the elder Wieland's character,—but to his death by spontaneous combustion, which deranged both son and daughter, particularly the son. Clara Wieland tells the story—how the mysterious voices around the temple her father had built, terrorize her brother and herself, separate her from her lover, Pleyell, and finally direct the brother to kill his wife and children,—which he does, being by this time quite insane. He is imprisoned, but escapes, intending to kill Clara; but the voices make him realize his crime, and he forthwith kills himself. Clara marries Pleyell, and the villain is allowed to go unpunished.

Perhaps the most bothersome thing in this strange story is the question why Carwin, the ventriloquist, acted his fiendish part. The author makes no attempt to explain. In all his stories there is what now seems indifference to motive, especially in the characters that do wrong. Yet Carwin, like other evil-doers in this type of story, is thoroughly fascinating. It is only in afterthought that the reader sees his devilishness. Artistically weak as a character so unmotivated, so preposterous in its career, might at first sight seem to be, Carwin is largely the attraction of the book, and other characters like him explain Brockden Brown's claim to remembrance. The author intended to give a complete account of Carwin's life, and the unfinished *Memoirs of Carwin the Biloquist* promised as good reading as any of the novels. In Brockden Brown's imagination he was an unusually gifted youth turning gradually into a fiend through the very possession of his gifts. This problem—the peril of life's blessings, if it may be so phrased—was in one form or another a favorite subtlety of the Romantic mind. It is not surprising that Brockden Brown, in the very center of Revolutionary movements, should have that faith in the possibilities of human nature and its gifts, which animated Burns and Byron and Shelley. But in such times of faith in man's intellect some philosophers are usually attracted to the darker speculation of man's destiny,—to that immoderate thirst for knowledge, or power, or both—which in other ages gave us the legends of Lucifer and Faust. Byron and the spirit over Europe which he so widely represented, chose to view such tragic personalities as passive in the hands of their fate, committing willingly no crime, but driven to evil by their natures, for which only Heaven was accountable. So the type is represented in Byron's *Cain*.

It is not to be supposed that Brockden Brown, exemplary Philadelphian, was laying Byronic charges at Heaven's door; he had his model, not in Byron, whose career began a decade later, but in Godwin, whose Caleb Williams is not only penitent but really entitled to pity, and Falkland himself, the arch-villain in Godwin's story, has moments of un-Byronic softening. But in the character of Carwin Brown was clearly developing the theme that the quest of knowledge is morally dangerous. What sympathy we have for him comes from the difficulties his father put in the way of his education, but the conclusion the author wishes us to reach is that his guilt, the deception he practiced on mankind, "was the offspring of a fatal necessity, that the injustice of others gave it birth and made it unavoidable."

A character which is so completely the creature of a ruling passion must seem doomed, set apart from the race. That theme of loneliness, which Shelley's heroes and Byron's illustrate, and the poets themselves illustrated in their lives; which was to find such splendid embodiment in the character of Leatherstocking, and which diffused itself through Hawthorne's genius,—here made its entrance into American literature. The loneliness in this book is not reserved for Carwin; all the characters, in different ways, share in it. The older Wieland is set apart from society by his religious mania; Clara Wieland, who tells the family tragedy, by those awful experiences is made peculiar—reserved, as she says, for a destiny without alleviation and without example; and her brother, of course, is completely isolated by his awful fate.

Brockden Brown lacked what may be called the social imagination; his temper and training prevented him from thinking of life in those complex relations which normally make up human intercourse. He cannot picture a family. But in imagining the psychological experiences of an individual, especially under stress of excitement, he has real power, and the fame of *Wieland* in its time was due to this quality of truth. The outward circumstances of the novel—the spontaneous combustion and ventriloquism,—are but slightly related to the author's main interest; Wieland's progress to insanity, step by step, is the real story, and any cause of that insanity is sufficient for Brown's purpose. Nor does the stilted, elaborate style conceal the keen penetration which distinguishes one gradation of Wieland's madness from the next. When he tells of his wife's death, Brown sees to it that the physical trick of ventriloquism is kept in the background; whatever doubts the reader has had, have been absorbed in the earlier part of the story; here both the madman and the reader are intent on the murder—realistic enough, to be sure, but not so much so as to interrupt the fascination of the madman's increasing disease. The scene illustrates the book, as a story of the mind:

"I raised my head and regarded her with steadfast looks. I muttered something about death, and the injunctions of my duty. At these words she shrunk back, and looked at me with a new expression of anguish. After a pause, she clasped her hands, and exclaimed:

"'O Wieland! Wieland! God grant that I am mistaken; but surely something is wrong. I see it; it is too plain; thou art undone,—lost to me and to thyself.' At the same time, she gazed on my features with intensest anxiety, in hope that different symptoms would take place. I replied with vehemence,—'Undone! No; my duty is known, and I thank my God that my cowardice is now vanquished, and I have power to fulfil it. Catherine! I pity the weakness of nature; I pity thee, but must not spare. Thy life is claimed from my hands. Thou must die!'

"Fear was now added to her grief. 'What mean you? Why talk you of death? Bethink yourself, Wieland; bethink yourself, and this fit will pass. O why came I hither! Why did you drag me hither?'

"'I brought thee hither to fulfil a divine command. I am appointed thy destroyer, and destroy thee I must.' Saying this I seized her wrists. She shrieked aloud, and endeavored to free herself from my grasp; but her efforts were vain.

"'Surely, surely, Wieland, thou dost not mean it. Am I not thy wife? And wouldst thou kill me? Thou wilt not; and yet—I see—thou art Wieland no longer! A fury resistless and horrible possesses thee!—spare me—spare—help—help—'

"Till her breath was stopped she shrieked for help,—for mercy. When she could speak no longer, her gestures, her looks appealed to my compassion. My accursed hand was irresolute and tremulous. I meant thy death to be sudden, thy struggles to be brief. Alas! my heart was infirm; my resolves mutable. Thrice I slackened my grasp, and life kept its hold, though in the midst of pangs. Her eyeballs started from their sockets. Grimness and distortion took place of all that used to bewitch me into transport, and subdue me into reverence.

"I was commissioned to kill thee, but not to torment thee with the foresight of thy death; not to multiply thy fears, and prolong thy agonies. Haggard, and pale, and lifeless, at length thou ceasedst to contend with thy destiny.

"This was a moment of triumph. Thus had I successfully subdued the stubbornness of human passions; the victim which had been demanded was given; the deed was done past recall.

"I lifted the corpse in my arms and laid it on the bed. I gazed upon it with delight. Such was the elation of my thoughts, that I even broke into laughter. I clapped my hands and exclaimed, 'It is done! Thy sacred duty is fulfilled. To that I have sacrificed, O my God! thy last and best gift, my wife!'

"For a while I thus soared above frailty. I imagined I had set myself forever beyond the reach of selfishness; but my imaginations were false. This rapture quickly subsided. I looked again at my wife. My joyous ebullitions vanished, and I asked myself who it was whom I saw. . . .

"I will not dwell upon my lapse into desperate and outrageous sorrow. The breath of heaven that sustained me was withdrawn, and I sunk into *mere man*. I leaped from the floor; I dashed my head against the wall; I uttered screams of horror; I panted after torment and pain. Eternal fire, and the bickerings of hell, compared with what I felt, were music and a bed of roses.

"I thank my God that this degeneracy was transient, that he deigned once more to raise me aloft. I thought upon what I had done as a sacrifice to duty, and *was calm*. My wife was dead; but I reflected, that, though this source of human consolation was closed, yet others were still open. If the transports of a husband were no more, the feelings of a father had still scope for exercise. When remembrance of their mother should excite too keen a pang, I would look upon them and *be comforted*.

"While I revolved these ideas, new warmth flowed in my heart. I was wrong. These feelings were the growth of selfishness. Of this I was not aware, and to dispel the mist that obscured my perceptions, a new effulgence and a new mandate were necessary.

"From these thoughts I was recalled by a ray that was shot into the room. A voice spake like that I had before heard,—'Thou hast done well; but all is not done,—the sacrifice is incomplete,—thy children must be offered,—they must perish with their mother.'"

Almost before *Wieland* was published Brockden Brown wrote his second novel, *Ormond, or the Secret Witness*, which with two other novels, *Arthur Mervyn* and *Edgar Huntly*, appeared in 1799. Brown is said to have worked at this time on five novels at once. *Ormond* is one of his inferior books; perhaps its chief right to remembrance is that Shelley admired its long-suffering heroine, Constantia Dudley, and used her name in one of his poems. The plot of the story shows the strong influence of Godwin, especially in the idea of an admirable villain. Ormond, a political and sociological enthusiast, who has revolutionary ideas about religion and marriage, but whose impulses are noble and generous, falls in love with Constantia. Other women have been susceptible to his fascinations, and Constantia realizes his magnetic influence, but her steadfast virtue withstands his pursuit of her. Ormond's remarkable character is turned gradually into that of a fiend; he murders Constantia's father, and compels her finally, in self-defense, to kill him. Constantia's patient and exalted virtues, such as Shelley could admire, make her, as a critic has said, a kind of Griselda, but the same critic has also said justly that she is a bore. "The contemplation of such a character in the abstract is more imposing than the minute details by which we attain the knowledge of it; and although there is nothing, we are told, which the gods look down upon with more satisfaction, than a brave mind struggling with the storms of adversity, yet, when these come in the guise of poverty and all the train of teasing annoyances in domestic life, the tale, if long protracted, too often produces a sensation of weariness scarcely to be compensated by the moral grandeur of the spectacle."

Ormond, the hero, is more interesting to the student of the novel; for impossible as he seems to be to the modern reader, he is one of the chief examples in America of that type of admirable villain of which Falkland, in *Caleb Williams*, and later Byron's heroes generally, are the standard. It is not usual to associate Byron with Brockden Brown, nor with this special character in fiction; what cannot be attributed to Godwin's influence has been connected, somewhat vaguely, with the popular notions of Freemasonry in Brockden Brown's time. It is said that Brown's evil heroes are permeated with the notion that the end justifies the means; they begin with noble ideals, which they deliberately choose to serve by moral short cuts, until they are entangled in their schemes; and their ideals and methods have been ascribed to the Illuminati, the secret order whose part in the American and French Revolutions is said to have been a large one. Reference to such a society is certainly made in the *Memoirs of Carwin*, but it seems more rational to ascribe his conception of the amicable villain to those sentimental idealizations of human nature which distinguished the age, and which later produced, and were further fostered by, Byron's heroic outcasts.

Wieland and *Ormond* were the first considerable romances produced in America. Their importance as pioneer work was recognized from the beginning, and they brought their hard-working young author a place of honor in the community, if not much pecuniary reward. In a letter to his brother James, dated from New York on February 15, 1799, he gives a hint of the quick vogue of *Ormond*, published only in that year:

"My social hours and schemes are in their customary state. . . . Up till eleven, and abed till eight, plying the quill or the book, and conversing with male or female friends, constitutes the customary series of my amusements and employments. I add somewhat, though not so much as I might if I were so inclined, to the number of my friends. I find to be the writer of *Wieland* and *Ormond* is a greater recommendation than I ever imagined it would be."

VI

No account of the art of Brockden Brown is complete without some notice of the book which served as his model, William Godwin's *Caleb Williams*, frequently mentioned in these pages. Godwin, it will be remembered, was the author of the *Inquiry Concerning Political Justice*, and more famous in literary history as Shelley's father-in-law. Philosophy and social problems, rather than literature, were his occupation, but he had an admirable narrative gift, and his great novel, published in 1794, made an immediate and lasting place for itself. Brockden Brown read it early, and for him it was always the standard of story-telling. Before *Alcuin* was published, while he was writing his first and unfinished romance, he says in his journal, of this attempt at fiction, "What is the nature or merit of my performance? This question is not for me to answer. My decision is favorable or otherwise, according to the views I take of the subject. When a mental comparison is made between this and the mass of novels, I am inclined to be pleased with my own production. But when the objects of comparison are changed, and I revolve the transcendant merits of Caleb Williams, my pleasure is diminished, and is preserved from a total extinction only by the reflection that this performance is the first."

Godwin intended, as he said, to show in his novel the modes of domestic and unrecorded despotism, by which man becomes the destroyer of man. Fortunately for literature the instinct to tell a thrilling story was too much for this didactic purpose. No one takes the persecution of Williams by Falkland as a typical record of society at the end of the eighteenth century, and no one cares whether the record is typical or not; it is engrossing, and in the given circumstances of the plot it represents character faithfully. Caleb Williams is a young servant in the household of Mr. Falkland, a man of generous virtues. Williams has every reason for gratitude to him, and comes to honor him, as does the reader also. But the servant's one fault, curiosity, leads him to inquire into the cause of Falkland's secluded life, and by wrong-headed persistence he discovers that Falkland once murdered a man. The ambition of Falkland's life had been to possess the honor and esteem of mankind, and he could not bring himself to acknowledge a crime committed in madness; he even allowed innocent men to suffer in his place. Up to this point in the story the author presents Falkland's character with so much sympathy, and so much justifying detail, that he rouses no harder feeling than pity, and the too curious Williams, who has violated his master's privacy, seems little better than a sneak. From this moment, however, the story reverses the situation of the characters.

Falkland confesses his crime to Williams, and binds him to secrecy with a terrible oath. But service to a confessed murderer becomes so unendurable to the youth that he tries to run away, and finds to his horror that he cannot; Falkland's emissaries hunt him down, spy upon him, keep him in prison or out of it, as they choose, until the wretched victim realizes that he is captive for life to the fears of his relentless master. The story must be read before one can appreciate the art by which Falkland is changed from an unfortunate recluse to a persecuting fiend, and Williams from an unscrupulous sneak to a pitiable victim of tyranny. The end of the story is masterly; Williams in desperation has his enemy haled into court, and breaking the oath of secrecy, accuses him of the murder; but the sight of Falkland, wasted with illness and a troubled conscience, brings back the old love of the man, and he wishes he had endured the persecution in silence. The effect of this scene is to remind us that we have been judging Falkland through Williams' imagination; when we see the unhappy murderer, we remember that he too has been persecuted. Falkland is therefore the model of the lovable villains in Brockden Brown, and he and Williams both illustrate the romantic loneliness which is the fatal product of a characteristic—Falkland being exiled from society by his desire for honorable fame, and Williams by insatiable curiosity.

The interest of the story is twofold. In the first part Godwin shows himself a master of that sort of psychological penetration that Brockden Brown emulated. We see with complete conviction just how Falkland came to be what he is; and though our attention is away from it at the moment, the persecution of Williams is prepared for and made a matter of absolute logic. In the second part the wanderings of the young servant afford opportunity for a realistic portrait of society; life on the highway and in the city, in the taverns and the prisons, is described with qualities of truth that Brockden Brown never commanded. From this part of the story comes the convincing power of *Caleb Williams*, and where Brown's work makes a feeble appeal the fault is chiefly in his disregard of external verities. Whether or not the story of Caleb Williams *could* happen in England at the end of the eighteenth century, we see, while we read it, that it *did* happen.

Arthur Mervyn, or Memoirs of the Year 1793, another novel published in 1799, is the closest imitation Brown made of *Caleb Williams*. The book had first appeared in the *Weekly Magazine*. It is remembered chiefly for its description of the yellow fever epidemic in Philadelphia, in 1793, which the author's family had happily escaped. In 1798, however, Brown saw the same pestilence at close range in New York, where he ran great danger himself, and where his friend Smith lost his life in an attempt to save a stricken foreigner, whom he took into his home. Some hint of Brown's temperament is in his letters to his brother describing the epidemic day by day. The account reads like a section from one of his books —no less unhappy, no less composed. Tragedy was his element. But this experience equipped him for his one accomplishment in realism. In the beginning of *Ormond* he drew a brief picture of yellow fever horrors; in *Arthur Mervyn* he drew the same picture at length.

The resemblances of the plot to *Caleb Williams* are at once obvious. Arthur Mervyn, a country youth, comes to Philadelphia to seek his fortune; his father's second marriage drove him from home. Rendered destitute by some surprising adventures in the city, he is rescued by a philanthropic man named Welbeck, who with his daughter lives in a lonely but sumptuously furnished home; evidently his wealth is great. He takes Mervyn into his service as a kind of secretary, but gives him little to do, and in his leisure Mervyn studies his employer's many peculiarities. His curiosity is aroused by the promise Welbeck demanded, never to speak of his own history to anyone he might meet. Of Welbeck's history he knows nothing. His distrust of Welbeck increases until one day he hears a pistol-shot in an adjoining room, rushes in, and finds Welbeck standing over the man he has murdered. The scene corresponds to Caleb Williams' discovery of Falkland, and is followed by a similar confession. Love of money is Welbeck's passion, as desire of public honor was Falkland's. Welback has committed forgery, and murdered the man who would expose him; the young girl in his house is not his daughter but his mistress, whose estate he has stolen, and whom he keeps in seclusion to prevent her from knowing the truth. This disclosure would seem to put Welbeck in Mervyn's power, but as in Godwin's story, the inquisitive young man finds himself in his employer's toils. From that moment his adventures are so complicated that Brown adds a second and inferior instalment of the story, to gather up the threads.

Here we have once more Godwin's attractive villain and victimized servant. Welbeck is less admirable than Falkland,—partly, it has been suggested, because his ambition is more sordid, and partly because we have to take the author's word for any charm he possesses. Godwin exhibits Falkland actually living an honorable and kindly life, but Welbeck takes Mervyn into his house merely in order to work out his plots, and his treatment of the heiress, Mlle. Lodi, is infamous; and lastly, Welbeck is never altogether frank, as Falkland is. Mervyn is intended to be far more admirable than Caleb Williams. His leaving home illustrates his high spirit, and the illness through which he enters the story, during the epidemic, gives him a claim at once on the reader's pity. He is less effective, however, than Caleb Williams; he is guilty of the same prying curiosity, to cover which he tells small lies, and throughout the book he lacks initiative.

The story is full of admirable situations, none of which are developed. The fact that Brown was writing four other novels at the same time indicates both the natural richness of his genius, and his lack of thoroughness. Mervyn's first adventure, in which he is shut up at midnight in a stranger's bedroom, suggests developments that would have done credit to a Stevenson, but it is sufficient for Brown to let his hero take off his shoes and go quietly to the locked door, which is not locked after all, and so make his escape to the street, stupidly leaving his shoes behind, for the surprise of the householder the next morning.

The power of the book, as has been said, is in its realistic account of the yellow fever epidemic. Brown had not the art to make his realism support the rest of the story; therefore Mervyn's fortunes in Welbeck's house are not a whit more convincing because of the pestilence, and the realism stands apart from the main plot. The introductory episode, in which the invalid Mervyn is taken into the home of the narrator, is based on Dr. Smith's similar and fatal generosity to the Italian Scandella, and those first pages of the book, though they are not usually praised, might well be so for their quiet record of natural and kindly manners. Two passages will illustrate Brown's skill in horror—one, a sketch of a burying party that echoes Defoe's *Journal of the Plague Year;* the other, a Hogarth drawing of the fever hospital, unforgettably terrible.

"I met not more than a dozen figures, and these were ghost-like, wrapt in cloaks, from behind which they cast upon me glances of wonder and suspicion; and, as I approached, changed their course, to avoid touching me. Their clothes were sprinkled with vinegar; and their nostrils defended from contagion by some powerful perfume. . . . Death seemed to hover over this scene, and I dreaded that the floating pestilence had already lighted on my frame. I had scarcely overcome these tremors, when I approached a house, the door of which was opened, and before which stood a vehicle, which I presently recognized to be a *hearse*.

"The driver was seated in it. I stood still to mark his visage, and to observe the course which he proposed to take. Presently a coffin, borne by two men, issued from the house. The driver was a negro, but his companions were white. Their features were marked by a ferocious indifference to danger or pity. One of them as he assisted in thrusting the coffin into the cavity provided for it, said, ' I'll be damned if I think the poor dog was quite dead. It wasn't the *fever* that killed him, but the sight of the girl and her mother on the floor. I wonder how they all got into that room. What carried them there?'

"The other surlily muttered, ' Their legs to be sure.'

"But what should they hug together in one room for?

" ' To save us trouble to be sure.'

"And I thank them with all my heart; but damn it, it wasn't right to put him in his coffin before the breath was fairly gone. I thought the last look he gave me, told me to stay a few minutes.

"Pshaw! He could not live. The sooner dead the better for him; as well as for us. Did you mark how he eyed us, when we carried away his wife and daughter? I never cried in my life, since I was knee-high, but curse me if I ever felt in better tune for the business than just then. ' Hey!' continued he, looking up, and observing me standing a few paces distant, and listening to their discourse, ' what's wanted? Anybody dead?' "

"I lay upon a mattress, whose condition proved that a half-decayed corpse had recently been dragged from it. The room was large, but it was covered with beds like my own. Between each, there was scarcely the interval of three feet. Each sustained a wretch, whose groans and distortions bespoke the desperateness of his condition.

"The atmosphere was loaded with mortal stenches. A vapor, suffocating and malignant, scarcely allowed me to breathe. No suitable receptacle was provided for the evacuations produced by medicine or disease. My nearest neighbor was struggling with death, and my bed, casually extended, was moist with the detestable matter which poured from his stomach.

"You will scarcely believe that, in this scene of horrors, the sound of laughter should be overheard. While the upper rooms of this building are filled with the sick and the dying, the lower apartments are the scene of carousals and mirth. The wretches who are hired, at enormous wages, to tend the sick and convey away the dead, neglect their duty and consume the cordials, which are provided for the patients, in debauchery and riot.

"A female visage, bloated with malignity and drunkenness, occasionally looked in. Dying eyes were cast upon her, invoking the boon, perhaps, of a drop of cold water, or her assistance to change a posture which compelled him to behold the ghastly writhings or deathful *smile* of his neighbor.

"The visitant had left the banquet for a moment, only to see who was dead. If she entered the room, blinking eyes and reeling steps showed her to be totally unqualified for ministering the aid that was needed. Presently she disappeared and others ascended the staircase, a coffin was deposited at the door, the wretch, whose heart still quivered, was seized by rude hands, and dragged along the floor into the passage."

VII

The year 1799 must have been a crowded time for Brockden Brown. Of the five novels he was working on, three appeared in that year. In June he did some traveling in Connecticut—an experience nearly as adventurous then as a trip to California now. He kept a note-book of the journey, to have, as he said, a scheme for preserving his impressions in a way that might serve a public and private purpose,—adding, that Connecticut had never been described, and surely it merited a description. Two months earlier he had published the first number of *The Monthly Magazine and American Review*, which ran for little over a year. The incomplete *Memoirs of Stephen Calvert* appeared in its pages, and part of *Edgar Huntly;* and the magazine shows, as might be expected, interest in the German literature which was influencing the romantic school from which Brown derived.

Edgar Huntly, or Memoirs of a Sleep-Walker, was the third novel to appear in this prolific year. The importance of this story is not perhaps greater than of some of the others, but it will receive more consideration because in it the American Indian begins, not unworthily, his career in our fiction; in part at least this is a border tale of adventure. The obsession which creates the mystery of the story is here sleep-walking, as the title implies; obviously the problems of the plot will be physical instead of psychological. Although this change takes Brockden Brown out of a field in which he had special interest, it is on the whole of advantage to the story. Even so, the plot breaks in the middle like most of Brown's work, following the example of *Caleb Williams*, but it would have been an outrageous insult to congruity if a psychological story had preceded the crude melodrama of the Indian adventures. Brown could always invent incident, though he was careless in working out his situations. He had the necessary ingenuity, though neither the poetry nor the art, to have been a true predecessor of Cooper, and whatever faults this novel has, it is not dull.

Edgar Huntly is a young native of the Pennsylvania frontier, who one night finds a friend murdered beneath a certain elm tree. His suspicions are accordingly directed to a strange creature named Clithero, whom he discovers several nights later digging under the same tree. When he approaches the spot, he sees that Clithero, for all his labor, is asleep. He is convinced that Clithero murdered the friend—that his conscience brings him in his dreams to the place of his crime. This opening scene is one of Brown's best strokes of craftsmanship; the situation is in itself striking, and the attention is diverted from the plausibility of the sleep-walking to the murder problem.

Huntly demands an explanation of Clithero, who—in a typical confession scene—tells of a murder he once committed in self-defense, long ago, which wrecked his life and preys still upon his reason. This explanation naturally does not account for his somnambulistic performance under that particular elm, and as he will tell nothing more, Huntly gives up his inquiries for the time. Clithero immediately takes to a wild cavern on the edge of the wilderness and hides; Huntly finds him evidently in a kind of insanity endeavoring to starve himself to death. Huntly's visits to him, for the purpose of saving him from self-destruction, are varied by encounters, more or less heroic, with mountain lions.

At this point the story turns in a new direction. One night Huntly awakes in agony, to find himself at the bottom of a cavern, open apparently only to the sky. Though the reader has not suspected it, he too, for the purpose of this predicament, is a sleep-walker, and has tumbled down the cavern while searching in his dreams for more mountain lions. Fortunately he has brought along in his sleep, and despite his fall still holds, the tomahawk that had been his defense against the panthers. In his attempts to get out of the cavern he finds a passage into a cave, which in turn leads up to level ground. But at the mouth of the cave he finds three Indians sleeping. Near them is a beautiful girl, bound captive, and just outside the cave a fourth Indian stands guard. Huntly glides through the sleeping group, brains the sentinel before the alarm can be given, unbinds the girl, and carries her away without waking up the other three Indians. In the fight that follows next day, when the Indians pursue, Huntly kills them all,—and to the end of the story the adventure keeps fairly well up to that pace. At the very last the author cheats the reader out of what little curiosity remains over from the first part of the story, by explaining that Huntly's friend had been murdered by the Indians, and Clithero was simply a lunatic.

But the part of the story that deals with the Indians is still interesting, even after Cooper has set a standard for the modern reader. How new the picture must have been, before Cooper's time, can well be imagined. Making all allowance for the melodramatic, sometimes juvenile, developments of the plot, the Indians in it are drawn with dignity and considerable truth. Brown had no natural love of the frontier, nor any experience of it; his attitude towards the red man is that of the dweller in the settlements, who sees the Indian only occasionally, when he comes in to spend his money or to make trouble; it is somewhat the attitude of Cooper's *Pioneers*. There is no attempt to idealize the savage morally. He is shown as the treacherous and wily foe, and he associates himself in the reader's imagination with the two panthers that had wandered in from the wilderness to trouble the farmers. Yet the ferocity and mysterious skill of the Indian in war, like the agility of the panther, gains a sort of unmoral credit; these savage raiders have the keen sight, delicate hearing and sure hand that rouses admiration for Cooper's Indians; and Brockden Brown is careful to make them neither too monstrous nor too successful,—they are simply half-tamed savages who break into murderous revolt and are put down by superior civilization and order.

Only one Indian is sufficiently characterized to seem an individual. That is the old hag, Deb, or Queen Mab, as the white people call her, who lives on public bounty and be-

cause of fancied grievances instigates her people to the raid.
Her realistic portrait seems to belong to a modern school—
she would hardly be found among Cooper's Indians; we suspect that Brown is here—and here only—describing the savage from observation. She originally belonged, he says, to
the tribe of Delawares, or Lenni-Lenape—the tribe of which
Uncas was the last chief.

"The village inhabited by this clan was built upon the
ground which now constitutes my uncle's barn-yard and
orchard. On the departure of her countrymen, this female
burnt the empty wigwams and retired into the fastnesses of
Norwalk. She selected a spot suitable for an Indian dwelling and a small plantation of maize, and in which she was
seldom liable to interruption and intrusion.

"Her only companions were three dogs, of the Indian or
wolf species. These animals differed in nothing from their
kinsmen of the forest, but in their attachment and obedience
to their mistress. She governed them with absolute sway.
They were her servants and protectors, and attended her
person or guarded her threshold, agreeable to her directions.
She fed them with corn and they supplied her and themselves
with meat, by hunting squirrels, raccoons, and rabbits. . . .

"The chief employment of this woman, when at home, besides plucking the weeds from among her corn, bruising the
grain between two stones, and setting her snares for rabbits
and possums, was to talk. Though in solitude, her tongue
was never at rest but when she was asleep; but her conversation was merely addressed to her dogs. Her voice was sharp
and shrill, and her gesticulations were vehement and gro-
tesque. A hearer would naturally imagine that she was
scolding; but, in truth, she was merely giving them directions.
Having no other object of contemplation or subject of discourse, she always found, in their posture and looks, occasion
for praise, or blame, or command. The readiness with which
they understood, and the docility with which they obeyed her
movements and words, were truly wonderful. . . .

"She seldom left the hut but to visit the neighboring inhabitants, and demand from them food and clothing, or

whatever her necessities required. These were exacted as her due; to have her wants supplied was her prerogative, and to withhold what she claimed was rebellion. She conceived that by remaining behind her countrymen she succeeded to the government, and retained the possession of all this region. The English were aliens and sojourners, who occupied the land merely by her connivance and permission, and whom she allowed to remain on no terms but those of supplying her wants."

Queen Mab is the only personality in this book, and a reasonable claim might be made that she is the only original character in all Brockden Brown's writing. His important work ends with *Edgar Huntly,* and when we look back upon the sum of his most representative writing, we see that his limitations in the creation of character as well as of plot, are great. He is never at a loss for an incident, and he can introduce any number of lay figures to fill his stage, but his hasty methods of composition were fatal to any structural development of plot, and curiously enough, with his great interest in psychology he pays little attention to character. In the case of his amiable villains, his charitable faith in humanity surrounds the hero for the time being in an atmosphere of sympathy, but when the book is laid aside, Ormond and Welbeck and Carwin fade into an unmoral bloodlessness, that seems more vital only in the course of the unusual incidents. It is almost impossible to imagine a character of Brockden Brown's as having further experiences after the book ends, though that is the simplest test of convincing character drawing. The motives, even of the villians, are weak or insufficiently stated,—which may explain why they pale in the memory. Carwin has no reason for his crimes, Ormond an inadequate one, and Welbeck is such a mixture of shrewdness and folly, and such a liar to boot, that we are inclined to give him up as the author gives up Clithero, for a lunatic.

But though these characters are frequently not characters

at all—mere lay figures, yet that they appeal to the imagination, in certain moods more common a hundred years ago, is not to be denied. The art of the Gothic romance at its best was essentially mechanical and scenic—the art of the theater. Stage, action, dialogue, character, all were represented in the rough, as so many stimuli of the audience's imagination; if you lost yourself in the tinsel and glare, you saw truth before you, but if you could not so lose yourself, you saw only the tinsel and glare. We have been sophisticated into a closer habit of scrutiny nowadays. The brook that tumbles its cascade toward the footlights must flow with real water, and the players who impersonate a family are chosen for resemblances of complexion or profile, so that the sluggish imagination of the house will not be overtaxed. Even Scott, our beloved romancer, now fails to create for many readers the old illusion of enchanted truth. Di Vernon poses on horseback before them, and the pose to them means nothing. If such a fate has overtaken Sir Walter, we need not be too hard on the achievements of the thinner-talented Philadelphia youth. An unjaded imagination can still fill out his theatrical hints, and for others less fortunate Queen Mab is a comforting promise of the modern photograph.

Wieland is the most typical of Brown's characters largely because he has so little character. We watch his actions and his psychological states as they are induced by Carwin's trickery; the process has its fascination, and it seems true; the deluded wretch, passing from too sensitive religiosity to murderous insanity, is an advance study of those mental transitions which Hawthorne was to trace so marvelously. But Hawthorne would have made Wieland a responsible character; he would have made the transitions result from resolves and actions, as in the changed nature of Roger Chillingworth. For Brockden Brown's purposes it makes no difference whether Wieland is morally good or bad, and in this separation of psychological and moral interests in character lies his resemblance to Poe and his difference from Hawthorne.

Brown never grasped the principle that character can be, or should be, exhibited by action. A less dramatic mind than his could hardly be imagined. Even in those actions which are intended to be admirable, where the actor is intended to have our praise, the author fails to make the proper connection between the act and the character. In *Edgar Huntly*, where the hero is enabled to kill the three Indians and save the girl, Cooper would have made the incident the direct result of character in Leatherstocking, or whoever it might have been; we should have had just one more illustration of his skill or courage, or some other virtue. As Brown tells it Huntly accomplished the rescue by sheer luck; he needs a freshly loaded gun for each Indian, and the author ingeniously puts a weapon into his hand whenever he needs one. We admire the author's foresight, not Huntly's. And when the book is closed, the scene, so far as Huntly is concerned, is distasteful; it seems far from an admirable thing to stand outside a door with a sufficient supply of loaded guns, and shoot down Indians as they come out.

VIII

In July, 1801, Brown started on a somewhat extended trip through New York, Massachusetts and Connecticut. As was usual with him, the journey was recorded and commented upon in his diary and letters. Though his note-books are not to be compared with Hawthorne's so far as literary quality or observation are concerned, yet they do one good service for Brown, as Hawthorne's do for him—they readjust our notion of his personality after we have been living in the atmosphere of his romances. He was not in general a good observer, but as he grew older he acquired a journalist's rather than a philosopher's alertness for material; the moralizing lessens, and the world he moved in enters the journal in matter-of-fact items. We are reminded that Brockden Brown was after all only a young man, handicapped by his precocity, and the change in the note-book is the welcome sign of experience and increasing poise. As he remarks at the beginning of this journey, he had been in New York only three or four years,— a small space into which to crowd so much work and suffering and pleasure as had been his,—and this had been his only education in the broadest sense. He had come to the city a provincial young pedant; already he was a reputable man of letters, an honored citizen, the first American novelist.

The journey began with a voyage up the Hudson, which Brown had never explored further than ten miles above New York. He was curious to see the Highlands and the "Kaats-Kill Mountains," which he described as of "stupendous" height; their elevation had already been ascertained, he says, but he does not recollect what it is. When the tide was against them, the passengers made excursions along the shore and bathed in the river. With a favoring tide, he goes on, "we left Red-hook at eight o'clock, but were obliged to anchor again before morning. At six o'clock my friend and I accompanied the captain ashore, in search of milk and blackberries. I have since seated myself on deck, watching the shore, as the breeze carried us slowly along. My friend is busy with his spyglass, reconnoitering the rocks and hay stacks, and surveying the wharves and store houses of Lunnenburg and Hudson, villages we have just passed. I have observed but little besides a steep bank, roughened by rocks and bushes, occasionally yielding to slopes of a parched and yellowish soil, with poor cottages sparingly scattered, and now and then a small garden or field of corn. A fellow passenger left us at Hudson. One only remaining, a Mr. H——— of Albany, a well behaved man, whose attention is swallowed up by Mrs. Bennet's 'Beggar Girl.'"

The captain's library consisted of a book on navigation, one on arithmetic, and Goldsmith's *Citizen of the World*. This last was evidently new to Brown, who tried to read it, for want of something to pass the time, but found he did not like it; the fiction is ill-supported, he says, "the style smooth and elegant, but the sentiments and observations far from judicious or profound."

At the end of his summer trip Brown returned to Philadelphia, which in this year had once more become his home. For a while he lived with his brother Armit, but he was already planning for a household of his own. In New York he had met the family of Dr. William Linn, a Presbyterian minister. John Blair Linn, the son, who became one of Brown's best friends, was like his father a minister, and had a church in Philadelphia. To this friend's sister, Elizabeth Linn, Brown became engaged, and they were married in November, 1804.

Had Brown's life been prolonged the influence of his love affair and his marriage might have appeared strongly in his work. His last two novels were occupied with studies of feminine character, to the neglect of masculine villains and horrors, and his other writings began to show broad human interests; from this time also his patriotism is seen in his concern for politics and for America's relations with Great Britain. Before he met Miss Linn, think of him as kindly as we may, he was in many respects a prig, and what he did not know about the course of true love in the human breast was complete. When he wrote *Alcuin* he had the usual contempt of over-intellectual young men for any but intellectual passions: "I know that love, as it is commonly understood, is an empty and capricious passion. . . . To thwart it is often to destroy it, and sometimes to qualify the victim of the delusion for Bedlam. In the majority of cases it is nothing but a miserable project of affectation. The languishing and sighing lover is an object to which the errors of mankind have annexed a certain degree of reverence." Constantia Dudley, in *Ormond*, and the frailer ladies in the same story, Helena and Martinette, sufficiently exhibit in different ways Brown's conscientious ignorance of the feminine mind. And shortly before his betrothal he perpetrated this delicious self-advertisement—"My conceptions of the delights and benefits connected with love and marriage, are exquisite. They have swayed most of my thoughts, and many of my actions since I arrived at the age of reflection and maturity. They have given birth to the sentiment of love, with regard to several women. Mutual circumstances have frustrated the natural operations of that sentiment in several instances. At present I am free."

Brown's changed attitude toward life is evident in *Clara Howard*, the last novel he wrote in New York, published in 1801. In plot this story much resembles *Edgar Huntly;* in both books a brother is intrusted with money, which after his death his sister inherits, supposing it to be a legacy, and then an embarrassing claimant of it appears. And in both stories the benefactor of the hero is an Englishman, who has had certain stereotyped adventures. The similarity of incidents partly explains the speed with which Brockden Brown turned out his group of novels, but *Clara Howard*, in spite of that similarity, is distinct from the preceding stories and marks the author's change of ideals. The plot is orderly and for the most part clearly worked out. The chief interest is focused on the characters of Clara Howard and Mary Wilmot, almost equally the heroines. Most significant is the new emphasis on character rather than psychology; the experiences of both girls are moral tests.

Edward Hartley becomes the friend of Mary Wilmot's brother, and through this friendship he comes to know the sister, who falls in love with him. Hartley's affection for her is no more than friendship, but he realizes her devotion to him, and when Mary's brother dies, they become engaged. The engagement is an offhand sort of provision for Mary's future. Mary then lives quietly on the five thousand dollars she has discovered in her brother's possession after his death, but at the end of six months a man named Morton appears, who says that he left the money in Wilmot's care. At about the same time Mr. Howard, Hartley's benefactor, returns to this country from England, where he has married a widow, an old flame of his; her daughter, Clara Howard, he hopes will be Hartley's wife.

Mary Wilmot, learning of this plan, unselfishly disappears, so that Hartley will be free. Hartley and Clara fall in love promptly, but Hartley feels bound to tell her his relations with Mary and his fear for her fate. Clara, equally magnanimous, gives up her lover and insists that he find the other woman. The situation viewed abstractly is rather funny, as Clara against her own wishes drives Hartley, much against his, to marry Mary, who has run off with another man. But the problem is real in the book, and Mary and Clara are fine characters. The difficulties are solved when Mary marries a former lover, Sedley.

This novel is quite lacking in those highly wrought incidents that give *Wieland* and *Arthur Mervyn* their fame; it is not surprising that its tameness has doomed it to obscurity. But it proves a capacity in the author for a broadened, normal point of view, which from his early mental habit could not have been expected. The plot gives him occasion also to comment on the differences between American and English social ideals, when Hartley, a country boy of humble parents, finds himself in love with the well-born Clara Howard. Though he had not visited England, Brown's comment is thoughtful and just, and in allowing Hartley to marry the English girl he illustrates consciously the triumph of those democratic ideals which, he says, are the proud distinction between this country and Europe.

It has been well said that in such characters as Mary Wilmot and Clara Howard, and earlier perhaps in Constantia Dudley, Brown was portraying a new type of heroine, and should have the credit for such pioneer work, no matter how crude it was. These women think and act for themselves, with all the newly discovered consciousness of woman's rights. They are not portraits, but social ideals, the concrete development of the theories in *Alcuin*. Too much credit can hardly be given to the author who conceived of this now common type so far in advance of its general acceptance. So early an example of the type as Diana Vernon was not to appear for nearly twenty years. Scott, and Cooper after him, were in general guided by eighteenth-century standards of the well-bred heroine, and their forceful women, like Norna in *The Pirate* or Judith Hutter in *The Deerslayer*, are exceptions, social outcasts. Brown was a thinker in a sense that Scott was not, and being less sane than Cooper, his speculations were more adventurous and in this particular more modern. It would be a not unprofitable fancy to trace the variations of type from Clara Howard or Mary Wilmot through Hester Prynne to Daisy Miller; not even so fanciful a descent can be traced from Scott's or Cooper's normal heroines.

In October of 1803 Brown inaugurated the *Literary Magazine and American Register*, which continued for five years. The pleasures of magazine editing were not great in those days, as Brown's letters show. He had to supply most of the material for the magazine himself—in one case writing the whole number, with the exception of one contribution. The fragmentary *Memoirs of Carwin* appeared in instalments until the busy editor could not find leisure to continue them. His health was not good at this time, partly because of overwork; the disease which was to end his life either brought about his invalid condition, or was encouraged by it. The humor of an unknown correspondent who proposed to make himself acceptable to his political party by publishing in Brown's periodical an invective against Adams and a eulogy of Jefferson, would hardly offset the business disappointments and embarrassments the editor had to complain of. How precarious any such venture was, may be gathered from Brown's letter to his brother Armit, in 1798, when he was planning his first experiment, the *Monthly Magazine*. How often again were American authors to indulge in such optimistic calculations! "Four hundred subscribers will repay the annual expense of sixteen hundred dollars. As soon as this number is obtained, the printers will begin, and trust to the punctual payment of these for reimbursement. All above four hundred will be clear profit for me; one thousand subscribers will produce four thousand five hundred dollars [*sic*], and deducting the annual expense will leave two thousand seven hundred [*sic*]. If this sum be attainable, in a year or two you will allow that my prospect is consoling." If this reckoning illustrates Brown's business capacity, perhaps it is no wonder that the first magazine failed, and the second had only a more lingering death. It is somewhat puzzling to explain how Brown supported himself at all, or could think of supporting a family. His novels brought him reputation, but no money; in one of his letters he says that the best an American author can hope for is to pay expenses. That he expected little from the *Literary Magazine* is intimated in terms more magnanimous than calculated to cheer the publisher, John Conrad, who financed the periodical and paid Brown a salary for editing it; "The project is not a mercenary one," writes the editor. "Nobody relies for subsistence on its success, nor does the editor put anything but his reputation at stake. At the same time, he cannot but be desirous of an ample subscription, not merely because pecuniary profit is acceptable, but because this is the best proof which he can receive that his endeavors to amuse and instruct have not been unsuccessful."

In this year, 1803, Brown published a political pamphlet entitled, *An Address to the Government of The United States on the Cession of Louisiana to the French; and on the Late Breach of Treaty by the Spaniards: including a translation of a memorial, on the war of St. Domingo and cession of the Mississippi to France, drawn up by a French counsellor of state.* The essay so formidably introduced is an argument, supposed to be drawn from a French document, to prove that the territory of Louisiana was an invaluable possession, and Brown pleaded for its acquisition by the United States. The pamphlet is a return to the debate as a literary form, such as *Alcuin*, but much more direct and mature in method. A second pamphlet, *The British Treaty*, begins with a discussion of Great Britain's treatment of this country as likely to lead to war—especially such incidents as the searching of the frigate *Chesapeake* in 1807. Brown then proceeds to examine in detail the terms of the treaty of 1806. His third pamphlet, in 1809, dealt with the embargo placed upon commerce with foreign ports, under the ponderous title, *Address to the Congress of the United States on the utility and justice of restrictions upon foreign commerce, with reflections on Foreign Trade in general, and the future prospects of America.* After expounding with considerable power the ridiculous futility of trying to retaliate for the French and English embargoes, Brown makes an excursion that does more justice to his patriotism than to his logic, and explains how desirable for internal commerce the embargo would be, were it otherwise desirable or possible. He saw the necessity of building up domestic trade and manufactures, and then uniting all sections of the country economically. Of all three pamphlets it may be said that they reflect broad patriotism and much economic sense, and the attitude of the author in each was in accord with later opinion.

In 1804, three months before Brown's marriage with Miss Linn, occurred the death of her brother John Blair Linn, then pastor of the First Presbyterian Church in Philadelphia. Dr. Linn was a poet in a harmless way, and for a posthumous volume of his verse Brown wrote a biographical sketch.

In Brown's last novel, *Jane Talbot*, published in England in this year, William Godwin's influence is turned to peculiar account; it is charged against the hero, by one of the characters, that he is a disciple of Godwin, and the charge is felt to be a serious one. The story is unworthy of its author, except that it is coherent and quiet in Brown's later manner. Colden, the hero, falls in love with Jane Talbot, an adopted child. Like the editor of the *Literary Magazine*, Colden has no mercenary ambitions,—in fact, he is so high-minded that he is hardly willing to support himself, let alone a wife. He and Jane discuss by letter the problem that naturally ensues; after a mysterious disappearance, which almost leads Jane to marry someone else, Colden returns, and with untypical promptness marries her himself. The letters which form the greater part of the book are intended as analyses of the heart, somewhat in Richardson's way. The method fits well with Brown's gift for debate and discussion, but it interrupts the flow of what narrative there is. It is the author who is speaking when Jane says, "I have always found an unaccountable pleasure in dissecting, as it were, my heart, uncovering one by one its many folds, and laying it before you, as a country is shown on a map."

In 1806 Conrad, the publisher of the *Literary Magazine*, brought out the first annual volume of *The American Register*, edited by Brown. The publication had considerable success, and it stopped only with the editor's death. It contained records of public events in America and Europe, of legislation, of the advances of science, and a review of literary publications. During this time—for the last years of his life—Brown worked on a geography, curiously enough reverting to that childhood interest which had mounted him on the parlor table. The book, which was left unfinished, was promising enough to make his friends wish to publish it as it was.

For some time Brockden Brown's friends had suspected that he was a victim of consumption. His temperament, perhaps his needs, did not allow him leisure for rest or recreation to fight the disease, and his constitution was always frail. Having the traditional optimism of consumptive people, he persisted in explaining away all his symptoms, until his condition was desperate. He was persuaded to try a sea voyage, and determined to visit his brother James in England. But during the summer of 1809 he made his last journey, a visit to New Jersey and New York. In November he was unable to leave his bed, and on February 22, 1810, he died.

In person Brown was tall and thin, but he gave the impression of much more strength than he had. His hair was black, and is said to have been straight, though in his portrait it appears to be wavy. His chin was weak,—in fact, none of his features were distinguished except his large and dreamy eyes, yet those who saw him were impressed by his remarkable personality, apparent at a glance.

IX

He was only thirty-nine years old when he died. If it is true that the great novels are all written after forty, we may think of his stories as 'prentice work, and speculate on the masterpiece he would have written had be lived. But there is no good reason for thinking of him as cut off in his promise, like Keats or Shelley. His early death is pathetic for other reasons; in literature there is no cause to doubt that he had said his say. He was not by temperament a novelist; he could neither tell a vital, coherent narrative, nor draw a true picture of manners. That he wrote stories at all was due to his need of a medium for his speculations about life, and as Godwin had used the novel effectively to attack domestic tyranny, it was easy for Brown to exploit his psychological notions through the same form.

The very real power that he is master of from time to time cannot be denied; his fame rests on it. But he was by nature a publicist, and story-telling only happened to be among his experiments. For that very reason, perhaps, he is a typical figure in his place at the beginning of American literature. Our great writers, especially in prose, have been public-spirited before they were artistic. *Uncle Tom's Cabin* is only one brilliant success among a thousand attempts to make a reform party of the Muses. It is to his credit as a citizen that Brown probably never wrote without the welfare of men, especially of his countrymen, in mind; whatever new truth he acquired, he made feverish haste to share with any who would read. The result is that he always has his eye on the reader whom he is instructing; he rarely loses himself in the story.

He is also prophetic of American literature in his readiness to welcome and absorb foreign culture. He is the disciple of Godwin, as he would have been of Scott, and he gave as cordial appreciation to the German and Italian literatures, though his education did not admit him to all their treasures. He is distinctly himself, as Cooper and Emerson in their separate ways are distinctly themselves, and equally American. All that he learned from other lands he transmuted into a native product, as he transferred the Gothic romance to Philadelphia. That use of a native stage, it has been said, is enough to earn our gratitude. He wrote of scenes he knew, and his tales lose no power by the setting.

He showed one great quality, in his brief literary career; he was quick to learn. In the preface to *Wieland* he had anticipated criticisms of the ventriloquism and spontaneous combustion—phenomena not generally credible—by remarking that "it is a sufficient vindication of the writer, if history furnishes one parallel fact." A mind so ignorant of art as not to feel instinctively the need of probability, seldom acquires the principle. But in a letter to his brother James, who appears to have been a sound and persevering critic, he wrote in 1800, "Your remarks upon the gloominess and out-of-nature incidents of Huntly, if they be not just in their full extent, are, doubtless, such as most readers will make, which alone is a sufficient reason for dropping the doleful tone and assuming a cheerful one, or, at least, substituting moral causes and daily incidents in place of the prodigious and singular. I shall not fall hereafter into that strain."

His was the realism of the journalist. He had an instinct for head-lines, with the gruesome details diagramed and illustrated. From this trait came his general inability to depict character. We find his art described by its opposite in the delightful plea Mr. Howells makes for his beloved realism, that "character resides in habit," and that "for the novelist to seek its expression in violent events would be as stupid as for the painter to expect an alarm of fire or burglary to startle his sitter into a valuable revelation of his qualities."

But in Brockden Brown's time the burglar and the fire alarm had their charms.

J. Fenimore Cooper

JAMES FENIMORE COOPER

I

COOPER is the great story-teller of American literature. He
was the first American to make a world-wide appeal, and to
this day he is one of the few who have taken and held a high
rank in the esteem of other nations. No single book of his has
had the universal popularity of *Uncle Tom's Cabin,* but on the
other hand that novel was not equaled by any other work of
its author, nor was its success due entirely to its value as a
story; whereas the Leatherstocking Tales belong to world
literature, and owe their immortality to the sheer delight they
give. Their recognition was as immediate and generous as
the welcome accorded the Waverley Novels, to whose author
Cooper is often compared. Perhaps the highest praise the
American ever received was from the author of *Henry Esmond,* who knew what was to be known about great novels;
in the Roundabout Paper entitled "On a Peal of Bells"
Thackeray follows a description of Scott's heroes with these
words: "Much as I like those unassuming, manly, unpre-
tending gentlemen, I have to own that I think the heroes
of another writer, viz:—Leatherstocking, Uncas, Hardheart,
Tom Coffin, are quite the equals of Scott's men; perhaps
Leatherstocking is better than any one in 'Scott's Lot.' *La
Longue Carabine* is one of the great prizemen of fiction. He
ranks with your Uncle Toby, Sir Roger de Coverley, Falstaff—heroic figures, all—American or British, and the artist
has deserved well of his country who devised them."

However well he deserved, Cooper received little from his

country in proportion to what he gave. Partly through his own fault, his career, though one of the most conspicuous, was one of the least honored in our literature. And since his death, when the common judgment of his personality has become kindlier, types of fiction more subtle than the story of adventure have led the fashion, and Cooper's novels have been in some measure consigned to the juvenile department of literature. Although the best criticism has lately been once more appreciative of the novelist who is not ashamed to tell an out-and-out story, who makes pretension to neither style nor wickedness, and never heard of the psychological or sociological problem, yet the admirer of Cooper, like the admirer of Scott, has still something of a case to prove; he has still a plea to make for that old-fashioned sanity which to the red-pepper palate of to-day is dullness; he must still set up the claims of a great imagination over against modern literary dexterity; and he must explain why the public honor that was Cooper's due was turned into public abuse,—why even to-day his greatness as a man is forgotten. For Cooper, in spite of his faults, was really a great man. He stands detached from his books, like Scott, a strong personality. He was one of the least provincial of American authors, and one of the most thoughtful, if not one of the wisest, of American citizens. For more than literary services he deserves well of his country.

He was born at Burlington, New Jersey, September 15, 1789. His father, Judge William Cooper, came of a Quaker family, who had settled in New Jersey a century before; his mother, Elizabeth Fenimore, was of Swedish descent. There were twelve children, of whom James was the eleventh. He got his middle name by dropping the hyphen in Fenimore-Cooper, the form to which the family name was changed in 1826, by act of legislature.

At the close of the Revolution the elder Cooper bought a large estate in New York, on the shore of Otsego Lake. A year before the novelist's birth he laid out what was to be the village of Cooperstown, and two years later, when the child was thirteen months old, the family removed to their new home in the wilderness. It was from his father, apparently, that the novelist inherited what were called his aristocratic tastes—his admiration for the manners of a traditional society, and here in the quickly gathering frontier settlement those tastes were strangely fostered; for his father built a pretentious house, and made himself, with considerable success, as it were the lord of the manor, dispensing hospitality and exercising a superior influence, as became the first gentleman of that region. The son passed his childhood under the influence of such a home, and as far as he could know, under such traditions. It would seem fitting to him that the exiled Talleyrand should visit his father's house; it would be natural in later years for the famous novelist to feel at home in the undemocratic society of the Old World, to the great scandal of his fellow-countrymen.

At the same time the childhood in Cooperstown developed in him that love of democracy which seemed to his enemies, considering his conservative tastes, paradoxical if not insincere. The little settlement contained men of every nationality and condition, but alike adventurous and hardy, or they would not have been there at all. What more delicious paradise could the heart of boyhood conceive, than this fellowship, on the very border of the mysterious forests, with hunters and woodsmen and trappers! The necessary roughness of the life which from his earliest memory he saw outside his father's house, had its own charm for one who was by temperament a man of action, and it developed in him that true valuing of the elemental in human nature which makes the democrat. Together with his love of a patrician mode of life, such as the North could rarely boast in his time, went always this other love of sturdy manhood. This dual interest was paralleled in Scott's life: and had Cooper but enjoyed also Sir Walter's genius for showing brotherly love in gracious conduct, he might to-day be similarly honored in the memory of his own people.

It is perhaps to be regretted that there is no record of Cooper's boyhood beyond what little he himself told, and what can be inferred from his matured character and his books. Undoubtedly the subtlest and perhaps the strongest influence of those years was nature, as it lay about him. Those particular regions, that peculiarly American landscape, took hold of him in a way quite unmatched in our literature—perhaps new in modern literature. If we had the inner record of his childhood we might find that he was as reflective and poetical as the American novelists have characteristically been. He had a poet's eye for the outward world, unsupported by the romance of human interests, and therein he differed from Scott. Apart from the moving accident by flood and field, which is his theme, Cooper paints indelible memories of the shadowy forests, the infrequent clearings, the crystal lake, with the pines and the heavens clear in its bosom. The pictures contain no other mystery than their own beauty; Cooper was guilty of no French sentimentalism over a savage world, nor was he in the slightest degree, as critics have pointed out, a Wordsworthian. He looked on the wild panorama with the detachment of a Greek, but in place of the ancient awe he felt the love of nature. It was in these scenes of his boyhood that he laid his greatest stories, because, as he said, he loved no other scenes so well.

The village of Cooperstown boasted a school, and there the future novelist had his introduction to learning. But the advantages of frontier scholarship proved limited, and he was soon sent to Albany, as a private pupil of the rector of St. Peter's Church. In this gentleman's household he first came in contact with those contemptuous English opinions of Amer-

ica, which in mature life roused his anger against the mother
country; at the same time he learned from his English tutor
Old World ideals of an established society and a traditional
church, which fitted well with his patrician tastes. In 1802,
on the death of his teacher, he entered the class of 1806, in
Yale College. He was then thirteen years old. His residence
at Yale lasted somewhat over two years. What little instruction the college could impart in those days, he managed to
avoid, nor did he find an equivalent in the familiar resort of
wayward genius—wide general reading. He occupied his
active mind partly with the enjoyment of nature, and more
largely with mischief; as a natural result he was dismissed
from college.

It has often been observed, justly, that Cooper—and American literature—suffered severely from his lack of systematic
training. His was a nature that could have profited from
mental discipline, and the little he ever had was limited to his
days in the rectory of St. Peter's. He had no hobbies or
amusements, as Scott had, to take the place of academic
training; he was neither a historian nor an antiquarian,—he
was not even a great reader. And as if to complete his separation from books, that natural school for his future art, he was
sent to sea in 1806, on the *Sterling*, a merchant vessel bound
for England and Spain. The long voyage of a year gave him
his first acquaintance with that ocean world he was to picture
with unique skill, and in particular he was fascinated by the
storms, which were unusually numerous and violent during
his first trip.

This voyage had been intended as a preparation for his
entering the navy. Accordingly he was commissioned mid-
shipman on January 1, 1808, and entered active service seven
weeks later. Little is known accurately of his movements
during the next few years. Curiously enough his most important duties were assigned on those frontier waters which

could not have seemed strange to him after his boyhood on Otsego Lake; he was sent to Lake Ontario in 1808 to assist in building a brig of sixteen guns, to be used in a possible war against England. The great lake and its shores he later embodied in the scenery of *The Pathfinder*. The next year, 1809, he was for a short time in command of the gunboats on Lake Champlain. The following winter he was on the *Wasp*, commanded by Lawrence, the future hero of the *Chesapeake*. A year later, January 1, 1811, his naval career ended with his marriage to a Miss De Lancey, at Mamaroneck, Westchester County, New York. His resignation from the navy was accepted the following May.

The family into which he had married were originally of Huguenot stock. His bride's father had fought on the British side in the Revolutionary war, and the family home was in the aristocratic Tory section, within the influence of the British armies. Affection for his wife undoubtedly was the chief reason for Cooper's just treatment of the Tories in his novels, but perhaps some credit should be given to his natural sympathy in general with the stately society that had held with the crown. Whatever he may have thought of the Tories originally, it should be remembered that before *The Spy* was written he had lived in Westchester County for six years, the only time in his life that he was subjected to those combined influences of history and landscape that made Scott's romance; and his own life as a country gentleman perhaps brought back and explained to him the point of view of the aristocrats before the Revolution.

For a year or so after his marriage Cooper lived at his father-in-law's home. After a second year in a rented house near by, he returned to Cooperstown in 1814, began to build a large home, and evidently intended to duplicate, as gentleman proprietor of the estate, the honored history of his father, who had died in 1809. But as his wife was discontented with the frontier, he returned to Westchester in 1817, and settled in Scarsdale.

II

Here in 1820 Cooper began his literary career by the inspiration of the merest chance. Having read a contemporary English novel which seemed to him rather poor, with characteristic self-confidence he remarked that he could write as good a book himself. The boast was carried out, though whether the novel he read could have been worse than the one he wrote, is fairly debatable. This first venture, *Precaution*, is sometimes treated with seriousness as an index to Cooper's qualities both as a writer and as a man, and in the limited respect that anything a man does, even chopping wood, may indicate his character, the view is not untenable. But the circumstances of composition and the subject-matter of the book prevented Cooper from showing a single spark of his genius, and his own judgment of his 'prentice work is the correct one—that it was altogether unworthy. He afterward realized the error of choosing an English plot, laid in English scenes he had not visited, and in a society he knew only from other novels; if he chose such a subject, not only in imitation of the model he had promised to excel, but with the knowledge that a volume of dukes and earls would satisfy a vulgar public, it is easy to understand the trouble his conscience gave him when his friends said it would have been more patriotic to write of American life; it was the charge of disloyalty that he felt, rather than a distinct consciousness that his theme was not one for his peculiar genius. The English country life in *Precaution* might have been treated with Miss Austen's exquisite satire, or with Trollope's emotional vigor; but Cooper was neither exquisite nor a satirist, and he lacked entirely the reflective penetration to reach the emotional crises of conventional lives. In the novel the Moseleys and Chattertons and Ives are occupied with nothing more critical than gossip and prearranged marriages, with a suspicion of a villain threatening to enliven the story, and throughout the dialogue a display of far more worldly wisdom than the narrow lives of the speakers can permit them to test in practice. The book made no impression in America, but in England it was received with complacence, as it was supposed to be by a British author.

Among his other resemblances to Scott, Cooper had great tenacity of purpose, and he was too sincere a critic not to realize that he had fallen somewhat short of his boast; in addition, as has been said, he was troubled by the charge of literary disloyalty to his country. Accordingly he began another story at once, determined to atone for his shortcomings, and on December 22, 1821, *The Spy*, his first great novel, was published in New York. He tells the history of the book in the dignified preface to a later edition in 1849. He had heard the experiences of a revolutionary spy, the original of Harvey Birch, and when the English quality of *Precaution* became a reproach to him, and he had chosen patriotism for the theme of a second book, the subject of which, as he says, should admit of no cavil, the tale of the spy naturally came to mind, and expanded itself into the famous plot. So much intention and care there was in the preparation of the novel; but Cooper tells an anecdote of its composition which not only illustrates the hopes of an American author in the first part of the nineteenth century, but also indicates that his craftsmanship, like Scott's, was haphazard. The first volume of the novel was in print several months before a line of the second was written. "As the second volume was slowly printing, from manuscript that was barely dry when it went into the compositor's hands, the publisher intimated that it might grow to a length that would consume the profits. To set his mind at rest, the last chapter was actually written, printed, and paged several weeks before the chapters that precede it were even thought of."

Cooper began *Precaution* with the simple resolve to write a novel. He began *The Spy* with the same resolve; but it was of immense advantage that he built it upon a legend already in his mind. His was the genius of the true story-teller, to whom inspiration comes in the form of plot rather than as an idea. He would have been as puzzled as Homer himself at the doctrine of the modern novelist that character is plot. His genius comprehended few subtleties, but he had the rarest of gifts, the ability to unfold a tale that happens before our eyes, and which seems to have been true always. The difference between Cooper fumbling with the vague problem of writing an English novel of manners better than an Englishman, and Cooper with the true task of his genius, telling a story of adventure,—affords one of the astonishing contrasts of literary history. From such a germ of plot as he now had to start with, he could always draw a fable to hold men from the chimney-corner, as Hawthorne's thought could blossom from a symbol; but without such a germ of action Cooper's genius was crippled, in more novels than his first.

The Spy grows from the history of one who served the Colonies in the Revolution by pretending to be in the British service. None but Washington knew his true character, and the deception was so thorough that the American troops more than once caught him, and all but succeeded in hanging him. At the end of the war Congress learned of his faithfulness, and voted him a sum of money, but he refused all recompense, having suffered peril and ignominy out of pure love of country. The patriotism of the character is what first appealed to Cooper; it is interesting, however, to trace the story-teller's instinct as it enlarged on the original sketch. The refusal of a reward is made more remarkable by portraying Harvey Birch by nature or force of circumstances a miser. The fact that he is in mortal danger from the countrymen he is serving, comes home with more tragic force through the portrait of his dying father, whom Harvey's heroic disguise has brought to disgrace and a pauper's death-bed; his father's need also explains, in part at least, Harvey's greed for gold. He is an outcast for his patriotism, but by nature, as Cooper is careful to show, he loves home life and gentle society; and the pathos of his resolve to leave a dishonored name to no children of his own, is further set off with effective irony by Katy Haynes' wish to marry him—Katy being the person she is. All this misery which Cooper naturally imagined for his spy, he turns to fine account by portraying Harvey without a heroic trait, save his one master purpose, and even his patriotism has become through too prolonged suffering less a thing of passion than of duty; he has neither mental ability nor personal prowess, and were it not for his strong will, he would show himself a coward. The character illustrates at once what has been thought Cooper's most remarkable gift, a perfect blend of romance and realism. Harvey's dangers and escapes are not less thrilling than those of the more heroic Rob Roy, yet while the page is still before him the reader sees no legendary glamor over Harvey himself; so actual does he seem, with his limitations and virtues, that the novel has often been mistaken for biography. Harvey also illustrates, as does Leatherstocking, Cooper's felicity in fixing a story upon a definite region, literally giving it a local habitation. This was Irving's great fortune too; 1819, the year of *The Sketch Book*, and 1821, the year of *The Spy*, gave American landscape, except for the Leatherstocking Tales, the only well-known legends it owns to this day.

The individuality of Harvey Birch is greater because he has no parallel in Cooper's writings. It is not surprising that he is sometimes mentioned with Leatherstocking and Long Tom Coffin, for like them he is the ultra-romantic hero of the novel he appears in, and like them is set apart from the surrounding characters in a peculiar isolation, more marked than the somewhat similar distinction of Rob Roy or Robin Hood. But in detail he has nothing in common with any of these heroes,—principally, as has been said, because he is in the personal sense not a hero at all. And he has none of the philosophy, the zest in life, the self-completeness, that are cardinal traits in Natty Bumppo and Long Tom. They have outward experiences, adventures of life and death, but they come before the reader with their minds from the beginning in the peace of an un-Byronic stoicism; Harvey Birch's sufferings are more of the mind than of the body, and his adventures have always the double interest of an outward and inward conflict. And whereas the isolation of Leatherstocking and Long Tom seems all-sufficient, as though they could have neither forefathers nor descendants, Harvey's loneliness is inherited from his race, in some inequality of power to aspiration; his dying father saw within the son that which would make him a pilgrim through life, and seemed to recognize it as the extension of his own destiny.

Whatever was his courage when he undertook his desperate career, Harvey shows little bravery after he has become a hunted outlaw. He is almost a coward, if the name cowardice can describe dread of a traitor's death, made terribly real on many a page. Indeed, the fear of hanging is a main theme in the story—in Major André's fate, and in the adventures of Captain Wharton, of Harvey, and of the miserable Skinner. The hanging of the Skinner, powerfully described in the last pages of the book, not only gets rid of the villain, but justifies in Captain Wharton and Harvey the fear of death, which the frequent escapes and rescues had made seem somewhat vague and unreal. With the terrible fascination of the Skinner's death Harvey's cowardice is, as it were, expiated. When he dies honorably on the field of battle in the War of 1812, his better self, his patriotism, has become a kind of mania, and with this passion blends a jealous pride in Washington's exoneration of his character. For the conventional conclusions of that curiously written last chapter Cooper might make apologies, but he was always singularly happy in imagining the old age of his best characters, and the convincing fitness of Harvey Birch's end could not be bettered.

The Spy is usually reckoned among historical novels, though strictly speaking there is no history in it. As a novelist Cooper has little interest in history for its own sake, nor for the elevation of the plot by testing the fictitious characters in the crucible of great historic crises. Those aspects of history which in the novel have to do with panorama, and, strangely enough, with action, Cooper usually neglects; though his genius is for the story of adventure, he had neither the interest in the past nor the scholarship to include a series of actual events in his romance. He goes to history only for the picturesque setting of past time. So in *The Spy*, though much that is told might have happened, and though the whole book has the air of history, none of it is historical in the same sense as the great episodes in *Kenilworth* or *The Abbot*. But Cooper had a genuine gift for historical portraiture. In *The Spy* he presented that picture of Washington which has seemed most authentic to the popular imagination. The benevolence and aristocratic reserve which distinguish the great patriot in tradition are here set forth with the conviction Cooper always gives to the characters he cares for; and if he himself showed in his later career a lack of tact and manner, he might vindicate his breeding by this picture, as fine a conception of gentleman as Thackeray himself could give.

The women in *The Spy* are on the whole as well imagined as any in Cooper's writing, and—with the forbearance of Professor Lounsbury and other severe critics of Cooper's "females,"—this is no slight praise. At their worst Cooper's heroines are unspeakable, but at their best they need no apologies. In this novel the objection of sentimentality or over-propriety is removed by the naturalness of the plot, which accounts satisfactorily for the traits in the ladies' characters that might otherwise seem excessive. Miss Jeanette Peyton, the mouthpiece of that social correctness from which no Cooper heroine ever escapes, is more acceptable because she cherishes her own dignified romance, and because Mr. Wharton, the head of the house, himself stands in no less dread of the proprieties; her character is made natural by the modes of thought about her. Sarah Wharton, the older niece, resembles her aunt so strongly that her idealization of Colonel Wellmere and the dignity with which she bears her disappointment are easily understood. The generous spirit of Frances shows her resemblance to her brother; she is as impulsive, as true, and as proud as he; it is to her, though she sides with the continentals, that he naturally turns, rather than to Sarah, who like him is loyal to the King. As the elder Wharton helps to explain Miss Peyton's character, so the son interprets the devotion of Frances to Dunwoodie; otherwise their love story might have been a mawkish affair, as they were betrothed at the very beginning of the book. Like Scott, Cooper tells no love story for its own sake, and generally he leaves it in the background, as a graceful incident, when time serves. But in *The Spy* the relation of Frances and Dunwoodie becomes vitally important, when Captain Wharton is captured as a spy by his future brother-in-law; whatever sentimentality there is in the situation is lost in the melodramatic interest. Miss Singleton stands somewhat apart from the story, the pathetic victim of love and fate; it is from her that modern sympathy has been furthest withdrawn by the changing fashions of thought; in the sentimental vogue which lasted well into Mrs. Stowe's work, she is the typical victim of life, beautiful and innocent, and cherishing a secret passion. Of course she must die prematurely, not only because that is the fate of the type, but because she is somewhat in the way. Her death by the bullet of the Skinner who is shooting at Lawton, makes it possible to hang the Skinner later with the reader's cordial approval. The thorough contrivance of the plot is further made clear by a comparison of Mrs. Stowe's summary method of disposing of her condemned heroines, Eva or Nina or Mara, with Cooper's careful preparation which makes perfectly natural the Skinner's attempt to kill Lawton and his accidental killing of Miss Singleton.

Maria Edgeworth praised the character of the Irish woman, Betty Flanagan, saying that the portrait could not have been bettered by an Irish writer. She is one of the best minor characters Cooper created, for he developed later a tendency to slight the unimportant persons in his narrative, unless he had a special interest in them. In this instance he imagined a genuinely funny character, and humor, as his hastiest reader knows, is not usually his strength.

Dr. Sitgreaves, the surgeon, belongs to a type Cooper must have loved, for they are represented in almost every novel. Some of the novelist's critics call the whole series "bores," using the word for both classification and description. It would be fairer to call them pedants, for invariably their infirmity is absorption in some department of knowledge. Dr. Sitgreaves inclines to the tedious when he continues to plead with Lawton for a more scientific sabering of the enemy; aside from this Dickens-like tag of his personality he is less unattractive than most of the type, and his humor, though unconscious, is not slight.

Well-made as is the plot of *The Spy*, and convincing as the characters are, the book leaves a strong final impression of two other qualities—the distinctness of the scene, and the rapid movements within it. It is remarkable that the plan of the fight, for example, should be so easily comprehended, considering the confusion of the field; not less distinct to the mind is the location of Wharton's last prison and the secret hut on the mountain. And the distinctness of the scene is not interfered with by the rapid movements of the soldiers and the Spy and the Skinners, nor by the two splendid chases that for some of us were the most exciting reading of our boyhood. Only an opulent genius could have described two such pursuits under circumstances so nearly identical; but whenever the situation involves rapid physical motion, Cooper has no superior in English, perhaps in any literature. His boy readers learn to look for the race or pursuit in every novel, knowing it will probably be the best moment of the story.

Cooper's fame is so linked with the Leatherstocking Tales that it is natural to look upon *The Spy* as a sort of practice piece for his more typical work. In comparison with that unique series it undoubtedly suffers, simply because it belongs in a well-filled compartment of the novel, and many of its fellows in the class are world masterpieces. But among the historical novels of adventure it takes a high place,—quite the highest place among American historical novels. Its popularity has been continued, as it was immediate. It was the first American novel to win the respect of the generally contemptuous English critics, and the American press, which had liked the book by instinct, was pleased with the mild praise, as though it were a national tribute. It would not have been surprising if the subject of the story had prejudiced English readers in those years of wounded feelings. After some difficulty an English publisher was found, in the man who had brought out *The Sketch Book*. In 1822 *The Spy* was translated into French, and afterward into most of the other European languages. Cooper had accomplished his purpose; he had written a novel on the theme of American patriotism, with American scenes and American characters, and with the minimum obligation to the old country that a man of culture

could owe; and the book had been welcomed by the civilized
world.

III

The reception of *The Spy* naturally gave Cooper confidence
in his powers, yet he began his next story with no false hopes;
he did not realize as yet what was his natural vein, and his
attitude toward his art was still experimental. His success,
however, had given him a certain right to choose his subject
without regard to the feelings of others, and having celebrated
his country in general, he decided to describe the scenes of his
childhood. The resolve was made out of pure love of Cooperstown and the lake, for he was too good a critic not to foresee,
as he says, that elaborate descriptions such as he purposed
would endanger the narrative interest. When *The Pioneers*
was published, in 1823, the eagerness with which it was
awaited and welcomed gave proof of the genuine success of
The Spy, and of virtue in the new story more than the author
had dared to hope. He had written it, as he declared in a
somewhat pugnacious preface, to please himself; but the
thirty-five hundred copies disposed of in the first half-day's
sale indicated that the public had not quarreled with his taste.

The Pioneers stands fourth in the complete cycle of the
Leatherstocking Tales, but being actually written first, it
has an added interest as illustrating the growth of his great
frontier characters in Cooper's mind. The scenery and the
general society of the novel were transcripts from his boyhood memories; the home of Marmaduke Templeton seems
to have been a less accurate reproduction of his father's house.
From this first novel as a document of his own life he later expanded and elaborated the Leatherstocking series, much as
he had evolved Harvey Birch from the anecdote of a Revolutionary spy. It is little to be wondered at, therefore, that *The
Pioneers* is in general far more crude than the later refine-

ments upon it; but it has singular merits, too often unrecognized. Cooper's realism is severely tested by this theme; the author who wished to set his country honorably before foreign readers, who wished to immortalize the home he loved best, might have found pardon for some rose-tinted exaggeration. But the story presents the unsoftened outlines of the new settlement, its pretensions to architecture and ceremony, the ignorance and recklessness of its inhabitants, the democratic confusion of its society. Cooper's Americanism, loyal as it was, never blinded him to the faults unavoidable in so new a country, and no later writer has portrayed with more merciless severity the meddlesome, officious sheriff, the quack physician who learns his profession by observing the results of his practice, the disreputable lawyer, and the incompetent builder. No single figure in the story escapes altogether the suspicion and pity inherent in such thorough realism; even Leatherstocking is here somewhat vulgar and narrow-brained, with none of the philosophy and dignity he exhibits in *The Deerslayer* or *The Prairie*. All the adventurous spirits that hold this outpost of civilization have some blight upon them, so that the reader half questions whether Cooper considers them social explorers or derelicts. Even the amusing Betty Flanagan, who lives on from *The Spy* as the wife of Sergeant Hollister, and who keeps the Bold Dragoon Inn, named in memory of Captain Lawton, is more canny and less impulsive than in her Revolutionary days.

Cooper described this society with such realism because he knew it perfectly; it may be doubted if he ever knew any other society so well. It was the school in which his youthful mind had learned democracy, and perhaps he owed to it, with good reason, the disillusioned suspicion of human nature which colors both his works and his life, and which has been charged against Americans as a national trait. It was not to such a community no matter what its good qualities, that the poetry in Cooper's temperament responded, but to the charm of the wilderness which the community had invaded. A settlement like Cooperstown represented to him, as to any good citizen, a necessary intermediate condition between the savage life of the forest and the civilized life of culture; but however much he approved of the end, his heart went back to the unspoiled woods.   Apparently this was his interest in nature from his boyhood; his earliest dreams must have been of such panoramas as Marmaduke Temple beheld when he first came to his uncleared estate.   The point is worth dwelling on; for the attraction of the Leatherstocking Tales is largely in the idealization of the disappearing wilderness, the pathos, as the old hunter felt, of the clearings and "improvements," of the wasted timber and slaughtered game.   Cooper reserves his realism for human nature; the poet in him delights in the woods and streams.   Because Leatherstocking and Indian John in this first novel were connected with this saddened romance of nature, they were transfigured in the popular imagination with all the poetry that Cooper, learning by the popular hint, later bestowed upon them.

Cooper's next story, like *The Spy*, took its inspiration from a random motive.   Before the publication of *The Pioneers* he had attended a dinner at which the authorship of *The Pirate*, Scott's latest novel, was discussed.   A gentleman present contended that Scott could not have written it, since he did not possess a knowledge of seamanship so minute as it showed. Cooper's naval experience led him to observe at once that *The Pirate* showed very little knowledge of seamanship on the part of its author, and that therefore Scott might well have written it.   Cooper did not convince his hearers, but the discussion directed his own thoughts to the ocean as an unworked realm of romance.   He acted upon the idea with characteristic energy, and *The Pilot*, the first great sea story, appeared in 1824.   It bore the date of the preceding year, but its publication had been delayed by the death of the author's son, Fenimore.

The Pilot is a tale of adventure at sea, but it also develops the theme of patriotism begun in *The Spy*, and to the same extent as *The Spy* it is an historical novel. It records no event of history, but it imagines the historical atmosphere, as the earlier novel had done, and it portrays one authentic person, Paul Jones, as *The Spy* had included a portrait of Washington. The materials of the story lent themselves to the most thoroughgoing romance,—the achievements of the American navy were among the country's proudest legends; the personality of Paul Jones was as mysteriously adventurous as the ocean itself; and the cause of liberty, ennobling the story above any other sea tale, identified itself poetically with the freedom of the great waters. The ocean also made possible more exciting chases than the land, and Cooper's genius for that kind of episode is at its best in the escape of the frigate from the shoals, and its battle with the English three-decker. In these manœuvers Cooper was exploiting the seamanship which *The Pirate* lacked, but no reader would suspect any other interest than the adventure itself, the genuineness of the excitement is so little interfered with by the technical purpose.

Scott had represented the ocean from the landsman's point of view, as a thing of terror. In reproducing the sailor's world Cooper had to show the preference for the deep sea and the actual fear of the coast. By laying his plot off the shores of Scotland he is enabled to bring his heroines naturally into the story, and what is more essential, he can introduce almost the only danger that belongs peculiarly to the water. The first scene of the story makes the reader fearful for the strange vessels so near the coast; the peril is brought home by the frigate's narrow escape from the rocks; and the wreck of the *Ariel,*—a scene of unusual energy and grandeur, even for

Cooper,—completes the tragedy, and by implication, gives the measure of the pilot's skill in saving the larger vessel. And in the portrayal of such moments of danger the author found opportunity to put the seaman's point of view into picturesque phrase, as in the conversation between Barnstable and Long Tom Coffin, under the cliff: "This is just such a place as one of your sighing lovers would dote on; a little land, a little water, and a good deal of rock. Damme, Long Tom, but I am more than half of your mind, that an island now and then is all the *terra firma* that a seaman needs."

"It's reason and philosophy, sir," returned the sedate cockswain; "and what land there is should always be a soft mud, or a sandy ooze, in order that an anchor might hold, and to make soundings sartin."

By laying the plot of his sea story near land Cooper has an additional advantage in the resulting complication of the incidents. The excitement of the storms and the fights would hardly sustain the interest through a whole novel, and the best episodes of *The Pilot* are occasioned by the movements on land. The treachery of Dillon leads to practically all the adventures except the first escape of the frigate from the shoals; he sends the expresses by land which bring the gunshot from the fort, fatally maiming the *Ariel*, and which summon the English fleet for the last battle with the frigate; and his recapture by Long Tom, under the very eyes of the Abbey guard, is not the least sensational adventure in the story.

The character that gives the book its title differs strongly from any Cooper had yet drawn, though it is repeated with variations in his later sea tales. Paul Jones, as Cooper imagines him, is no such idealization of romance as Leatherstocking, nor such a hero as he is in popular memory. Cooper represents him as an adventurer, whose remarkable ability for the time was used for the cause of liberty, but whose motives were not altogether noble; vanity weighs with him more than patriotism, of which indeed he has none, since he owns no country, and he would serve a flattering tyrant as quickly as he would the Continental Congress. It is surprising that Cooper can make so much of a hero he has so little sympathy for; in the comments of Barnstable, and in the meetings of Paul Jones and Alice Dunscombe, it is perfectly evident that the Scotch fighter did not meet the author's measure of a great man. As a character, the pilot is most effective on the first reading of the story, while the mystery in which he delights gives its own interest; on a second or third reading he becomes a little tiresome. Except at sea, and then only in moments of extreme peril, he is hardly a man of action; he seems paralyzed by some hidden griefs, that remain hidden, and at times his behavior is childish if not unbalanced, as when he gives incorrect and unintelligible answers to Boltrope's hail, on approaching the *Alacrity*, and then boards the cutter with a "proud and angry eye," because he has not been recognized. What saves him to the sympathy of the reader is the efficiency he does show in moments of extreme peril, and the private romance that dignifies and excuses his foibles by its unmistakable note of tragedy. His skill is employed not for his own profit, nor even for his fame; and when Griffith and Barnstable carry off their rescued loves to the frigate, the pilot loses Alice forever.

A large part of his behavior might be called Byronic, since it appears to be learned in the general school of the Giaour and the Corsair. For the most part Cooper is too healthy minded to be influenced by the more mawkish currents of Byronism, but here, as in *The Red Rover*, the secret past of the chief figure pursues him like a fury, and especially induces moods of irrelevant abstraction just when a clear, decided mind is needed. The pilot has a way of folding his arms and gazing into space at the precise moment when the captain or some other officer has asked for the instructions that are to save or lose the ship. And these theatrical attitudes come so often that it is easy to understand his slight popularity with the crew. It is hard to see why Cooper so represented Paul Jones, as he shows clearly, in the disgust of Griffith and Barnstable for such sentimentalism, that he knows how the average man would criticize the pilot. Yet the trait is unmistakable, even exaggerated. When the frigate was in the shoals and the captain suggested heaving the lead, Paul Jones' "head rested on his hand as he leaned over the hammock-cloth of the vessel, and his whole air was that of one whose thoughts wandered from the pressing necessities of their situation. Griffith was among those who had approached the pilot; and after waiting a moment, from respect, to hear the answer to his commander's question, he presumed on his own rank, and leaving the circle that stood at a little distance, stepped to the side of the mysterious guardian of their lives.

"' Captain Munson desires to know whether you wish a cast of the lead?' said the young officer, with a little impatience of manner. No immediate answer was made to this repetition of the question, and Griffith laid his hand unceremoniously on the shoulder of the other, with an intent to rouse him before he made another application for a reply, but the convulsive start of the pilot held him silent in amazement.

*   *   *   *   *   *   *   *

"' This is not a time for musing, Mr. Gray,' continued Griffith; ' remember our compact, and look to your charge— is it not time to put the vessel in stays? Of what are you dreaming?'

"The pilot laid his hand on the extended arm of the lieutenant, and grasped it with a convulsive pressure, as he answered:

"' 'Tis a dream of reality. You are young, Mr. Griffith, nor am I past the noon of life; but, should you live fifty years longer, you can never see and experience what I have encountered in my little period of three-and-thirty years!'"

The contrast to the pilot is found in Long Tom Coffin, the

only character in Cooper's work that can be ranked near
Leatherstocking or Harvey Birch. He is the creature of the
same aspects of Cooper's genius, showing the same qualities
of truthfulness, picturesqueness and self-reliance. The spy's
pack and the hunter's rifle, the labels of their individuality,
are matched by Long Tom's harpoon and his cannon, and he
is localized to the imagination in the *Ariel*, as the other heroes
are fixed in the landscape. For all that, Long Tom differs
from both Harvey Birch and Leatherstocking. He represents no tragic sacrifice, like the first, nor any of the pathos
of advancing civilization, like the second. Strongly individu-
alized, he yet suggests a class, as Birch and Leatherstocking
do not. He is proud of his Nantucket ancestry and of his
Nantucket comrades, and is careful himself to say that their
skill is greater than his. The mention of the old mother for
whom he provides a comfortable home, gives him a place at
once in normal society. Cooper represents in him the highly
developed resourcefulness and the equally marked idiosyn-
cracy to be found in a crude society,—and, for the same reasons, in the American navy during the Revolution. It is evident, however, that Long Tom would be out of place on the
frigate; he belongs with the little schooner, on which discipline is apparently superseded by the efficiency of individuals,
and his death in the wreck is most fitting. He is no wizard
of the sea, like the mysterious pilot; his force is from his character,—his simplicity and his loyalty. By these two qualities
he is ennobled to a poetic degree, chivalrous in his rough way
to womanhood, and terrible to his foes. He alone in the story
belongs entirely to the sea. He therefore satisfies the imagination more than Paul Jones and is more clearly remembered;
he is the true hero of the book.

The nautical realism of *The Pilot* has been practically un-
questioned. Cooper tried some of the early pages,—the description of the frigate in the gale,—on a professional sailor,

who visualized the episode so sincerely that he said the jib
would not stand so long in such a wind. Cooper took the advice and blew the sail out of the bolt-rope. But the story has
great realistic force in directions that the untechnical landsman can appreciate. A genuine atmosphere of physical danger is sustained at a higher pitch, with fewer moments of
relief, than elsewhere in Cooper, who is the master of such
effect. Yet the climaxes of terror are both adequate and in
good taste. The abject cowardice of Dillon, and his death,
are matched as mental pictures by the physical horror of the
English captain's fate, harpooned to the mast. The good
taste which restrains these portrayals, by a master-touch of
art left Long Tom's last moments entirely to the imagination.

Cooper wrote other sea tales, some of them admirable, but
the only one that at all approaches *The Pilot* in merit or fame
is *The Red Rover*, published in 1828. Its plot is laid entirely
at sea, the land serving only as a place to start from and end
on. The immediate result is the necessary elimination of all
land manœuvers and of those coast dangers that stiffened the
plot of *The Pilot*. Since the story is not historical, the theme
of patriotism is almost debarred, though Cooper by a loyal
effort inserts a flavor of it. The interest is in pure adventure.
The Red Rover, a Byronic corsair of superhuman adroitness,
inexplicable moods, and detached virtues, is strangely drawn
to a young American, a disguised officer of the British navy,
who is at the moment plotting to deliver the pirate to justice.
The unsuspecting Red Rover takes the officer into his confidence, and to further his piratical purposes, puts him in
charge of a merchant vessel just leaving port. On this vessel
there are two ladies, with the younger of whom the officer is
in love. The conflict of so many demands upon his honor
bids fair to make this lover, rather than the pirate, the hero
of the book, but a balance is struck by the Red Rover's skill
in capturing his prey and defeating an English man-of-war,

and by his magnanimous treatment of the prisoners. His surprising forbearance is due to a wholesale "discovery" of relationships between himself and the ladies and the young officer, such as quite equals the most optimistic "recognitions" of the old drama. His career is saved to patriotism by the statement that it was the scorn heaped on him in the British navy for his American birth that made him a pirate. As a proof of his personal lovableness he is attended by a Byronic mistress, disguised as a boy.

Cooper tells his story with so much singleness of impression that *The Red Rover*, as a whole, has been ranked higher than *The Pilot*, though the excellence of that story in its separate scenes is undisputed. It is only by esoteric standards, however, that *The Red Rover* can be considered by the side of the masterpiece. The number of available incidents in a deep-sea story is so few—limited practically to storms, mutinies, fire and battle—that Cooper actually repeats one device, the carrying away of the masts, to account for the capture of both ships,—though a single experience would have taught the American officer caution. The device at the beginning of the story, by which the officer is put in charge of the merchant vessel five minutes before she sails, is too impossible even for a pirate story, and the Rover's skill and influence border on or overlap the miraculous; the reader sees none of the steps by which the evolutions of the pirate ship are accomplished, nor is any convincing cause assigned for the Rover's hold on his men. Yet the plot favored Cooper's genius in the opportunity for long pursuits and for storms, and here the interest rises to a high pitch. The Red Rover's vessel is a second version of the *Ariel*, miraculously speedy and graceful. Cooper's keen love of sea things makes the boat attractive, though independently of the story; no human interest adds to her charm, as Long Tom's presence enriched the *Ariel*.

IV

It was Cooper's intention to write a cycle of romances dealing with the colonies in the Revolutionary War. The first and last of these *Legends of the Thirteen Republics* was *Lionel Lincoln, or the Leaguer of Boston*, published in 1825. The careful preparation of this novel has been contrasted with the desultory composition of *The Spy*. Although the same ardor of patriotism inspired Cooper in this new historical novel, the consciousness of faults and of the lack of sound history in his first success persuaded him to more accurate researches for the background of *Lionel Lincoln*. But the result was most unfortunate. That the book was not an entire failure was due to his general popularity at the moment. The disappointment must have been great to the author, who had done what care could to insure its worth. The historical scenes—the fights at Concord and Lexington and Bunker Hill—have received the praise of qualified critics, and still are interesting. The main plot, however, an extremely complicated domestic intrigue, not only is ineffective in itself, but it has no necessary connection with the history. The average reader would find little in the book to suggest Cooper's familiar qualities; it is the more unfortunate, since the historical background is elaborated with such unusual truth and effect.

Cooper's next story, *The Last of the Mohicans*, 1826, came into a fame so immediate and permanent that the failure of *Lionel Lincoln* and that novel itself were speedily forgotten. In 1824, while on a visit to Glens Falls, he had his attention called to the caverns in the river as a suitable location for a romance. From this hint grew the famous episode of the fight on the island, and the rest of the exciting story. If *The Pioneers* gave Cooper a footing in his peculiar realm, *The Last of the Mohicans* established his sovereignty for all time.

Here Leatherstocking, or Hawkeye, appears in his prime, with his distinct traits well developed; and the Indians fill the story with that fascination, which, according to some critics, is more of romance than of reality.

Of all the Leatherstocking Tales, this, the second in the final series, can most easily stand by itself; yet something must have been gained for its initial success by the public's acquaintance with the hunter and his Indian comrade in *The Pioneers*. Like Cooper's other masterpieces, *The Last of the Mohicans* has serious faults, or rather improbabilities, of construction; it has been easy to point out the folly of summoning the heroines to a fort about to be captured, and no good reason is given for sending them by an unknown and dangerous route, when they could have had the escort of the regiments. The woodcraft of this story has been an amusing target for Mark Twain's criticism. But none of these questions touch the book's real power, which lies in its wealth of adventure. The rapidity of the incidents has been justly called breathless. And the adventure takes place in an atmosphere of true poetry, an unsuspected source of delight to many an uncritical reader.

The plot divides into two sections. The first gives the adventures of Heyward, the sisters, and their guides on the perilous journey to Fort William Henry. The second deals with the pursuit of Le Renard Subtil and his captives after the massacre. With the exception, therefore, of the brief pause in the doomed fort, the novel tells of a race or pursuit—that type of adventure Cooper excelled in; and along the chase the interest is furnished by the woodcraft of Hawkeye and the Indians. This latter element gives the tale its attraction to boy readers, as the character of Leatherstocking is its charm for older people; there are so many other veins of interest, however,—in the story of Cora and her Indian admirers, in the portrait of Montcalm and the historical element generally, and in the unusual description of landscape,—that the novel is fairly sure of its readers among all types of mind.

The *Last of the Mohicans* is the only one of the Leather-stocking Tales devoted especially to the Indians. Though Hawkeye dominates the story by the more general interest of his character, it was evidently Cooper's chief intention to picture the Indian and his customs, his peculiar strategy, his faults and his code of honor. Chingachgook and his son Uncas are idealized within the limits permissible to any heroes of romance, yet the portrait concedes so much to actual Indian character that Parkman's well-known objection to their unnatural virtues has been almost entirely discarded by later critical judgment. All that Cooper can fairly attribute to Indian nature he bestows upon the chieftain and his son; they, rather than Hawkeye, know the woods, and the hunter defers to their superior skill on all occasions. Their ideals of courtesy, which more than anything else, perhaps, make incredible the chivalry of the Mohicans, are probably not overdrawn, if we are to believe modern champions of the red man. And it should be said for the credit of Cooper's subtlety, a quality rarely attributed to him, that he has here treated the ominous theme of race-conflict with more absolute fineness than any other American writer. Hawkeye draws a careful line between the Indian's "gifts" and the white man's; from his philosophical standpoint the murder of the French sentinel is inevitable, since the Mohican is what he is,—yet he does not approve the treachery, nor does the reader. At no time in the story does Cooper allow the reader's sympathy to go out unreservedly to any Indian, even to Uncas. The red man, whether Mohican or Huron, is represented as of a race that cannot share the white man's ideals, and is therefore doomed. It has been pointed out that Le Renard Subtil and Uncas fall in love with Cora because she has negro blood; that significant touch marks the barrier between Uncas and all his civilized admirers. Had he declared his passion, Cora would probably have rejected him with pity, but with little less horror than she felt for Le Renard Subtil. Cooper does the Indians justice; a little reflection shows that he has not neglected their savage traits, even in Uncas, who he confesses frankly is a romantic ideal.

Hawkeye is here a much nobler figure than the old hunter of the settlement. He exhibits at its best that philosophy, mingled fatalism and optimism, which is inseparable now from his memory. He shows no surliness nor discontent, as in *The Pioneers*. In fact, the only important trait common to both books is his miraculous skill with the rifle. But what raises him to heroic proportions in this story is his love for Uncas, a master passion that quite exceeds his faithful friendship with Chingachgook. With Uncas dies the hope of the Indian race, and the cause of his death is his hopeless worship of the white girl. With him dies also the only social tie that could have bound Hawkeye to any society; for Uncas, as he so often says, is almost his own son. As Uncas is enlisted in Cora's service by his love for her, so the scout follows, more for the youth's sake than for any other reason, and few passages in romance record more perfect chivalry than Hawkeye's return to the Huron camp to die with Uncas,—or his offer to give his life to Le Renard in exchange for Cora—an offer that had in mind the happiness of Uncas as well as of the girl.

The pedant that Cooper likes to introduce into these stories is in this case a strangely effective figure. In David Gamut, the singing teacher, Cooper produces a travesty on the New England character that in certain picturesque details of physique and horsemanship recalls Ichabod Crane. Neither of the two great New York writers had much insight into the Yankee nature; perhaps it is natural that they should treat it with most tenderness in their most exaggerated burlesques of it; it is natural to make amends with a little sympathy, in the midst of so much ridicule. David Gamut is an admirable foil for Hawkeye, whose contempt for the pitch-pipe, "that useless we'pon," at first blinds him to the singer's few and simple virtues. But in scenes of danger a constantly strengthened impulse to take up real arms and fight, at last wins the scout's respect. Gamut also brings out in both the Mohicans and the Hurons the Indian reverence for the mentally infirm, and Hawkeye himself is not unawed by the singer's phraseology and his rhapsodies. A large share of the romance of the story settles about this uncouth figure as he stands in the massacre at Fort William Henry, actually protecting Cora and Alice by his song.

" ' If the Jewish boy might tame the evil spirit of Saul by the sound of his harp, and the words of sacred song, it may not be amiss,' he said, 'to try the potency of music here.'

"Then raising his voice to its highest tones, he poured out a strain so powerful as to be heard even amid the din of that bloody field. More than one savage rushed towards them, thinking to rifle the unprotected sisters of their attire and bear away their scalps; but when they found this strange and unmoved figure riveted to his post, they paused to listen. Astonishment soon changed to admiration, and they passed on to other and less courageous victims, openly expressing their satisfaction at the firmness with which the white warrior sang his death song."

It would have been hard to improve on the portraits of Munro, the English commander, and Montcalm. The first is largely a fictitious person, elaborated according to the needs of the plot and Cooper's idea of the British soldier of the period. The conflict in his heart between his duties as commander and his love for his daughter gives him a place of dignity in the romance, which otherwise, in view of his defeat and his helplessness, he could hardly hold. As a soldier he is of course brave, but not astute; Cooper lets him stand for the usual British incapacity to cope with the Indians, which Braddock so fatally illustrated. Only such a man would have summoned his daughters to the besieged fort, or would have neglected to insist on Montcalm's promised escort. In sharp contrast is the portrait of the Frenchman,— a beautiful conception of old-world grace and courtliness, which Cooper must have drawn with affection. Yet with all Montcalm's adroitness, his management of the Indians and his tact in treating with a conquered foe,—the reader is made to feel the moral slipperiness which the hearty Englishman resents with a national distrust of French traditional perfidy. The trait is not too strong, however, for the charm of the character, and Cooper, with the reserve of a good historian as well as artist, pronounces no final judgment on Montcalm's conduct.

The massacre, the historical point about which the romance revolves, has natural opportunities for picturesqueness, almost for pageantry in Scott's vein. But the bent of Cooper's genius for actual rather than for imagined scenes is illustrated by the superiority of such pictures as he could remember from his visits to Lake Champlain, over even the description of the massacre. The ruins of the fort, revisited by the scout and his party, are truer to the mind than Heyward's first glimpse of the stronghold. So also the adventure in the old burying-ground and the encounter with the unfortunate French sentinel by the bloody pond,—such pictures as the imagination would build upon actual sight of those places,— belong not to history at all, but to poetry and romance. In these two latter scenes, as in most of the night descriptions, the landscape becomes an element of great power, almost an actor in the story. Cooper is nearer here than anywhere else to the classical awe of nature, or the Wordsworthian sense of its personality. At such moments he is most the poet; he makes the dim moonlit forest seem to close in upon the human adventure and supplant it; had his temperament been less sane, so much susceptibility would have endowed the northern pinewoods with sylvan deities out of hand.

V

In 1822 Cooper had left Scarsdale and taken up his residence in New York, that he might be near the literary world. The first years of his success had brought many changes in his family and his affairs. His mother was dead, and his older son, Fenimore, had died in 1823. The next year his second son, Paul, the last of his children, was born. There were also four daughters living, and one had died in infancy. His father's estate, through various causes, had depreciated until its value was too little to provide comfortably for the novelist. The returns from the stories, however, had placed Cooper in a secure financial position. Just what his profits were is not known, but with such popularity as he enjoyed, they must have been great. Had he been able to control by copyright the sales in foreign countries, his income would have been enormous; for as fast as they were written the novels were published in thirty-four different places in Europe, and were on sale in every European bookshop. It is not known, however, what arrangements Cooper made even with his American publishers; he resembled Scott in the ability to keep his secrets. He brought out *The Spy* at his own expense, since no one else would run the risk, and his share in the returns of that book at least must have been large.

It was natural for a person of his mental energy to turn his thoughts to travel on the first opportunity. His naval experience had afforded him little knowledge of England and less of the Continent, and his devotion to his family, a distinguishing trait, for some time prevented him from going abroad alone. On June 1, 1826, he sailed for Europe with his household, family and servants, intending to remain away

for five years; he did not return, however, till November, 1833.
These years of travel were of the deepest influence upon his
later career, providing him with material for those criticisms
of the old world and the new, which he made with so much
more vigor than tact, and which accordingly brought him
into general dislike. Even before he sailed he had laid a few
lasting foundations for unpopularity. His sudden rise excited the envy of the small fry of letters, and his peculiar sensitiveness to adverse criticism served to encourage rather than
suppress attacks upon him. The original preface to *The
Pioneers* had referred to the race of critics in a passage which
illustrates his strange facility in making enemies: "I should
think criticism to be the perfection of human acquirements,
did there not exist this discrepancy in taste. Just as I have
made up my mind to adopt the very sagacious hints of one
learned Reviewer, a pamphlet is put into my hands containing the remarks of another, who condemns all that his rival
praises, and praises all that his rival condemns. There I
am, left like an ass between two locks of hay; so that I have
determined to relinquish my animate nature, and remain
stationary, like a lock of hay between two asses." For the
time, however, this sharp challenge produced no uncomfort-
able effect for Cooper; his greatness as an author was a matter
of pride to his countrymen, and before he sailed for Europe a
literary club founded by himself gave him a dinner in New
York, at which Chancellor Kent, DeWitt Clinton and other
notable guests bore testimony to the esteem in which he was
held. That occasion practically ended the purely literary
part of his career,—the happiest part.

His time abroad was passed in France, Italy, Switzerland
and Germany, but chiefly in France. The generous admiration of his genius which the French showed from the first, of
itself would have made his stay among them pleasant, but he
was still more attracted by the courtesy and grace of their

national character, and especially by the polished life of Paris. If the French admired him as a sort of romantic expert in savagery, he found in their capital the aristocratic exquisiteness of breeding that had always been his social ideal, though his own manners may not have realized it. For the two years following 1826 he was consul at Lyons, but the post added little to his knowledge of the French, or to his literary equipment. Though he made his longest stay in France, Cooper, like all American men of letters since, lost his heart completely to Italy. It is perhaps proof of the poet in him, that his devotion was so entire to a country that then had so few of the institutions which appeal to an ardent democrat.

Cooper's stay in England was very short, but unfortunately it was long enough to make him unduly sensitive to insular ignorance and prejudice, and to start him on the campaign of controversy which was the curse of his later life. Among the most cultured Englishmen he found a cordial reception, or at least a sincere intention of it; but the English attitude at that moment toward America and Americans was so condescending, as Cooper knew in advance, that it would have required more than British tact to keep his temper unruffled. He came to England on his travels with a love of his own country and a resentment of English injustice that must have been quite unparalleled, even in years of angry feeling. On his first voyage, in 1806, two American-born comrades had been seized and pressed into the British service, and one such act of tyranny was enough to inflame Cooper for the rest of his life. Even the praise his own work received from the English was usually couched in terms to annoy rather than please him; knowing the individuality of his own genius, he naturally did not like to be called the "American Scott." And at times English criticism of him, and treatment of him too, passed quite into the manner of insult.

That his unpleasant experience was in part at least his own

fault would be proved beyond question, even if we had no other evidence, by Washington Irving's far more delightful relations with the English. Nathaniel P. Willis also, though he made himself less lovable than Irving, was equally happy in England. Cooper was undoubtedly looking for quarrels, and he had a strange gift for finding them. His habitual championing of his country, not always perhaps in the best taste, gave him the reputation of being prouder of American citizenship than of the authorship of his novels. It became somewhat dangerous in his presence, as later in Lowell's, to introduce the United States as a subject in any degree for controversy, but he had not Lowell's wit nor his grace to keep the argument from bitterness. In 1828 he published his *Notions of the Americans, Picked up by a Traveling Bachelor*, a work intended to set Europeans right in their judgments of the republic. It has been well pointed out that no American would learn anything new from this treatise, nor would the prejudiced foreigner be convinced of his ignorance by the extreme praise of the author's country. Cooper's statements, as far as they go, show an unusual knowledge of America, and unusual wisdom in the predictions of her future, but the whole work defeated its purpose by its partisanship. And some incidental disparagement of English society was the probable cause of the ill-feeling shown towards him later by the English press. In all the novels he wrote at this period he very unnecessarily went out of his way to defend America or to attack its critics. This practice became for a while so unpleasantly common with him, that an illustration of it from *The Heidenmauer* will not be without value. The passage is one of the least offensive of its kind, though Cooper's satire is never subtle or delicate:

"Should we unheedingly betray the foible of national vanity—that foul and peculiar blot of American character! we solicit forgiveness; urging, in our own justification, the aptitude of a young country for falling insensibly into the vein of imitation, and praying the critical observer to overlook any blunders in this way, if perchance we should not manifest that felicity of execution which is the fruit only of great practice. Hitherto we believe that our modesty cannot justly be impeached. As yet we have left the cardinal virtues to mankind in the gross, never, to our knowledge, having written of ' American courage,' or ' American honesty,' nor yet of ' American beauty,' nor haply of ' American manliness,' nor even of ' American strength of arm,' as qualities abstracted and not common to our fellow-creatures; but have been content, in the unsophisticated language of this western clime, to call virtue, virtue—and vice, vice. In this we well know how much we have fallen short of numberless but nameless classical writers of our time, though we do not think we are greatly losers by the forbearance, because we have sufficient proof that when we wish to make our pages unpleasant to the foreigner, we can effect that object by much less imposing allusions to national merits; since we have good reason to believe, there exists a certain querulous class of readers who consider even the most delicate and reserved commendations of this western world as so much praise unreasonably and dishonestly abstracted from themselves."

From this habitual defending of his country against British criticism Cooper's evil fate brought him to defending himself against his own countrymen. There were many Americans then as now, who for various reasons were not so sure as he of republican superiority over older forms of government. And in 1831, when Cooper took part in a public discussion of the relative burden of taxation in France and America, these critics made their opinion of him fairly plain. Lafayette, whom Cooper honored out of patriotic gratitude as well as friendship, had referred to the United States as a model of inexpensive government. His opponents in French politics claimed that the average Frenchman was taxed less than the average American. Cooper felt obliged to support his friend in the *Letter to General Lafayette*, a pamphlet which stated in detail the low cost of the American government. Some polite interchange of argument followed, but the interest was suddenly shifted for Cooper by the interference of a Mr. Leavitt Harris, an American long resident in Russia, who for some unexplained reason felt impelled to rebuke Cooper by denying the accuracy of both his premises and his deductions. The American government, interested in the discussion, began collecting information from the different parts of the Union, without distinction between Federal and local taxes. Against this method of investigating the subject Cooper protested effectively, on the ground that the taxes compared in the two countries should logically be the same. This protest took the form of an open letter, printed in a Philadelphia paper in December, 1832. It ended the controversy as far as Cooper was concerned, but it furnished occasion for his American critics to complain that his patriotism was too strenuous and his self-appointed guardianship of the United States egotistical. He could well feel that his countrymen had failed to appreciate his devotion. The years abroad had been passed in a kind of unofficial service of democracy,—service rich in zeal, if not in tact; the end of his travels brought him home cruelly wounded by what he considered democracy's rejection of him.

VI

During his residence abroad Cooper wrote two groups of stories, one dealing with American themes, the other devoted to an attack on monarchical institutions. In both groups the grade of excellence varies greatly. By far the most famous novel is the first of the American group, *The Prairie*, published in May, 1827. This is the conclusion of the Leatherstocking Tales, describing the last days of the hunter, as *The Pioneers* described the last days of his comrade Chingachgook. In artistic value, however, there is no comparison between the two books; *The Prairie* is a masterpiece, though the solidity of its qualities prevents it from becoming as popular, perhaps, as the more brilliant stories. Cooper's happy skill in tracing a character into old age, for which only Thackeray in one instance, Beatrix Esmond, gives a parallel, is exhibited here in the portrait of Hawkeye, now a venerable trapper, but undeniably the same person who years before had protected Heyward and the Munro sisters. This character alone sustains the popular interest in the story. But an imaginative reader finds also a poetical rendering of the prairie landscape, a kind of group-picture of elemental man with nature for a background, that has hardly been excelled in American literature.

The plot is of the simplest. Ishmael Bush, the squatter, is moving across the plains to find a home suited to his lawless nature; like Hawkeye, though for a different reason, he is crowded westward by civilization. Abiram White, his villainous brother-in-law, has persuaded him to kidnap Inez, whom Middleton, her lover, pursues; and the bee-hunter follows for love of Ellen, who lives with Bush's family against her will. This simple story is complicated to a slight degree by the murder of Asa Bush and the temporary suspicion under which the trapper falls, by the hostile Indians, and by the prairie fire. As usual in the Leatherstocking Tales, Leatherstocking himself stands outside the action, lending his aid only as occasion demands.

Ishmael Bush's journey gives the plot the ground plan of a pursuit and rescue, already familiar in Cooper's method. But in this story there is a central theme of rest instead of motion. The main plot is framed in, so to speak, between the vast stillness of the deserted prairie, and the no less heroic calm of the trapper's age. Bush has almost reached the end of his pilgrimage when the story begins; at its close he is retracing his steps to the east. The solidity of nature, massive rocks

and wide reaches,—an effective if not accurate idea of the
prairie,—take the place of the stirring witchery of the forest,
as Bush and his stalwart sons supplant the lithe frontiersman
of the earlier stories. The movement necessary in the picture for the sake of contrast is furnished by the Sioux and
Pawnee bands on their horses, and by the fire; but in both
cases the effect is a pictorial illusion of motion,—the somber
plot unfolds in practically one place, without haste and without change.

The squatter and his family are perhaps the most Titantic
figures in Cooper—at least on the physical side; they seem to
be magnified in the enchanted prairie light, like rude gods of
the early world, dim-souled, misty and vast. Had they represented anything in the story commensurate with their imposing stature, they might have taken their place with the un-
forgettable peasant-figures of French painting. As it is, their
huge clay is informed with dignity only when they are roused
by their brother's murder; until that time they are open to a
suspicion of meanness, even viciousness. Cooper redeems
the whole family by Ishmael's belated sense of justice to the
girls, no less than by the elemental force of the execution
scene.

Aside from the novelty of putting them on horseback,
Cooper says nothing new of his Indians; Sioux and Pawnee,
they are the familiar Iroquois and Mohican, Le Renard Subtil and Le Gros Serpent, come to life again. Hard Heart is
clearly an idealized savage, no more typical than Chingachgook or Uncas, but equally legitimate in a romance—as Washington or Paul Jones is a legitimate character, but not average, of their race. The Pawnee chief gains this much over
Chingachgook, that he enters the story unannounced, and
unprotected by the good name of Hawkeye; like the Mohican, he serves as the measure of Hawkeye's character, giving
a savage's testimony to absolute honesty and wisdom; and he

is necessary in the plot to show how much more at home the old hunter is with red men than with white. Leatherstocking would like to be passive in any struggle between Bush and the Sioux, little as he likes the latter, because to his high sense of justice the Indian owns the land; and much more does his heart go to the young Pawnee, whose principles are as just as his own, and who reverences his age.

In the Doctor, Owen Bat, Cooper gives us another of his pedants—perhaps his most tiresome one. He and Middleton and the bee-hunter, and Ellen and Inez, are involuntarily neglected in a final mental summary of the story. The mind holds simply to the picture of the prairie, with the group of Bush's caravan, and the two bands of Indians, and in the center of the picture the aged Leatherstocking. It is a picture of elemental man,—the white man seeking breathing-room in the wildness, and the Indian warring in his native savagery, and the best of the elemental of both races united in Leatherstocking. It is also a picture of age; the squatter has been driven to the wall by progress, and he sees the end of his kind in the death of his favorite son; the Indians, though mounted on the wild horses of the plains, are already overtaken, as Leatherstocking sees, by the landhunter; and Leatherstocking himself dies beaten in his long flight from the influence of the "settlements." The future is with the less significant characters—the pedantic scientist, the bee-hunter, and the young army officer.

Age makes Leatherstocking more effective in some of his traits, thought it takes from him his skill and his physical prowess. The tendency to sermonize on all occasions seems natural in so old a man, and the slight self-conceit of his youth and prime are buried beneath a touching humility, that confesses age and infirmity with shame. With the instinct of genius Cooper has stripped from his hero's character all but the rooted fibers that time could not touch; he is brave, simple and honest,—and nothing more. And his dying answer to the imagined roll-call is a master-stroke that Thackeray imitated, but did not equal, in Colonel Newcome's "Adsum!"

Cooper's instinct for plot seems to desert him more or less when he chooses subjects apart from the Leatherstocking frontier or the sea. In the novels dealing with those themes and in *The Spy*, though his constructive art is open to much criticism, he usually avails himself of all the possibilities of the story; there may be insufficient motive or explanation of the incidents, but little could be added to the incidents themselves. In other novels, however, and in his later work generally, there is often a rich suggestion in plot or character that goes undeveloped or is allowed to die by the way, as though the author were not aware of its significance. *The Wept of Wish-ton-Wish*, published in November, 1829, a year after *The Red Rover*, illustrates such a failure to make the most of a story. The plot is laid in New England, in King Philip's war, and its simple elements might have given Cooper the material for a very striking romance. In an attack upon a Puritan household the Indians carry off a little girl. An Indian boy, who has been kindly treated by the child's father, falls in love with her, and when they both grow up, marries her. He becomes a powerful chief, in league with King Philip, and in the war happens to attack the long-forgotten parents of his white bride. In gratitude he protects them and offers to restore their daughter, but she has become an Indian at heart, and prefers her husband's life. This is the intended theme of the story, and the title refers to the heroine, the child whose loss was bemoaned in the valley of Wish-ton-Wish. Many white children were captured by the Indians and adopted into their tribes; had Cooper elaborated his story with this theme in mind, he would have portrayed a phase of the early Indian warfare which has not yet been used with effect in romance. But from the capture of the little girl, in the beginning of the book, to her reappearance at the end, nothing is said of her; the story occupies itself with a picture of Puritan life in the New England frontier—a subject Cooper was eminently unfitted to deal with. Even if he had been fitted, however, the result would have been the same; it is difficult to find any direction in the movement of the plot, and the story has apparently neither hero nor heroine. This uncertainty of interest is reflected in the various titles of the novel,—in England, *The Borderers*, and in France, *The Puritans of America*, or the *Valley of Wish-ton-Wish*.

Something has been said already of Cooper's deficient sympathy with the Puritan character. His biographer has explained this by the paradox that he was himself too like the Puritans to do them justice. The explanation is not completely satisfactory, for in an essential quality of Puritanism Cooper was as completely lacking as Irving; he was in no respect a visionary nor a dreamer. In so far as Puritanism coincided with his nature, he portrayed it admirably in this novel; he lets the reader see the practical vigor, the exalted piety, and the domestic affection of Mark Heathcote and his comrades, for these virtues he can recognize, as he could recognize the common piety and the common sense of *The Pilgrim's Progress*. But the mastering vision that burns like flame in the Puritan temper, impelling it to strenuous action, was entirely hidden from Cooper, if we can judge by his writings. Mark Heathcote, living in the wilderness to enjoy freedom in his beliefs, is presented as a fanatic, whose only claim on our sympathies is his efficient soldier-quality when there is fighting to do. So little did Cooper understand the type, that he actually divorced warfare and religion in his conception of the Puritan, as though Cromwell and his men fought for earthly purposes, which they would try to regret when they went to church. It is in this Quaker-like aspect that Mark Heathcote is described: "Even the gentle and ordinarily little observant Ruth might trace the kindling of the eye, the knitting of the brow, and the flushing of his pale and furrowed cheek, as the murderous conflicts of the civil wars became the themes of the ancient soldier's discourse. There were moments when religious submission, and we had almost said religious precepts, were partially forgotten, as he explained to his attentive son and listening grandchild, the nature of the onset, or the quality and dignity of the retreat. At such times, his still nervous hand would even wield the blade, in order to instruct the latter in its uses, and many a long winter evening was passed in thus indirectly teaching an art that was so much at variance with the mandates of his Divine Master."

Grave as is this misunderstanding of the Puritans, Cooper does the type a more serious injustice in the virtual betrayal of the Indian chief who had brought back his wife to her parents. The hypocrisy of the white men, led by their pastor, the Reverend Meek Wolfe, inspires a horror that would have prevented the popularity of the story, even if it had been founded in truth. The only portion of the novel that repays reading now is the description of the attack on the blockhouse, and the escape of the defenders by hiding in the well.

The last of the novels on American subjects written abroad, was *The Water Witch*, published in December, 1830. It has the merits of Cooper's other sea stories, to a moderate extent, and in the destruction of the burning warship and the adventures of the survivors on the raft, it has a moment of grandeur, but neither its plot nor its characters are at all important. Evidently it is a tame replica of *The Red Rover*, with the substitution of a smuggler, the Skinner of the Seas, for the pirate. There is the same phenomenally fast and graceful outlaw ship, the same magic in its handling, a secret relationship to be discovered in the final chapter, and a girl in love with the outlaw, disguised in his ship as a youth. Since the hero is a smuggler, not a pirate, the story would be quite bloodless if the patriotic element were not introduced,—with some effort,—by arranging a fight between the British and French cruisers. The main interest is in the smuggler's skill in eluding his pursuers, at sea and in the harbor waters of New York; it might be added that this real interest is lessened by the mummery which is meant to wrap the outlaw's ship in mystery.

The second class of novels Cooper wrote in Europe includes *The Bravo*, published in November, 1831, *The Heidenmauer*, published in September 1832, and *The Headsman*, published in October, 1833. These stories represent old world forms of government or social conditions, in contrast with the republican ideals of America. All three suffer from the purpose that inspired them. Cooper could tell a story, apparently, only when he gave himself up to it without reserve; to make it serve a didactic purpose was for him to confuse and enfeeble the plot. Further, he had chosen to write about times well back in history, trusting to his reading and to his acquaintance with the scenes to make the stories faithful pictures of the past. But he was by nature no scholar; he was neither widely nor deeply read; and the Venice and Germany and Switzerland of these three books are more convincing of his trust in the democratic ideal than of his competence to judge old institutions. Especially is this true in the second and third of the series; in the first he could make so general a use of the modern Venice as a stimulus to the imagination, that he seems to speak with considerable authority of its medieval condition.

On other accounts also *The Bravo* is to be reckoned the best of these novels. Its subject, the despotism of a city pretending to freedom, could easily be embroidered with striking scenes of palace, prison and lagoon,—and the pictorial sense in Cooper's genius was never appealed to in vain. As a panorama of Venetian life, then, the story has undoubted power, though the portrait, as far as it includes human character, may be quite incorrect. The social fabric of the city, under-mined in all directions by treachery and concealed distrust, makes a consistent picture; its effect lies not only in the pub-licly recognized career of the assassin, in the dark figure of the Bravo and the foul murder of the fisherman, Antonio, but still more in the unstable household of Signor Gradenigo, who sets spies on his own son, for good reasons, and is himself dis-covered in his designs on his ward. In the treatment of all grades of society Cooper is here unusually successful; the gondoliers, the shopkeepers and minor citizens, are realized as faithfully as their lords, and the Doge and the Council of Three are portrayed in their official state with a remarkable effect of actuality, whatever they may owe to imagination. But the chief power of the story is in the tragic plot. The in-evitable fate of the Bravo, used by all rivals to spy on each other, and safe from them only by virtue of the secrets he knows, becomes plain to the reader by a gradual enlighten-ment, so that the story gathers gloom as it proceeds; and the realization that the course of life so surely fatal was never his choice, but was the price, vainly paid, of his innocent father's freedom, completes the indictment against a social system that sacrificed him to its selfish fears. The Bravo, in his pa-tience and the injustice of his evil fame, is akin to Harvey Birch; for patriotism is substituted in his case hatred of his city, a natural result that Cooper means to indicate as a very real part of his tragic fate. Not to examine too closely a novel which has no claim to be considered masterly, it is enough to mention its chief fault for modern readers, the tedious extent to which Cooper explains to his ignorant countrymen the characteristics and customs of Venice. It seems improbable that even in 1831 the average American reader needed to be told that Venice is built practically in the water, with canals for streets and gondolas for vehicles; nor did he probably need to be told how a gondola is propelled. It may be suspected that those of Cooper's countrymen who did need his instruction, never read his book.

The Heidenmauer is among its author's most complete failures, though it is not the least readable of his books. It deals with the monastic orders shortly after Luther's attacks, when the church of Rome had still a strong though a failing grasp on Germany. In plot the story is feeble, its only important incident being the destruction of a monastery by a heretic baron. One of the baron's followers, the hero, if the story has any, is supposed to have perished in the burning chapel, and the most moving scene in the book tells of his stricken mother's vain pleadings with the church for prayers for his soul. As he has not been killed at all, however, the church's pride suffers an anticlimax. The only original character is the hermit, who having committed sacrilege in a youthful enthusiasm for Protestantism, is haunted by the wrath of God, a lifelong prey to remorse. In so rambling and ineffective a story it is hard to see the author's intention, but the hermit brings into relief the failure of the religious order about him, both by his superstition, and by its inability or unwillingness to recover such a penitent to the sane uses of life.

The Headsman is an excellent example of wasted opportunity in plot. Intended to record the tyranny of local customs in an undemocratic society, the story unfolds, after a somewhat tiresome introduction, in strong outlines which admirably develop its theme, and which promise to be as logically relentless as a Greek tragedy. The canton in which the plot is laid has a hereditary executioner. The office, once considered an honor, has become an unspeakable disgrace, and the unhappy heir to it in each generation would escape it if it were not compulsory. In spite of his tediousness, Cooper makes the horror of the headsman and his family entirely

convincing in the first chapters of the novel; from this point
the plot begins. A young soldier saves the life of a beautiful
girl and her father, winning the girl's love and the father's approval. All three are present at a wedding which terminates
abruptly in the discovery that the bride is the headsman's
daughter. Unwilling to bear the public disgrace of union with
the family, the bridegroom jilts her at the altar. The young
soldier, strangely disturbed by the incident, tells his betrothed,
as a matter of honor, that she cannot marry him, for he is the
headsman's son, supposed dead, but really seeking to avoid
the dreadful inheritance. With this information, when the
unchivalrous bridegroom is found murdered, suspicion naturally falls on the young soldier. Had he been guilty of the
crime and been beheaded by his father, or had his father been
the murderer, for him to execute, the plot would have been
complete. But at this point Cooper seems to lose sight of his
original purpose. It turns out that none of the important
characters had anything to do with the murder, and the young
soldier is discovered to be, not the headsman's son, but the
heir of a noble family. The story is worth reading for the
excitement of this rapid descent in the last chapters.

VII

Cooper returned to America November 5, 1833, and took
up his residence again in New York. His unfortunate experiences with his countrymen while abroad made false impressions inevitable to his oversensitive disposition, and he
probably threw away the one chance he had to recover a
friendlier point of view. A public dinner was offered him, a
compliment similar to that he had received at his departure;
but prompt as the invitation was—within two weeks of his
landing—he had already fancied himself slighted or treated
with coldness by his old friends. Perhaps for this reason he
declined the honor now sincerely offered. It is hard to under-

stand his state of mind. Apparently he had brooded upon American criticisms of him until he could accept nothing but aggressive warfare with his countrymen. He was so much a political and social idealist that he mentally severed all connection between those fellow-countrymen whom he had come almost to despise, and his country, which he worshiped. It has been well said that the rapid changes in the United States during his absence were of a nature to estrange him; on his return he found great commercial activity,—and very naturally, no proportionate advance in culture or art. But the willingness he had shown in the preface to *The Pioneers* to start controversy and to rouse permanent enemies, makes other explanations unnecessary. The most ardent admirer of Cooper must admit that even if he had not gone abroad, and if the country had not changed, he would probably have got himself into trouble. It is impossible to form an accurate idea of his personality, so far as details of manner are concerned, for the most reliable of those who described him were usually critics or admirers, and the accounts contradict one another. Scott, whom he met in Paris, thought him rude, and the English record in general follows Barry Cornwall's impression that he was boorish. Yet the reverse was said of him by English acquaintances, and there were many friends in America to bear witness to his warm heart and his generous loyalty. It is fairly safe, however, to concede that he was unpleasantly rough in manner when he returned to his country, and few men, if any, were attracted to him through a personal encounter. And in his polemical writings he had a mania for expressing disagreeable truths; that they were truths, cannot be denied, for his sense of justice was admirable. Indeed, he distributed his energies equally among all nations and parties which he was in position to know—a kind of muck-raker at large. If in his later years he becomes an unpleasant figure, to which national pride would prefer not to point, it is well to keep in mind, as compensating virtues, his real love of justice and his high ideals for his country.

Most of the physical descriptions of him date from about this time, when he was abroad or soon after his return. He was tall and stalwart, the most athletic of American authors. In the foreign accounts of him some allowance must be made for the disposition to find the frontiersman in every American, but even with that allowance we can well believe that he did appear somewhat out of place in continental drawing-rooms. The impression which he gave of great strength and energy made him seem as restless as a wild animal yearning for out-door freedom. The familiar portrait of him is in accord with the written description; his eye was deep, slow moving and not very bright, and his heavy features, in repose almost stolid, suggested a peasant ancestry.

His actual warfare with the American public began in his *Letter to His Countrymen*, which appeared in June, 1834. This pamphlet was a reply to adverse criticisms in several New York papers, of *The Bravo* and others of his books. In addition to the uselessness of such a reply under any circumstances, it was not at all clear that Cooper had a good case. But his evil star led him by a surprisingly roundabout course to include a discussion of the quarrel then in progress between President Jackson and the Senate, and he managed by an adroit exhibition of his impartiality to wound the feelings of both legislature and executive. This letter made the author a subject of national debate. The press turned on him the disgraceful vigor of its denunciations, at once squaring all old scores, and his onslaught upon the politicians made for him a generous harvest of really powerful enemies. The sale of his books is said to have fallen off, though even his bitterest opponents occasionally honored the genius apart from the man. But whatever might be the personal loss, Cooper had now committed himself single-handed to the unequal struggle, and he opened a general attack on all enemies in *The Monikins*, in July, 1835.

This satire, describing the visits of John Goldencalf and his comrades to the countries of Leaphigh and Leaplow—England and America—has been pronounced unreadable. It is certainly tedious on the whole, and there is no reason why it should be read to-day. It is surprising, however, that it was not read when it appeared; the excitement of the moment would naturally have caused Cooper's opponents to look into it. The fact seems to be, however, that it was a flat failure. Cooper had no gift for satire, and his conversation is invariably the weakest thing in his novels; as most of his satire is conveyed through the discourse of Dr. Reasono and Noah Poke and Goldencalf, and as much of their discussion has no interest to-day, the book is generally dull. But when Cooper drops the conversation and hits out in his Brobdingnagian vein of satire, the result is often funny and makes excellent reading. The introduction contains what ammunition was left over from the volume, and its painstaking thoroughness is delightful.

Having passed from a serious difference of opinion with some of his countrymen to a condition of conflict with all of them, Cooper now had the misfortune to localize the conflict in his native village. On his return from Europe he had spent a few winters in New York, but during the summers he restored his father's house, which had fallen into ruin, and when the repairs were completed he took up his residence at Cooperstown for the rest of his life. His father had owned a piece of land called Three Mile Point, a convenient excursion place, which with the permission of the estate had been used by the public until they had forgotten it was private property. Cooper, as executor of the estate, took occasion to remind his townspeople of the true ownership of the Point, though he interfered in no way with their use of it. They paid no attention to him, and in 1837, when a building erected by the community needed repairs, they sent workmen to the Point without asking his permission, and incidentally they destroyed a tree that he especially prized. He sent a notice to a local paper, protesting against the destruction of trees on the property, but making no objection otherwise to the public use of it. Before his notice was published the attitude of the community on the subject proved so hostile that he substituted a plain warning against trespassing, in which he stated his rigid intention to enforce his title to the estate. The village had actually got it into its head that the Point had been given to it by Cooper's father. A mass-meeting was called, at which a series of ridiculous resolutions were passed, in which the public ownership of the Point was claimed, Cooper's conduct was described as such as to render him odious to a great portion of the community, and the trustees of the Franklin Library, in the village, were requested to remove from the building all books of which he was author. Cooper replied in two letters which completely ended the dispute so far as Cooperstown was concerned. The citizens soon perceived their mistaken position, though they thought no better of Cooper personally; he on his part considered the mass-meeting as in no respect representative of the good sense of the village.

Out of this insignificant quarrel grew the libel suits against the press, which form such an interesting if not very profitable episode in Cooper's career. The *Chenango Telegraph*, in Norwich, Chenango County, published an account of the dispute, with uncomplimentary references to Cooper. The Whig newspaper of Cooperstown reprinted the article, with the addition of the village's side of the case, stated without regard to the facts that Cooper had made plain. The editor refused to investigate the truth of his own statements, or to retract them, and the novelist brought a suit for libel, which he won in May, 1839. He conducted his own case in this and most of the later suits, with the assistance of his nephew, Richard Cooper; and he discovered a skill in persuading a jury that was nothing short of remarkable. It was typical of his courage that he made his hard fight alone, with no assistance or encouragement from any public sympathy; the juries that gave him the decisions did so reluctantly, as the small damages in each case showed. He won simply on the justice of his plea.

The details of the famous suits cannot be given here. It is enough to say that Cooper brought suit against the *Chenango Telegraph;* the *Oneida Whig*, of Utica; the *Evening Signal*, of New York; the *Courier and Enquirer;* the *Albany Journal;* the *Tribune*, of New York; and the *Commercial Advertiser*, of the same city. All of these suits Cooper won, with the exception of that against the *Courier and Enquirer*, in which case the jury disagreed on two trials. The suits that attracted most attention were those against the *Albany Evening Journal*, The famous editor, Thurlow Weed, committed himself to a reckless policy of reprinting attacks on Cooper from other papers, and Cooper systematically won damages from the *Journal* for every libellous reprint. Such a proceeding was too expensive even for the editor's enmity toward Cooper, and in December, 1842, he retracted all that he had published against the novelist. These suits, extending over three or four years, proved Cooper's fighting capacity and his sound sense in legal matters, but they set him completely outside the sympathy of the country at large, and the editors whom he convicted of libel were apparently unconvinced of any essential untruth in what they had said. His very success naturally increased their prejudice.

During the Mile Point episode Cooper determined to write a story which should present a frank picture of American society as he saw it. The work was not to be a satire, but as it was inspired by the author's quarrel with his fellow-townsmen,

it would hardly be pleasant in tone. At first the plan included only the introduction of a group of foreigners to the
United States, and their unbiased impressions of the land;
but the author's friends advised him to describe the voyage to
America at some length. The suggestion resulted in the publication of two books, one in August, 1837, *Homeward Bound*,
dealing with the voyage, and the other in November, *Home
as Found*, giving the study of the country. The characters
are the same in both, and the series makes practically one
story, telling of the return of Mr. Edward Effingham, his
daughter and his cousin to their home at Templeton Hall, on
Otsego Lake. The story of the voyage is an admirable tale
of adventure. The ship is pursued by an English war vessel,
is disabled in a storm, drives on the African coast and is in
desperate peril from Arab brigands. So exciting are the
events, that the interpolated discussions of America do not
seriously interrupt them, and the novel stands quite distinct
from its sequel, as one of the most interesting of his minor
writings. *Home as Found*, however, is among his least fortunate works. Not only does it fail to interest as a story,
but it betrays a temporary lack of all reason and sense on
Cooper's part. His fellow-townspeople had long ago called
his father's house *Templeton Hall*, in compliment to his description of it in *The Pioneers*, and when he called the Effingham home by that name, and described it as exactly the same
house, even to its interior decoration and furniture, it is incredible that he should not have expected his readers to
identify the Effinghams with himself. It is needless to say
that this identification, which was made at once, completely
nullified whatever force the book might have had, and made
the author, for the first time in his life, indefensibly ridiculous.
The impression that men like Thurlow Weed and Horace
Greeley must have derived from the book explains perhaps
their later unchanged contempt for Cooper's character.

This capital error in the book makes its other shortcomings insignificant. Yet in spite of the unreasonableness that marks almost every criticism of America in both volumes, there is a kind of surface cleverness here and there which must have been exasperating to the subjects of the attack. Mr. Steadfast Dodge, the editor, is such a composite portrait of his profession as Cooper's wrath could picture; his name was significant, for "there was a singular profession of steadiness of purpose and of high principle about him, all of which vanished in Dodge at the close." He is the chief direct subject of the satire, and the ruthless treatment he receives at Cooper's hands is illustrated by this conversation with Mr. Blunt, the Englishman in *Homeward Bound*.

"'If one man be as good as another,' said Mr. Blunt, . . . 'will you do me the favor to inform me, why the country puts itself to the trouble and expense of the annual elections?'

"'Elections, sir! In what manner could free institutions flourish or be maintained, without constantly appealing to the people, the only true source of power?'

"'To this I make no objection, Mr. Dodge,' returned the young man, smiling; 'but why an election; if one man is as good as another, a lottery would be cheaper, easier, and sooner settled. Why an election, or even a lottery at all? Why not choose the President as the Persians chose their king, by the neighing of a horse?'

"'This would be indeed an extraordinary mode of proceeding for an intelligent and virtuous people, Mr. Blunt; and I must take the liberty of saying that I suspect you of pleasantry. If you wish an answer, I will say, at once, by such a process we might get a knave, or a fool, or a traitor.'

"'How, Mr. Dodge! I did not expect this character of the country from you! Are the Americans then all fools, or knaves, or traitors?'

"'If you intend to travel much in our country, sir, I would advise great caution in throwing out such an insinuation, for it would be apt to meet with a very general and unqualified disapprobation. Americans are enlightened and free, and as far from deserving these epithets as any people on earth.'

" 'And yet the fact follows from your own theory. If one man is as good as another, and any one of them is a fool, or a knave, or a traitor,—all are knaves, or fools, or traitors!' "

Equally clever in a superficial way is some of the satire in *Home as Found*, though the tone of the book is too polemical and ill-natured for the few bright spots to be noticed. But there is a coarse kind of truth in the description of the Fourth of July oration, containing "the usual allusions to Greece and Rome, between the republics of which and that of this country there exists some such affinity as is to be found between a horse-chestnut and a chestnut-horse, or that of mere words; and a long catalogue of national glories that might very well have sufficed for all the republics, both of antiquity and of our own time. But when the orator came to speak of the American character, and particularly of the intelligence of the nation, he was most felicitous, and made the largest investments in popularity. According to his account of the matter, no other people possessed a tithe of the knowledge, or a hundredth part of the honesty and virtue of the very community he was addressing; and after laboring for ten minutes to convince his hearers that they already knew everything, he wasted several more in trying to persuade them to undertake further acquisitions of the same nature."

The unfortunate thing about this kind of satire is that it hits an unworthy foe; the hypocrite who is also a fool, and the country orator who talks nonsense in platitudes, hardly need to have a book written to point their defects. And as the author so avowedly undertook to lecture his countrymen on their faults, it is not surprising that many who were neither editors nor orators felt his presumption in an almost personal way.

The enemies that his many quarrels had brought him made one last attempt to crush the militant man of letters,—and of all the battles he fought, this seems the most to his credit. From the time of his first success as a writer of sea tales, he had planned a history of the United States navy. It was a work in which both his professional pride and his patriotism found every incentive, and when he was at last free to undertake it, he spared no pains to make it authoritative. It was published in May, 1839. Competent critics attest its thoroughness, and the court before which it came in the process of the quarrel it aroused, vindicated its fairness. But its very fairness made trouble for Cooper. There had been for some twenty years a bitter quarrel over the facts of the battle of Lake Erie. Shortly after the victory a report was in general circulation that Elliott, the officer second in command, had been treacherous to Commander Perry, failing to assist him in the critical part of the fight. Perry at first exonerated Elliott from the charge, but some four or five years later changed his mind. The popularity of the Commodore, and his death in 1819, left Elliott with little means of righting himself in the public opinion. The course he adopted was very unwise, as it appeared to be self-assertion rather than defense; he allowed a life of himself to be published in which the victory at Lake Erie was attributed to his skill and courage. He had indeed this support of his view, that Perry, in his first approval of Elliott, had written, "I consider the circumstance of your volunteering and bringing the smaller vessels up to close action as contributing largely to our victory." Whatever bias Cooper had when he began to investigate the subject is said to have been against Elliott, but apparently he found no proof of the charges of treachery, and in his history, while giving due credit to Perry, he said nothing to disparage the other officer.

The attack upon the book was general, and the critics directed their fire against this one passage, claiming that in refraining from passing judgment on Elliott, Cooper had been unpatriotic, and adding personal reflections upon the author. Some of the offensive reviews were written by prominent men,—one in particular, appearing in the *Commercial Advertiser*, of New York, by ex-president William A. Duer, of Columbia College. Cooper brought a suit for libel against the editor of the paper. The peculiar conduct of the case shows not only Cooper's skill, but also the high motives that impelled him to go to law. At the request of the defendant he agreed to have the case tried, not before a jury, but before three judges, who were to decide whether the review was libellous, and whether the history was fair and truthful. At the trial in May, 1842, in New York, Cooper conducted his own case, with a triumphant effect well described by a spectator:

"On the one hand his speech was a remarkable exhibition of self-esteem, and on the other, a most interesting professional argument; for when he described the battle, and illustrated his views by diagrams, it was like a chapter in one of his own sea-stories, so minute, graphic, and spirited was the picture he drew. The dogmatism was more than compensated for by the picturesqueness of the scene; his self-complacency was exceeded by his wonderful ability."

The judges were asked to give their decision upon different aspects of the case, making eight points in all. Every point was decided in Cooper's favor, the five chief ones being decided unanimously. Some minor litigation followed, but Cooper had vindicated his honor as a writer and had come to the end of his public imbroglios with this victory.

VIII

It is not to be wondered at that during this period of turmoil most of Cooper's writing suffered in quality. He had been preoccupied with controversial ideas—never the best material for artistic literature; and with him more even than most authors a conscious message was fatal to the story. Yet in the midst of the libel suits he wrote two of his most notable books, showing an almost incredible detachment from his other interests of the moment. In *The Pathfinder*, published in March, 1840, and *The Deerslayer*, published in August, 1841, he completed the Leatherstocking Tales in his best vein of sympathy with nature, and in his richest poetic mood: in the second novel particularly, the reader finds no hint of a mind disturbed by petty litigation.

In *The Pathfinder* Cooper attempted, as he said, to bring the Indian and the sailor together,—in other words, to combine his two most successful veins of romance. His naval experience on Lake Ontario gave him the needed basis in fact for his tale; he laid the plot on that inland water, in the French war, with one British cutter, the *Scud*, and Indian canoes for accessories. The plan of the story is in some respects weaker even than that of *The Pioneers*, since it has less coherence, though occasionally more action; and in several places, as when the cutter is in danger off the cliffs, there are feeble echoes of earlier novels. But the poetical rendering of the frontier, the forests and the waters, is as magical as ever,— indeed it sometimes reaches effects of unusual power, especially when the characters first reach the lake, and the seaman, Uncle Cap, brings out, by the contrast of his loyal praise of the ocean, the unique charm of the inland sea. In this one respect the book holds its place among the Leatherstocking Tales; in other ways it stands quite apart from them.

Cooper himself suspected that the juxtaposition of the sea-interest with woodcraft might not have the happiest effect, and his purpose to describe the movements on the lake naturally compels him to shorten that portion of the book in which his genius was surest. The adventures of the scout and Chingachgook, while bringing Mabel Dunham to the fort, of necessity suggest the finer journey in *The Last of the Mohicans*, but the situation loses no interest in the repetition; such

pursuits, calling for ingenious woodcraft, never exhausted
Cooper's invention. But the episode is far too brief. At its
end, when the evolutions of the British force begin, the plot is
uncertain, Chingachgook practically disappears from the
story, and Leatherstocking ceases to display almost all his
characteristic virtues, save his sense of honor and his skill
with the rifle. So important to the reader of the famous series
- are the hunter and his Indian comrade, that when the peculiar
interest in them is relaxed, hardly any compensation redeems
the story; and in this case the great charm of Mabel Dunham
and Dew-of-June, the Indian girl, and the consistent humor
of Uncle Cap, the pedantic sailor, fail to make up for the rare
appearances of the Great Serpent or for the inferior portrayal
of Leatherstocking.

In this novel as well as in *The Deerslayer*, Cooper shows the
hunter in love. It goes without saying that any love-affair
in Leatherstocking's life would need the most delicate treatment, if the peculiar quality of his character were to be preserved. In the first attempt Cooper's skill is inadequate;
Leatherstocking betrothed to Mabel Dunham is a highly
interesting and in the end a noble figure, but he is no longer
Leatherstocking. He has lost his poetic isolation from society, in the need he is made to express for "a house and a
furniture and a home." The wish so expressed, in terms of
the conventionalities he never had known, contradicts the
portrait of him in the other stories. And his wooing of the
beautiful girl so much younger than he, makes him seem less
sensible in human things than he is known to be at all other
times. In more than his love-making, however, he is changed
in this story. Cooper makes him much nearer to civilization
than in any other novel of the series; the fact that he is habitually employed by the army, and has command of the other
scouts, gives him a false bearing of discipline and coöperation, quite in contrast with the detached self-completeness

that makes him attractive to the imagination. And with his nearness to society goes a surprising acquaintance with its ways; his notable piety here takes the form of quotations from Scripture, though elsewhere he is illiterate, and nature is his Bible. Undoubtedly his renunciation of Mabel's hand when he discovers her love for Jasper, is the action of a great-hearted character, and the long and trying scene is one of the most effective in Cooper. But in its prolixity and its elaborate courtesy it is unlike Leatherstocking, who in the other stories showed latent tact whenever a delicate situation called for it. And the final picture of him, cherishing for years the sad memories of a blighted love, is completely out of tone with his lack of sentimentality wherever else he appears.

The wonder is that Cooper should have written such a book at all in those years of worriment. No less remarkable as a tribute to the fascination of the story is the legend that while the author was suing him, Thurlow Weed sat up all night to read it. Only a comparison with the other novels of the series makes this one seem tame. But such a comparison is inevitable now, and the modern reader perceives the effect of distracting worries in the author's reworking of old material,—in the escape to the fort, less effective than in *The Last of the Mohicans;* in Arrowhead, less convincing as the villain than Le Renard Subtil; in the cowardly Muir, so clumsy a traitor after Dillon; and in the figure of Leatherstocking standing with his rifle on the deck of the cutter,—so idle and out of place in the contrast he there suggests with Long Tom Coffin.

In *The Deerslayer* Cooper recovered his old skill tenfold. Parkman thought this the best of the Leatherstocking Tales, and for once his judgment of Cooper can hardly be questioned. The beautiful story of the hunter in his youth, loyal to his friend, and just beginning to make his fame, shows the author's powers at their highest. To have represented the Deerslayer so convincingly in his days of inexperience, working backwards as it were from the character as shown in *The Pioneers*, is no less an achievement in art than to have brought the character to its logical old age. As the Leatherstocking Tales are now read, in their proper order, the mysterious youth, already separated from the habitual society of his race, and leagued with the Delaware chief, has certain virtues in a crude form, which elevate and explain his actions in the later books. His love of truth is here most complete and most important to his welfare, from the moment when he refuses to alter his speech though Hurry Harry threatens to strangle him, to his last words with Judith—a parting that brought out his delicacy as well as his honor. And in his first encounters with the Indians, here described, the process by which his truthfulness and his skill became established among them as a proverb, is made to seem more natural and less a matter of fiction than several later exhibitions of his prowess; and what boy reader, or what reader who still knows the secret of the joy of adventure, would give up the history of Killdeer and the account of its coming into the hunter's possession!

The Deerslayer's inexperience is charmingly used to describe the beautiful lake as he first sees it. The fresh joy in nature, which gives the story a peculiarly youthful zest, is felt through the character of the hunter, who has never before met with such a panorama of water and forest, and whose delighted amazement has no opportunity of abating before the story closes. Hurry Harry, in his rough way, notices the Deerslayer's admiration of the lake, and at the other end of the book Judith has it in mind when she would persuade the youth never to leave the region. But Cooper manages to let us feel a finer taste in his hero, parallel to his loftier moral sense, which makes his enjoyment of the perfect scene unshared to any great extent by his companions. Hurry Harry and old Hutter, with their villainous commercial schemes, represent the opposite extreme of susceptibility; in between come the Indian and Judith and Hetty, but their private interests for the time are more to them than fine landscape. Chingachgook wins his bride, and Judith's passion finds a tragic end; but the Deerslayer is shown falling in love with nature, and through him the reader sees the lake and the forest in a transfigured charm, through a lover's eyes.

Like the last of the Leatherstocking Tales, this first story, though full of action, is confined to one spot, and there is, properly speaking, no chase or pursuit. As in *The Last of the Mohicans*, there is very little woodcraft. The plot busies itself with the characters in the "castle" on the lake, and with those in the Indian camp; the escape of the ark from the river, the pursuit of the girls in the canoe, and Deerslayer's attempt to flee from the Indian camp, are subordinate episodes, and are felt to be such in the reading. But the lack of movement on a large scale is more than compensated for by the personal prowess of the characters in hand-to-hand encounter. The courage of all the men in entering the Indian camp—though the motives vary with their different natures—gives a certain credit even to Hutter and Hurry Harry. Chingachgook's exploit in carrying off Hist is breathless, and the excitement takes on a noble interest when the Deerslayer assures the venture of success by the sacrifice of his freedom. And hardly less interesting is Hetty's simple trust, which makes her an unharmed visitor at the Indian camp-fires, or Judith's audacious strategy, that sought to rescue the Deerslayer by the sheer force of her great beauty. Of all the Leatherstocking episodes, none is worked out with greater variety of effect, or with more sustained power, than the fight with the Iroquois in the castle. From the moment when Hist discovers the floating mocassin and suspects the ambush, the suspense is terrific, and the actual events which follow the powerful premonition of danger, are more than sufficient for a satisfactory climax; the rescue of Harry, and the discovery that Hutter has been scalped, have the true thrill of romance, for all their melodramatic traits. And the final scene of the book, the charge of the soldiers and the destruction of the Indian force, is one of the most telling closes in Cooper's plots; all the picturesque possibilities of the situation have been exhausted,—Deerslayer at the stake, Chingachgook appearing in the midst of his enemies, bringing his friend's rifle, and Judith in her superb beauty masquerading as a queen, have brought the story to a point where only a big effect will not seem anticlimax,—and the steady tramp of the redcoats, in final contrast to the undisciplined fighting throughout the plot, ends all the picturesque dangers with a still more picturesque display of justice and order.

When Cooper made much of the Deerslayer's first mortal combat, describing at length his talk with his dying enemy and his assuming of the name Hawkeye, he was guided by a true artist's sense. In all the other books of the series Leatherstocking's rifle brought certain death to his Indian enemies; though he takes no life willingly, his skill in his prime is chiefly shown on human victims. However satisfactory such skill might seem in the experienced Indian fighter, it would have prejudiced the other virtues of his character to show him so deadly a fighter in his youth. The impression Deerslayer, so represented, would have made upon the reader is made in the story by Hurry Harry, who has the true frontiersman's faith in a dead Indian. We see the hardening process of experience, which compels the peaceful-minded hunter to put aside his qualms of conscience, and for his own safety become a slayer of men, in the rough world his destiny leads him to. The temper in which he accepts the necessity is highly fatalistic, partly as a result of a frontier environment, and partly as his peculiar nature dictates; we see him here in process of learning to accept the inevitable race-conflict, as in the later books we see that acceptance become habitual. But in this picture of his youth the adjustment to inevitable conditions is accompanied by much disillusion. Along with Deerslayer's discovery of these special charms of nature, comes his discovery of the cruelty of Hurry Harry, the sordidness of old Hutter, and—most tragic for him—the evil that has cursed Judith's beauty. The integrity of his simple character could not be permanently shaken by the knowledge of good and evil, but Cooper, whose skill in analyzing the soul is not usually great, makes it quite clear that Deerslayer did not come through the ordeal unscathed; he returned to the Delaware village "in a sorrow that it required months of activity to remove." In all the other Leatherstocking Tales the hero gives his services to the deserving and the good, young or old; here in the flush of youth he is the protector of the most beautiful woman, who is at the same time the most unworthy, he ever met. He is more perfectly humanized as a hero of romance by his encounter with Judith than by his love for Mabel Dunham, and it must be regretted that Cooper attributed to him the second and unconvincing passion.

In Hurry Harry and Thomas Hutter are depicted again the adventurous forerunners of civilization, such as were shown in *The Pioneers*. But in *The Deerslayer* these waifs of society gain by being fewer in number, and their characters are more firmly and completely studied. Hutter is one of Cooper's most interesting minor characters—interesting for his strange dwelling and his amphibious habits, but still more for the mystery of his past and for his unknown relation to Judith and Hetty. For once Cooper finds the frontier romance, not in the frontiersman's prowess on the line of civilization, but in the hidden circumstance that impelled him to leave established society. This vein of romance is more frequently worked, of course, in Scott; a somewhat similar mystery surrounds Mertoun, in *The Pirate*. But Cooper keeps the frontier note of truth by disclosing nothing of Hutter's secret, even at the end of the story; as Hurry Harry makes plain to Deerslayer, it is the etiquette of the border to ask no embarrassing questions.

IX

With the publication of *The Deerslayer* Cooper's best work was over. Indeed, it is hardly too much to say that no book he wrote afterwards has even a slight hold on fame, with the exception of *Wing and Wing*. It is supposed that the prolific succession of novels continuing almost till his death were intended to make up certain financial losses he had suffered in investments and cotton speculation. To what extent they succeeded in this purpose, it is now impossible to tell, but they clearly suffered from the marked speed of their production. Then, too, Cooper's genius was aging fast; he had exhausted his vein, and he was too old to find a new one. The mere mention of the titles of his last books is in most cases all the notice they deserve.

To the end of his days, Cooper had the faculty of fixing on rich themes, though he no longer could work them out. *Mercedes of Castile*, published in November, 1840, is an historical romance, with the first voyage of Columbus for its main incident. Cooper was quick to see the possibilities here for a sea-story, and for a picture of the Indians as white men first knew them. But the voyage does not begin until one quarter of the volume is past, and the part played by the Ozema, the Indian whom Columbus brings back to Spain, does not rank the character with his earlier work. For all its fine idea, the story is tiresome. Much the same criticism applies to *The Two Admirals*, published in April, 1842. The long and tedious introduction spoils the story for most readers, though it should have proved interesting. Cooper here attempted to describe the manœuvers of large fleets, rather than the adventures of single ships, and in the moments of real action the plot becomes as exciting as he alone could make such ocean adventures. But in his best sea tales the interest is focused upon one vessel, often upon only one part of it; the difficulty of keeping whole fleets before the reader's attention would be great for any author, and particularly for Cooper, whose genius lacked much organizing faculty. The result is that the story is at its best only when the fleet as a whole is neglected for a single ship, as when in the last battle the fight on the *Plantagenet* is described.

In *Wing and Wing*, which appeared later in the same year, Cooper repeated with variations the sea-story told in *The Red Rover* and *The Water Witch*,—that is, he gave once more an account of an outlaw vessel of great speed, with a commander of personal charm and miraculous skill. The plot is laid off the shores of Elba, and the outlaw captain, Raoul, is a French corsair. The loss of the lugger and the death of its commander give the story a tragic end, and the figure of Nelson in command of the English fleet raises the narrative to a place of some importance among Cooper's historical romances; but the familiar elements of chases, running fights and wrecks, can be found to far better advantage in *The Pilot* or *The Red Rover*.

In September, 1843, appeared *Wyandotte; or the Hutted Knoll*, one of the most curious experiments that poor judgment could allow an author to make. In this novel Cooper actually attempts to tell another story in the same scenes and almost in the same period as *The Pioneers*. Wyandotte deals with the settlement of a claim in the neighborhood of Otsego, just before and during the Revolutionary War. Of course there is no Leatherstocking to give his peculiar interest to the story, and the society pictured is not only less interesting than that of the earlier book, but it is entirely different; it has the effect not only of failing to justify itself, but of casting some suspicion upon the historical accuracy of the account of the frontier in *The Pioneers*. The novel has never been read enough, however, to be reckoned with seriously. Nor is there need to mention the following stories, published in 1844, *Afloat and Ashore*, and its sequel, *Miles Wallingford*, except to say that the hero tells his own adventures, and the autobiographical manner is so pleasant as to offset somewhat a long and tiresome tale. In all these later novels Cooper's piety took the form of dogmatic references to church and religion, and his heroes became frankly prigs. His life had not been such as to enrich his nature with charitable sympathies, and his opinions were not softened in his last years, as Scott's were, by universal love and admiration.

The three following novels, *Satanstoe*, in June, 1845, *The Chainbearer*, in November of the same year, and *The Redskins*, in July, 1846, though worthless as stories, illustrate admirably Cooper's patriotism and his love of justice. The series pretends to follow the fortunes of the Littlepage family through several generations, and the subject of all three books is the relation of landlord and tenant, with direct reference to the anti-rent troubles in New York State in the years following 1839. If there is any difference, the last of the series makes the most hopeless reading, for in that volume Cooper concentrated his main discussion of the economic question, but all three books are fatally enfeebled by the author's ethical purposes. In the prefaces, however, he writes most effectively of the question itself and of his object in dealing with it, and perhaps he has nowhere better stated his personal ideal of good citizenship than in the conclusion of the preface to *Satanstoe:*

"For ourselves, we conceive that true patriotism consists in laying bare everything like public vice, and in calling such things by their right names. The great enemy of the race has made a deep inroad upon us, within the last ten or a dozen years, under cover of a spurious delicacy on the subject of exposing national ills; and it is time that they who have not been afraid to praise, when praise was merited, should not shrink from the office of censuring, when the want of timely warnings may be one cause of the most fatal evils. The great practical defect of institutions like ours, is the circumstance that 'what is everybody's business, is nobody's business,' a neglect that gives to the activity of the rogue a very dangerous ascendency over the more dilatory corrections of the honest man."

Cooper's last stories were *The Crater*, October, 1847, a study of social conditions as illustrated by a handful of adventurers on a Pacific island; *Jack Tier*, March, 1848, a sea tale of the *Red Rover* type, with changes that may be imagined from the circumstance that the mistress of the Corsair, disguised as a boy, is here represented by the deserted wife of Stephen Spike, who to find her husband adopts the character of Jack Tier; *The Oak Openings*, August, 1848, a story founded on a western journey Cooper had made the year before; *The Sea Lions*, April, 1849, a tale of Antarctic adventure; and *The Ways of the Hour*, April, 1850, an attack upon the system of trial by jury. In these years Cooper also finished less important pieces, and in 1850 he wrote a comedy, *Upside Down; or, Philosophy in Petticoats*, which was acted for three nights in New York.

His last years were spent happily at Cooperstown. Some of the old rancour had begun to fade, and before he died a movement was on foot to honor him with a public dinner; already his fame was mellowing with the gratitude of a world of readers. In 1850, in the summer, he went to New York City, where his splendid appearance was remarked and remembered. Early in the next year his health began to fail. On September 14, 1851, he died at Cooperstown. His wife, who had made his home a lifelong world of happiness, outlived him only four months.

X

It is not difficult to see now why Cooper, in spite of his great services to his country,—"deserving well of it," as Thackeray said,—has enjoyed little personal honor. His character has become fixed in a tradition of tactlessness and love of quarreling, which has rendered him with much injustice, a somewhat unlovable figure. It is probable, as time goes on, that the sterling worth of his Americanism will win a broader credit, and the lofty ideals of the man will atone, as they should, for the excess of militant criticism that bred up detractors from his fame. That he was almost invariably on the right side can hardly be disputed, and no other American man of letters, not even Lowell, gave his genius so passionately and so continuously to the welfare of his country and the prospering of the cause of humanity.

It is clear, however, that Cooper's fame now rests on practically seven books—*The Spy*, *The Pilot* and the Leatherstocking Tales. Whatever he wrote with specific purpose, in behalf of justice or for the glorification of national pride, is now allowed by the general reader to rest on the shelves undisturbed; but Harvey Birch, Long Tom Coffin and Leatherstocking still delight the world, and probably will continue to do so as long as the novel is an acceptable form of entertainment. In these seven books is the real Cooper, untroubled by a conscious purpose; here are displayed best his love of nature, his zest for physical adventure, his admiration for sturdy manhood; and here unconsciously he finds expression for the rich vein of poetry that colored his practical knowledge of life.

The term "artist" hardly applies to Cooper, in whatever aspect his writing is considered; his great successes, artistic as they are, follow from intuition more than from conscious control of the effects. Yet any writer so prolific must for economy's sake follow beaten paths, even in his intuitive moments, and these seven best novels show as a whole Cooper's "methods,"—if the word may be used of the natural habit of his mind in dealing with narrative material. Whatever literary influence appears in this habit, comes from Scott, though in many respects the very use of similar methods and material usually emphasizes Cooper's originality.

These seven novels follow the general plan of such romances as *Waverley* and *Ivanhoe* and *Rob Roy*. Perhaps the most important resemblance is in the ultra-romantic hero, touched with the extreme individuality that marked the first years of the nineteenth century, and became fixed in the typical isolated hero of Byron or Shelley. As Robin Hood and Rob Roy and McIvor stand apart from the main interests of the plot, fatally yet not altogether disagreeably detached from society, so Harvey Birch, Long Tom Coffin and Leatherstocking are lonely men, whose relation to their race, for some inward reason of the spirit, is limited and casual. The restless aspiration of the new age found its image in wanderers and explorers of the frontiers of thought—in the hero of *Alastor*, and in *Childe Harold;* and in America it found its expression in these prose parallels of Cooper's. But however else the imaginative exiles in the English poems may have superiority, Birch and Coffin, and especially Leatherstocking, excel in a certain effect of permanence, not matched even by Robin Hood or Rob Roy. It was Cooper's unique fortune to place his lonely wanderers, explorers along the frontiers of the spirit, on an actual frontier, which actually represented in our national history those forces of democracy and civilization which Shelley dealt with in a dream world. The American frontier, moving westward from Leatherstocking's youth in New York to his death on the prairie, is the only frontier in modern times marking the progress of the race mind; its consequent advantage in dignity over the delightful

frontier Mr. Kipling has pictured for us, or the newer frontier
of Africa, as the novelist of to-day uses it,—hardly needs mention. Robin Hood and Rob Roy are the most attractive of
border ruffians; but the vast human destinies flooding along
the American border make such types trivial in comparison.
Cooper belongs to the new day; the America he loved was
of the future; he never represents the frontier without a faithful picture of the men who were leading the race westward.
Only it should be noticed that he paints such men as they are
—Harry March, or Marmaduke Temple and his cousin the
sheriff,—rough and incomplete men, heroic merely by virtue
of the great causes they unconsciously serve. The heroes he
idealized are the finer spirits, that feel the unrest rather than
the achievements of progress—who wistfully contemplate the
final evolved perfection, but feel hopeless agony in the process. This is the mood of Shelley's hero and Byron's; it is the
mood of Harvey Birch, and most of all, of Leatherstocking,
and if the old hunter at his best seems ill-equipped intellectually to fill a place beside the poetic types, after all it is in mood
and spirit, not in brain, that a character is one with his age.

If Leatherstocking and his fellows suggest in their loneliness Scott's border chiefs and outlaws, there is at the same
time a striking difference. To Scott the border was a fixed
thing, an unchanging zone through centuries of stirring incident; though the edge of progressing society was the scene of
danger and conflict, the romance of it accumulated in one
spot, and came to suggest long-memoried age rather than
the eternal novelty of youth. The American frontier moved
rapidly, never pausing long enough for its legends to take deep
root in any one place, and changing its character as it moved,
so that the legends of it in any two places are different. In
each of the Leatherstocking tales a special and distinct
world is pictured, and no one of them resembles the frontier
that Bret Harte knew. There was hardly time for more than

one writer to record any one phase of the American border life before it underwent its next transformation; so that the fortunate chronicler of it is master of an unassailable realm. But the shifting line brought Cooper a special advantage. His genius was at its best when dealing with a changing scene, with the rapid movement of a chase or pursuit. He alone of novelists has sought to represent the frontier, not in a stationary cross-section, but in its natural passage from change to change. The whole series of the Leatherstocking Tales is therefore a pursuit—civilization in its uncouth outworks overtaking the beauty and innocence of nature; and the eternal embarrassment of the human heart between love of the unspoiled world and approval of civilized progress, is made into a living person, Leatherstocking. Virgil, the nature-poet of the Old World, felt the sorrow of the problem in the spoiling of his beloved Italy, and personified it in Camilla. Far as the distance seems from Rome to Otsego Lake, it would be hard to find a third figure, equally significant and poetic, between the Italian Amazon and Leatherstocking.

Cooper's frontier had another advantage in the presence of the Indians at practically every stage of it. Scott had his Highlanders for picturesqueness and loyalty, but they represented to the mind only a lower stage of civilization,—not a distinct race, and the ultra-romantic hero, wedded to a Quixotic cause, was usually one of their number. The American Indian has these important qualities for romance, that he is quite distinct from the race advancing upon him, and yet in some of the best qualities of that race he is undeniably superior. And the circumstance of his fate—condemned by the rapidity of the frontier's approach to accept and digest all of civilization at once,—to pass in little more than a generation from ignorance of an alphabet to the use of electricity,—invests him with a romantic pity as well as admiration. So tempting is the subject, that from the appearance of Parkman's famous essay Cooper's Indians have been charged with unreality; they have been called creatures of romance, or at best, of improbability. Their wonderful fascination could not be denied even by Parkman, for his own remarkable studies were inspired by his youthful enthusiasm for Cooper. But even more than that, it is fortunately becoming the fashion among critics to see that Cooper said little, if anything, of the Indians that was not strictly true. He paints the savage's treachery and cruelty in unequivocal colors; even his "good Indians" have the traits that set them off from the white man's complete sympathy. And the good Indians themselves, Chingachgook and Uncas, are shown to be singular exceptions. By portraying the moving border, Cooper is able to show the changes in Indian condition, parallel to the changes among the white frontiersmen; so the Sioux are different in many ways from the Iroquois, and within the single nation of the Delawares, the aged Tamenund represents an already forgotten type of character. And in the individual Indian, Chingachgook, who in his own race stands for the same isolation, the same devotion to an ideal, as Leatherstocking, the remorseless picture of drunken ruin ought to convince the most fastidious critic that Cooper did not idealize the red man.

Besides his ultra-romantic hero, Cooper, like Scott, has a moderately interesting hero—Duncan Heyward, for example, to correspond to Frank Osbaldistone or Waverley. These young men are frankly in Scott's vein. They are chivalric, energetic and manly, but not clever, and their part in the story is never one of great initiative. They are simply admirable citizens, born to ornament a settled, polished society, and their presence on the frontier serves both for a foil to the mental isolation of the ultra-romantic hero, as in Scott, and for encouragement to a faith in the advancing civilization which they represent. That they do represent the future, is felt in the sense of vital youth which Cooper manages to give them, which always makes Leatherstocking seem in comparison old and outdistanced. It must have been by the intuition of genius that the novelist drew no such character in *The Deerslayer*, where he wished Leatherstocking to seem young; the comparison would have been to his disadvantage.

Cooper's heroines, too, have much resemblance to Scott's, though Parkman also set the fashion to see little true or interesting in the American writer's ideals of femininity. Professor Lounsbury in his admirable biography gives Parkman's point of view better support than it deserves, holding that these ladies are insufferable bores with their correctness, their stilted talk, and their insipidity. Mr. W. C. Brownell in his recent acute essay on Cooper takes the other side with convincing power, pointing out the genuineness of feminine portraiture in the novels, the real though quiet charm of Cooper's ideal, and the occasional grandeur of a character like Judith Hutter,—who Parkman himself admitted was the finest woman Cooper drew. It must be confessed at once that Cooper portrayed no such glorious creatures as Di Vernon or Catherine Seyton. He had known no such women in life, and his ideas were always founded strictly on the society he knew. But he had known women of strong character and charming manners, and he drew them in Katherine Plowden, Sarah Wharton and Cora Munro—a list which could be lengthened, and which hardly needs defense against criticism. It is evident, however, that Cooper's knowledge of feminine character is limited to very few types. He follows Scott in representing an ultra-romantic heroine, such as Alice Dunscombe, in *The Pilot*, or Isabella Singleton, in *The Spy;* like Flora McIvor, they have a mysterious career and a tragic end; they probably owe their existence to Cooper's reading, for he could hardly have met them in the America of his time. They are the product of the Byron influence in Scott, in whose romantic world they are natural and intelligible, but in Cooper, whose sense for the real is so strong, they never quite ring true. His best heroines, on the average, belong in a second type to be paralleled in Scott—girls of much sense and strong emotions but without any abnormal brilliancy, like Frances Wharton. This type of womanhood had been glorified in Scott's novels to the same extent as the corresponding sort of hero, full of sense and energy, but not unusual. Since it represents the normal character, Cooper must have known many examples of it; at least we can indulge a conviction that the type had his admiration, from the prominent place it usually holds in the center of his stage. It seems, however, that Parkman, and Professor Lounsbury after him, would have us believe that Cooper's preference was for the fragile, clinging creatures, ranging in the scale of intelligence from Alice Munro to Hetty Hutter. The extreme type of innocence, usually shown in a younger sister or close relative, does occur frequently in Cooper's novels, and is represented with a charm not to be lightly regarded even to-day by the reader who admires old-fashioned gentleness and breeding. But Cooper is too good a story-teller to put the weight of the plot upon such delicate creatures, and he knew his subject too well to picture them as average examples of American womanhood. His best heroines have more initiative and a more passionate interest in life. By far the best is Judith Hutter, whose complex nature he has drawn with power and delicacy. No discriminating reader can pass lightly over the great scenes in which she tells her love to Deerslayer. No modern analyst of the feminine heart could indicate with more skill and dignity the effort that went to her self-confession, or the agony she endured from the hunter's rejection of her offer.

Cooper follows Scott and the other romancers in his invariable use of the villain. If he portrays no elaborate wickedness to match Rashleigh's character, in *Rob Roy*, at least his villains are unmistakably bad, and in one or two instances they have as great individuality. In the portrayal of evil, as in everything else, Cooper's genius works most effectively on the frontier, and Le Renard Subtil, the Indian enemy in *The Last of the Mohicans*, is easily his most successful embodiment of wickedness. He availed himself of the Indian qualities of shrewdness and treachery, to paint a figure which should be almost diabolical, and yet perfectly natural,— which perhaps is more than can be said for Rashleigh. Le Renard's cruel determination to possess Cora, his device for luring her into the forest by carrying off her sister Alice, and the satisfaction he has in stabbing Uncas, are nothing short of devilish, yet the circumstances of his race, and his treatment at the hands of Cora's father and Chingachgook, make his conduct inevitable rather than incomprehensible. He is the finest of Cooper's villains because the evil in him is joined with a great capacity and a noble scale of action, and he is not a coward. The original injustice of the harsh treatment that made him the Englishman's foe, almost turns the reader's sympathy to him, and in places the general sense Cooper has of the rights of the Indians to the land, serves to render Le Renard, as well as Chingachgook, an object of pity; and the ethical poise of the story becomes unsteady,—as a greater mind than Cooper's once found, when he sang of Satan's defiance of the eternal justice. In *The Spy* the Skinner is an even more picturesque villain, if possible, than Le Renard, but he is a coward, and his wickedness has no excuse. Dillon, in *The Pilot*, stirs some pity by the very meanness of his nature, but the strongest interest he excites is through his relation to Long Tom Coffin.

The element of horror, of mental and physical fear, had a large place in the early romances, and literary skill in dealing with it shows a steady increase from the *Mysteries of Udolpho* to the morbid triumphs of Poe. Scott's sturdy mind accepted horror only as it came in the natural way of adventure, as one of the incidents of a romantic life. So the drowning of Morris, in *Rob Roy*, gives the effect of horror by actual physical events, in broad daylight—something to be seen and, as soon as possible, forgotten,—not brooded upon. Scott's good taste as an artist led him to limit this effect to one occurrence in each story; otherwise the force of it would be blunted. Cooper follows Scott's custom in making the effect through physical means, and in limiting himself to a rare use of it, but his skill in making the scene real was greater than Scott's, and some of his earliest critics found fault with him for a too dreadful facility in inspiring terror. Though we should not now care to give up such powerful scenes, we may concede some truth to the criticisms, remembering such haunting episodes as old Birch's death, the hanging of the Skinner, the execution of Abiram White, the harpooning of the English captain, and the retreat from Fort William Henry.

Cooper's pedants, or bores, of whom enough has been said already, are also direct descendants of the talkative, officious pedants Scott loved to draw. Bailie Jarvie, in *Rob Roy*, is the model of the class,—yet as soon as the name is mentioned, the lover of Scott feels the superior richness of character which he discovers in his bores. The type perhaps appealed to Cooper because of its satire upon officiousness. In his imitation of it, much of the sweetness is lost, especially as the years of controversy embittered his opinion of the race; only Gamut and Dr. Sitgreaves, of all their class, are really pleasant companions. But to say this is only to repeat that Cooper had little humor and no delicacy of satire.

In one respect Cooper differs widely from Scott, and loses by the comparison. In common with most American novelists, he had little gift for dialogue. His unconsciousness of the defect is one of the chief causes of his occasional tiresomeness in his inferior novels, where he tries to indicate character by conversation, or to reproduce dialect. All his characters speak a stilted literary prose, not to be disguised by Indian interjections, nor by Leatherstocking's formal breaches of grammar, such as his "used to could." The voice and the style is Cooper's throughout: if there is any difference in the novels, the preference in this respect must be given to the earlier ones, for in the later stories the talk becomes constantly more ponderous and undistinguished.

An ultra-romantic hero, and a more commonplace hero, matched by the ultra-romantic and the more normal heroines; a villain; and a pedant,—these are the people to be met in the best Cooper stories, and as the types are named over, his resemblance or indebtedness to Scott is clear. The world he describes is the frontier, and the plot involves a chase, with one moment of horror. The simplicity of these elements is the index of the writer's character. The inventory of his literary equipment is short; he is neither a great bookman, nor a philosopher, nor a historian; he is nothing but a story-teller. After the fashion of practical minds, he observed and represented life as an experience not necessarily complex; in private life he recognized no situation that a prompt application of the ten commandments would not solve. But he had for humanity at large a vast sympathy, for the expression of which his intellectual equipment was inadequate; and he loved his country with a fervor hardly matched again among American men of letters. It was his patriotism that made his success in literature. Whatever he learned from Scott was changed into something new by the complete Americanism of his mind, and the American landscape, his lifelong passion, colored even his pictures of the Old World. To say that he was not an artist, or that he had no style, is to leave his quality untouched. He had American character, which he stamped on everything he wrote, and which he made familiar to all peoples. Through his pages our gaunt pine forests, our charmed lakes, and our mysterious prairies were added once for all to the geography of the human imagination; in his stories a romantic and fast dying race were rescued to the remembrance of every reading nation, so that through him boyhood the world over "plays Indian"; he created the most typical figure in the novel of his age, the frontiersman, and setting him on the most romantic border our civilization recalls, endowed him with American ideals of justice and efficiency, and with something of American fatalism.   Leatherstocking is one of the heroic figures of the world's fiction,— one of its prizemen; Thackeray spoke truth when he said that Cooper deserves well of us.

W. Gilmore Simms

WILLIAM GILMORE SIMMS

I

WILLIAM GILMORE SIMMS, like Cooper, is a story-teller. He did for the Southwestern border what Cooper did for the Northern frontier and what Bret Harte was later to do for California. Simms has suffered somewhat in the rating of critics because he so strongly resembles Cooper,—just as Cooper has suffered for his resemblances to Scott. The two American writers have this in common with the great romancer, that they were masters of story-telling rather than thinkers or scholars, they were poets in their idealism, and they used their immediate country and its history for the scenes and plots of their tales. Beyond this it is uncritical to press their similarities. Simms was ready enough to acknowledge his indebtedness to Cooper. The admiration he expressed for him when the New York writer was not personally beloved by his countrymen is chivalry at its best. But Simms had a personality of his own—a noble one, and it is much to the interest of American literature to remember him in his own right.

His boyhood, in its way, was as romantic and as favorable to the fostering of genius as Scott's or Cooper's, having a large element of that not unhappy loneliness which seems reserved for imaginative boys destined to be great. His father, after whom he was named, was an Irish semi-genius of much temperament, who came to Charleston, South Carolina, just after the Revolution, and in 1804 married a Miss Harriet Ann Augusta Singleton, some twenty years his junior. Their second child, William Gilmore, was born in Charleston, April 17, 1806. Two years later the mother died, shortly after the death of the first child. The father had been overtaken by business troubles which ended in bankruptcy, and in a fit of desperation, apparently, he disappeared into the wilderness of Tennessee, leaving his surviving child to the care of its maternal grandmother.

This Mrs. Singleton, left a widow, had married again and was now Mrs. Gates. It is extremely unlikely that any calculation ever prompted the more than Celtic actions of the elder Simms, but if he had been the coldest and shrewdest of men he could hardly have left his infant son in better hands. As the boy grew up he heard from his grandmother's lips stories of the great war for freedom, which she had witnessed, —stories which in her fashion of remembering and telling had perhaps already assumed the quality of legends. Mrs. Gates was a generous woman and brought up the child to think well of his wandering father, who wrote few letters, but those always full of border adventure. Scott himself can hardly have absorbed more stories in his childhood, nor gloated over tales of adventure nearer in family history.

When he was six years old the boy was sent to a public school, which from his own account was not all that a school should be. An old Irishman who taught him to spell, read tolerably, and write a pretty good hand, was the best teacher he had, "and he knew little." There was no one who knew enough to teach arithmetic. After two years of this system, which Simms in later years described as "worthless and scoundrelly," he had a few years more in private schools, and so ended his formal education. But the meagerness of this training was balanced by a great love of books, which reacted as it usually does with such natures, in a love of writing. Before he was thirteen he wrote verses on the war of 1812, and by that time he was enthralled by Scott, Byron and Moore, and probably by many others of the English poets. In prose *The Pilgrim's Progress* and *The Vicar of Wakefield* were early and lasting favorites. When his school days were over he was apprenticed to a druggist, with some idea that he might study medicine. But his real studies were conducted at night after he was supposed to be asleep, when he read good books by the light of a candle stuck in a box,—this not very black deception being made necessary by Mrs. Gates' disposition in favor of early hours.

About this time his father returned, making his coming felt in a startling way. He evidently wanted to see his son and doubted if the grandmother would part with him, so to make sure, it is said, he tried to kidnap the boy on the street. The attempt failed, more formal negotiations were opened in court, and young Simms had his choice of going or staying. He wisely enough chose to stay with his grandmother, and the father, in complete good humor, paid them a visit in 1816 or 1817. What the visit meant to the boy can easily be imagined. The father whom he had idealized as borderer and Indian fighter was now for a while his companion,—a handsome man, with wit and the gift of verse-making, and with innumerable adventures to tell, both of the general frontier life and of his fighting under Jackson against the Creeks. The drug shop must have been a dreary place when the meteoric father returned to Florida and Jackson.

When his apprenticeship was up young Simms entered the law office of Charles R. Carroll. The pleasant relations between his father and himself suggest that the father may have been contributing something to his support. The study of medicine had been abandoned,—if for no other reason, because the fates so often decree that in America a great writer must have first tried to be a lawyer. Simms filled out the tradition completely by dividing his time between law-books and verse-making. Probably not all his odes celebrated pub-

lic men like Lafayette, for in a short time he was engaged to
be married to Miss Anna Malcolm Giles.

Studies and poetry and love-making were all interrupted
by a visit he paid his father near Georgeville, Mississippi, in
1824 or 1825. The journey was adventurous and his stay in
the border country must have been the realization of many
of his boyhood's day-dreams. He visited numerous settlements with his father, unconsciously storing up material for
his romances, and he wrote poems on Indian subjects inspired by visits to the Creeks and Cherokees. Once in the
wilderness he found he had been resting by a grave, which
in spite of his father's skepticism he liked to think was the
burial place of some follower of De Soto.

This visit of several months was of great importance in the
young man's development. It was the first traveling he had
done, and it took him through varied and picturesque scenes
to a romantic world. But at the time he seems to have been
chiefly stirred by his father's suggestion, occasioned by the
visit, that he should remain in the Southwest. The elder
Simms had no happy memory of Charleston and he prophe-
sied vehemently, after his fashion, that his son would not
succeed there. Perhaps the young man's admiration for his
father was tempered with some distrust of his judgment in
practical affairs, or he may have inherited the paternal determination; in any case he decided to make his career in his
native city and accordingly returned. He never saw his
father again. In 1830 he probably visited Mississippi after
his father's death, on March 28th of that year.

II

The career that Simms began upon his return from visiting
his father was in some ways as sad as Poe's, though it was of
perfect honor. He lacked the social position necessary to
win a hearing in his aristocratic city; he was doomed always

to lack an appreciative audience in the South; and he came so late in the troubled decades before the Civil War that neither North nor South had much attention to spare for his type of story. Cooper's fame was achieved in the most established parts of the country during the most peaceful years between the Revolution and the Civil War; before Simms began to write Cooper had preëmpted the audience that cared for his kind of romance. Simms was evidently facing as many difficulties as possible when he entered the same field in troubled years and in a section of the South whose quietest moments politically were but intervals in volcanic spasms. There was something immensely heroic in the vigor and astounding copiousness with which Simms dedicated his genius to his own times and his own section—writing to make a place for himself in the South and especially in Charleston, and writing equally to give the South the place in literary esteem which he believed its ideals deserved. The motive of patriotism was no more compelling in Brockden Brown or Cooper than in Simms; he certainly paid a bitterer price for his patriotism than any other American writer,—wasting his genius in limitless heart-breaking journalism, that the losing cause might have a voice.

But of course he was untroubled by any glimpse of his fate when in 1825 he returned to Charleston. In August died General Charles Cotesworth Pinckney, still remembered for his reply to the French commissioners, "Millions for defence, but not a cent for tribute." On September 14 the Charleston *Courier* noticed a monody on the dead statesman. The poem was anonymous and in spite of the friendly notice it achieved an early and complete oblivion; no copy of it has been found. It was Simms' first noted appearance, though some of his more youthful verses had filled space in the newspapers. Before his visit to his father he had written a tragedy on Roderick, the last of the Goths, and he now offered it to a Charleston manager,—who accepted it and would have produced it, had not Simms withdrawn it as the result of some quarrel. These initial disappointments were no more than young writers by tradition are heir to, but in the case of Simms they seem to be tragic omens.

In January, 1827, Simms published his *Lyrical and Other Poems*, the first volume in which he formally laid claim to the laurel. For thirty-five years he was to put forth books of verse, convinced of his authentic election to Parnassus. Of that conviction it is not necessary to speak here, beyond registering sincere regret that verse and magazine writing kept him so largely from training his story-telling genius. But from his own point of view, no matter what posterity thinks of it, Simms was justified in his verse-writing; nothing else gave him, perhaps, a pleasure quite so keen. And any exercise which fostered his idealism should be gratefully thought of, for altogether too many incidents of his life were of a nature to darken his ideals, as writer and man.

Late in 1827 he published a second volume of verse, entitled *Early Lays*, more interesting than the first because of certain pieces based on the legends of his region—material he was later to use advantageously in prose. In September of the following year he joined a fellow-poet named Simmons in publishing and editing a magazine—the first of his many adventures of that sort—called *The Tablet, or Southern Monthly Literary Gazette*. Simms' lifelong sacrifices to supply the South with a magazine are pathetic. This first attempt, after a few numbers, was a failure, and the two editors bore the loss. Perhaps Simms gained something in local fame not easily commensurable. On the Fourth of July, 1828, he had delivered an oration before the Palmetto Society, at the celebration of the battle of Fort Moultrie; evidently he was to be a marked man even in his unappreciative city. His biographer makes the interesting suggestion that among his audience at Fort Moultrie may have been Edgar Allan Poe, stationed there at the time as E. A. Perry in Battery H, First Artillery.

The largest part of his attention was given, while it lasted, to his magazine. It is self-evident that his law studies were well in the past. He had indeed been admitted to the bar on April 17, 1827, had pleaded his first cases with much skill and energy, and had made in the first year six hundred dollars—no bad beginning for that profession. But his heart was set on literature, and in his optimistic temperament practical considerations did not count. That he had reason enough to be practical may be inferred from his marriage to Miss Giles on October 19, 1826—six months before he had been admitted to the bar. In November of 1827 was born a daughter, Anna Augusta, the only child of this marriage. His wife apparently had no money, and how they managed to get on at all is not clear.

Simms may have been living on the capital of a small legacy from his mother. Upon the extinction of his magazine he invested the remnants of this little fortune in a daily paper, the *City Gazette*, which in 1830 he began to publish, in partnership with E. S. Duryea, a printer. The editing of this paper was destined to launch Simms into the political maelstrom of those days,—to lead him as far as possible from the literary pursuits for which he had abandoned the law. As if to recover his balance, he published towards the end of 1829 a volume of verse, *Cortes, Cain, and Other Poems*, in which appeared his best known poem, *The Lost Pleiad;* and in 1830 democracy had its say in *The Tri-Color, or The Three Days of Blood in Paris*, a book of verse that had the luck to be reprinted in London before the year was out.

He was soon to have experience of mob democracy at home. When he assumed control of the *Gazette*, South Carolina had for some years been in the throes of the nullification movement—the movement led by Calhoun, which strove to establish the right of a state to reject or ignore any Federal legislation which it did not approve. The point of debate at the time was the tariff, which almost caused South Carolina to secede; but the real issue, as thoughtful men foresaw, was not nullification but secession—the question whether a state under any circumstances had the right to leave the Union. Simms held consistently through his life that a state had no such right except in the very last extremity—a position which made secession logical for him when slavery was at stake, but which now held him as logically on the Union side. A matter of tariff rates did not in his opinion justify nullification or secession. On the Fourth of July, 1831, he read a *National Ode* at a Union celebration, and his editorials were firmly against the nullifiers.

At first he happened to be on the winning side in the local elections, and in what is supposed to be the spirit of Southern journalism he allowed to appear in his paper certain personal attacks, which provided him with enemies against the day of adversity. In 1831 the followers of Calhoun were victorious, and celebrated with a torch-light procession which passed the office of the *Gazette*. Simms was standing outside the door. The crowd hissed him, and he retorted by calling them cowards, whereupon he almost lost his life. His unmoved courage when the crowd made a rush at him, awed them or at least gained their respect, and they were persuaded by cool-headed leaders to march on. It was the most spectacular appearance Simms ever made in his own city; the only profit of it, as of most of his appearances there, was a very empty glory. His paper immediately began to feel the effect of his unpopularity. Subscriptions declined steadily until on June 7, 1832, he published a notice that the paper was now in the hands of William Laurens Poole. Duryea had died in March. The notice in the *Gazette* made it quite clear that Simms was a bankrupt.

He had suffered heavier losses. His first little home had been burned down—a foretaste of his final domestic tragedy. His father had died in Mississippi; Mrs. Gates, his beloved grandmother, had died soon after; and on February 20, 1832, he buried his wife. A strong nature might well have been crushed by this tragic sequence. That Simms bore his fate and lived to know sufferings that make these seem light, is at once a measure of the man and of his sorrows. His father's doleful prophecy of a career in Charleston had come true. Simms stirred himself to begin life afresh, and leaving his daughter presumably with his wife's relations, he came North.

III

How unfortunate Simms was in the particular time in which he lived is illustrated by his attitude toward the North. It was there that his genius was appreciated and his books published; his literary career would probably have been impossible, even in peace, without the support the North from the first gave him. But his political sympathies—his patriotism, as he would have said—withheld him from the full enjoyment of what the North offered. Many years later, in a book that is not without strong sectional prejudice, he writes pleasantly of his first days with Bryant and the other appreciative spirits who gave him welcome. "When I first visited New York, Hoboken was as favorite a resort with me, of an afternoon, as it was to thousands of your citizens. Its beautifully sloping lawns were green and shady. Now! Oh! the sins of brick and mortar! There, I first knew Bryant and Sands, and wandered with them along the shores, at sunset, or strolled away, up the heights of Weehawken, declaiming the graceful verses of Halleck upon the scene." The contrast with the scenes he had left behind him in South Carolina speaks for itself, and one wishes his fate had here given him a period of high-minded leisure in which to concentrate and organize his powers.

But his recent losses impelled him to an active life even in those summer days that he remembered so pleasantly. On his arrival from the South he had found the cholera raging in New York, and for a time had stopped at Hingham, Massachusetts. In this village he had worked on his long poem *Atalantis, a Story of the Sea*, which was published in New York a few months later, in 1832. When the cholera scare was over, Simms met Bryant, as he says, and began a friendship that was ended only by his own death. Through this fortunate introduction to literary New York he seems to have met most of the interesting men, and he had an opportunity to indulge his love of the theater. He heard Fanny Kemble and met George Holland, and later became the intimate friend of Edwin Forrest.

When his ambitious poem was safely through the press, Simms returned to Charleston, much cheered by the visit. But there was nothing for him to do in the South just then, except to visit his little daughter and hear generous friends praise his new poem; so in 1833 he was North once more, this time settled in New Haven. He was ready for any profitable literary enterprise, and finding among his papers a murder story which he had written for his *Gazette*, he elaborated it into his first novel, *Martin Faber*. This book was put into print by a New Haven publisher, but the Harpers accepted it and put it on sale, and it had an immediate success. Much of the author's satisfaction was spoiled by the charge that the book was imitated from an English novel, published at the same time; and though the charge was easily answered, it induced in Simms a frame of mind that almost led to a duel with a gentleman who had spoken slightingly of him. The only completely satisfying result of the book was the money it brought, and Simms was not the type of man to consider that a substitute for the honor he desired to win by his pen. This first novel, however, is of little literary importance beyond the fact that, as its sale proved, it was very readable. So were all his stories. Here he was attempting simply a tale of horror, common enough at the time, as the suspicion of plagiarism showed; and though he had a natural bent toward realistic horrors, he was never an artist in his management of such effects, least of all in his early attempts. Simms felt this himself, and omitted *Martin Faber* from the revised edition of his works.

In the meanwhile he had been doing various kinds of magazine writing, some of it interesting, the rest of it mere hackwork. Several stories written in this way he now collected into an unimportant volume published in Philadelphia, in 1833, under the title *The Book of My Lady : a Mélange.* In the same year he found time to start a new magazine in Charleston—at least he brought out one number of it. The wide experience from publishing in so many cities perhaps encouraged him to call this paper *The Cosmopolitan.* It failed at once.

In July, 1834, Simms published in New York his first notable book, *Guy Rivers.* The reception of this story was the most encouraging that the author had yet enjoyed. The Northern critics fell completely under the charm of a new scene and a new genius in the perennial romance of adventure. The book was published the next year in England. One curious result of its popularity was an offer from a Charleston merchant to send Simms to Europe—an opportunity for study which the author greatly desired but was too proud to accept.

Guy Rivers belongs to the group of novels known as "border romances." It is not perhaps the best of them; certainly it is not among the best of all Simms' stories. Its merit is that it begins the series of books that the author and his admirers were glad to recognize as his; if *Martin Faber* may be passed over, *Guy Rivers* is the first of his stories. That it is a tale of adventure, with a Scott hero, normally stupid, and a villainous outlaw for the secondary, romantic hero, and with a correct heroine to console the proper youth at the end—is sufficient characterization of it. But the scene is laid in the frontier region Simms knew, and therefore the book was accepted by his countrymen as a new discovery of the romance they had overlooked, at their very doors. In this they were right; and if Simms has grave faults of structure and style, if he indulges at times in a species of the romantic that almost spells itself claptrap, he is still entitled to remembrance as a true discoverer, in less degree but no other kind than Cooper and Scott. His hero and his heroine were the pattern of youth in his own state, as they appeared to his romancing ideal. The scenes in Georgia which he clothed with these adventures were easily recognizable, and doubtless he had some thought that they would hold the tradition of his story, as the Scotch landscape holds the Waverley novels, or Sleepy Hollow, the ride of Ichabod Crane. That Simms failed in any such permanent results is explained by those faults of writing which mar this and all of his books, and which can be studied to greater advantage in his next novel, his masterpiece.

Immediately after the success of *Guy Rivers* Simms began *The Yemassee*, and in a year it was published in New York. Its success was complete. The same showers of praise fell upon it that had greeted *Guy Rivers*, but the critics were learning wisdom and their judgment of this story was discerning. No other story of the author's is now so much read, and common opinion holds that none other is so good. If it were worth while to attempt to disturb the tradition which is kindest to Simms' fame, one might challenge this opinion in favor of some of his shorter, livelier tales; but it is fairer to examine the book as it stands, with the author's genius and limitations written large in it.

Perhaps the legends that Mrs. Gates used to tell her grandson now proved his inspiration, or his knowledge of the Yemassees may have been gained from his wide reading in the history of his state. In 1715, when Charles Craven was governor of Carolina, the Indians planned a wholesale insurrection against the settlers. They were partly incited by the Spanish in Florida, and partly by their own fears, as we are told in the story, that the white men would possess their lands and drive them into the swamps. Their rising was terribly successful on the borders, but when they advanced towards Charleston they were met and totally defeated by the governor and his army of twelve hundred. The Indians were dispersed and took refuge in Florida.

These facts Simms used as the basis of his story, and Governor Craven, masquerading gratuitously as Gabriel Harrison, is his hero. The Indians he drew from observations made among the Creeks and Cherokees, while he was visiting his father. The scenery in the book was that of his native state, described as carefully as though he had been writing history; the rivers and places were accurately named, so that the natural illustration for the volume is a map. Only such episodes as the defense of the blockhouse were complete romancing. In short, he set out to write an historical novel, which by virtue of the quality of his genius became a tale of adventure.

It is the solid intention of the story which has made it permanent. History was not the author's end in the border romances, and without an organized ground-plan of fact, his too facile incidents resulted always in chaos. But in this book he seems to have denied himself many a thrilling episode, and it is our business to be grateful; as it is, the story contains enough adventure to furnish an artist like Cooper with several plots. Simms also appears to have turned resolutely away from the Cooperesque portrayal of the Indian, probably because he could not have reproduced that aspect of savage life from observation; for this reason *The Yemassee* is peculiar among Indian stories for the infinitesimal amount of "woodcraft" it contains. *The Last of The Mohicans*, published nine years before, had set the tradition of Indian craft which still has authority with us, though later frontiersmen would call Cooper to account for excessive romance; yet Simms gives his red men superior acuteness in only one place, and there Sanutee's keen hearing is compared with nothing sharper than Richard Chorley's common shrewdness. The savages are susceptible to panic, as white men might be; Harrison and his dog put one section of the Indians to rout before the blockhouse. Nor are they of superhuman strength—otherwise Chorley would not have had Sanutee at his mercy.

Yet the true romance of the story is in the Indian part of it. More heroic, certainly, are Cooper's red men than Sanutee and his tribe, but Simms endows his warriors with a natural humanity that has its own charm. Sanutee, the last of a proud race, his wife Matiwan and his son Occonestoga, call to mind at once—and the comparison is illuminating—that other Indian family, Chingachgook, Hist and Uncas. The early death of Hist and the tragic killing of Uncas save those two most poetic characters for a kind of immortal youth. It was the poet in Cooper that thus visualized the extinction of the Indian race. To depict Chingachgook as the drunkard in *The Pioneers* was also a poet's work, recognizing an ugly truth with the greatest economy of ugliness. If any of the three must be degraded, Chingachgook could best be spared. Imagine the horror of besotting Hist or Uncas with whisky from the settlements! Yet Simms is fully aware that when the savage encounters civilization, it is his son who is lowered by the contact, since the younger nature is less fixed and more easily lured. The commonest tragedy for the Indians must have been always, as it is now in the reservations, the fading of the race's ideals in their young men. Occonestoga, in the story, is the only son of the great chief. He has his father's prowess and all the fineness of his noble descent; he is tender as well as brave, and his devotion to his mother, Matiwan, lights his character even at its worst; his friendship for the English also indicates his quick-witted appreciation of the civilization that fascinates him. But he is enslaved to drink, and every fine inherited trait, every purpose of his own, wastes in him like water poured upon the sands. The truth of the picture is at once made darker and brighter, so to speak, by the fact that Occonestoga is powerless to resist his beset- ting vice; he thereby loses in respect, but gains much in pity, and his mother's love for him is more touching.

Something is gained further for the reality of Sanutee's character by making him an exceptional figure among his people; he is unable to persuade the other chiefs not to sell their lands to the English. Perhaps it is more romantic to think of the Indian as making forlorn stands against encroach- ing civilization, driven to the wall against his will; but it is probably truer to show such a race as Simms does, inclined to accept the worst side of civilization first, selling the graves of their fathers, as Sanutee says, for gold and whisky. That a fine minority, a romantic aristocracy should survive, is easier to believe than that all should be heroes; and therefore Sanutee in his companionless nobility is a convincing good Indian.

In one sad respect Simms is but too probably a follower of Cooper; he tries to be humorous. It might seem in general hard to establish any literary imitation by so common a phenomenon, but the reader who knows Cooper's peculiar attempts at sprightly witticism or humor of character can never be in doubt when he tastes that fare again. Simms even takes over Cooper's stock comic character, the pedantic bore, who monopolizes the talk with set speeches on his one topic. In *The Yemassee* Dr. Constantine Maximilian Nichols, who parades his patriotism at every turn, asserts his readiness to die for his country, yet is always safely in the background, is the very worst type of the Cooper bore. Both Cooper and Simms were too serious and in a way too elaborate to be masters of the lighter shades of character drawing. Simms here suffers also from a faulty sense of structure, which allows him to add an irrelevant personage simply for the purposes of his supposed humor; Dr. Nichols is in no way necessary to the plot, nor does he really enter it.

Like Scott and Cooper Simms makes a contrast to his romance by occasional scenes of horror—horror in all these stories being the one legacy from the Gothic school. The scenes of horror in *The Yemassee* are among the best that Simms pictured, because they are not too grimly realistic, and they have a certain right to the room they take. The best of them is the great scene of the book, in which Matiwan kills her son to save him from disgrace. Second in importance artistically, though better known, is the description of Bess Matthews' encounter with the rattlesnake. Finely wrought as this scene is, it is cheap artistically because it is unprepared for and has no consequences. Some credit is due to the author for refraining in one place from the sort of crude, even revolting horror he too often indulges in; when the Indians are swimming after Harrison's canoe and are themselves pursued by alligators, the reader with any experience of Simms' habit nerves himself for a bit of gruesome tragedy; but Harrison escapes the Indians, the Indians escape the alligators, and the reader also is spared.

The easy solution of this scene is typical of a certain fault in this novel, which can be said to mar most of Simms' work. His imagination is extraordinarily fertile in incident, so much so that he has not time in any book to develop the situations that fill the story to overflowing. Rapidity is well enough in plot, but sequence counts for something too, and it is a sort of disappointment to any but a boyish reader to find the hero, even in a book of melodramatic adventure, plunged into a new dilemma in the beginning of every chapter, and lifted into safety bodily in the last line. The rescuing angel is overworked and sometimes not sufficiently agile. When somebody has somebody else by the throat and the victim already sees the knife or the tomahawk starting on its almost instantaneous descent, the reader learns to know that either a shot will ring out from the forest and the fierce eyes of the murderer will be observed to lose their fierceness in the glaze of death, or somehow that knife will obligingly delay its stroke till a figure leaps upon the murderer's back and chokes him off. The rattlesnake charms Bess, and Occonestoga happens along at the last moment and transfixes the reptile with his arrow. Harrison's negro attendant is captured and taken to the Spanish ship, but Harrison immediately captures the Spanish captain and trades him off for the slave. Harrison is fettered in the Indian lodge, but Matiwan simply walks in, holds an animated conversation, unbinds him and goes out with him—both stepping carefully over the sleepy figures of the Indians on guard. The reader is surprised that those Indians wake at all, even when Harrison steps on one of them.

But the worst illustration of this too facile solving of dangerous situations is the whole episode of the fight around the blockhouse—the part of the story which is usually counted, along with the rattlesnake scene, as most effective. Certainly the fight is described vividly, and the sally of the smith gives a true thrill, but when the Indians set fire to the blockhouse and there is no apparent escape for the white people, how does the author save them? He has neither the patience nor the ingenuity of Cooper in a similar predicament, to let his garrison wait in the bottom of a dry well until the house is burned

over their heads and the foe have retreated. He simply tells
us that the Indians at this moment were obliged to go somewhere else to fight another foe, and the garrison, much relieved, opened the door and walked out.

Simms is too good a story-teller, however, to seem ridiculous even in these solutions while his book is in our hands.
The very rapidity of the incidents leaves no opportunity for
too minute examination at the time. It is only when the book
is closed that we reflect soberly on the waste of undeveloped,
undisciplined material. And one episode, which has been
justly said to be the great moment of the story, is a shining
exception to all this criticism. The chapter in which Matiwan
brains her own child with her tomahawk so that his soul will
not be lost is in every way greatly told, though other less admirable sections of the story are better known. What gives
the episode its quality is that the problem is carried through,
for once, to a logical conclusion. The reader hardly expects
Occonestoga to be executed, or excommunicated from his
tribe; the previous experience of the book suggests that some
escape will open to him. When his mother kills him the solution is felt at once to be both logical and true, since it is the one
thing she would do, and the paradox of such a deed as the
work of sublime love lifts the episode into something higher
than mere adventure.

The faults that have been suggested in *The Yemassee* may
appear to sum up into a severe charge, but they indicate the
condition of Simms' genius rather than the worth of the book.
Simms was a prodigious worker,—reckoning by the volume
of his work. He was not a careful writer, nor did he ever
listen to criticism. He lacked the artist's conscience and perseverance; he might have been richer in such polishing virtues,
had he been poorer in ideas and themes. But a story may be
out at elbows so far as art is concerned, and still be memorable,—as some of Brockden Brown's work would indicate.

And *The Yemassee* is a fine story, true in scene and character, rich in incident, and filled with noble conduct such as we ask of romance.

IV

After *The Yemassee* appeared Simms went on immediately to other work which, if not quite so good, is at least among his best.   In August, 1835, a new romance from his pen was advertised, and at the end of the year *The Partisan: a Tale of the Revolution* was published in New York.   A legend attaches to the composition of this story, almost too fabulous for belief, but showing the conception Simms' contemporaries had of his working methods.   His biographer tells the incident, as recounted by James Harper.   Simms came North with the manuscript half finished, and all he had written was soon in type.   He was going out of town for a few days, when Mr. Harper objected that the printers had nothing to work on in that period.   Simms asked for pen and paper and a quiet room, and in half an hour produced enough copy to keep the type-setters busy till he returned.   With proper allowances this tradition probably does justice to the speed of the Southerner's pen, and explains numerous defects in his art.   On the whole the incident, if it were quite true, would be no more remarkable than Cooper's writing and paging the last chapter of *The Spy* before he knew how the plot was to end.

In 1836 appeared *Mellichampe: a legend of the Santee*. Fifteen years later Simms published *Katharine Walton, or The Rebel of Dorchester*, but in spite of the interval these two books were intended to form a sort of trilogy with *The Partisan*, and it is convenient to consider them together.   The third is the true sequel of the first; *Mellichampe* has little in common with either.   But Simms was not too conscientious about his own plots, and the series, no matter how loosely bound, represents a solid kind of romancing.   The scene is laid around

Dorchester, where Simms had delighted as a boy to trace the movements of Marion's men, or to hear an old inhabitant tell some of the local legends. His material was therefore well in hand, and his historical conscience was roused; in most of these patriotic romances a desire to be accurate in his facts and his geography was his best substitute for artistic discipline.

There is much in these stories to remind one of Cooper's *Spy*. The historical atmosphere, the shifting movements of the troopers, the daring bands of partisans, at first seem much alike in both. A close comparison, however, brings out Cooper's art—a quality too often denied him, and emphasizes also the larger scene, the more humorous and spectacular events that distinguish Simms' work. Simms had more history at his command than Cooper had. It is not simply that he writes three long volumes to Cooper's one, but he has an old and interesting society to reproduce, independently of the battle scenes and war motives, and the period the three stories cover includes important fights, whereas *The Spy* depicts only skirmishes. Simms has no central historical figure like Washington; on the other hand, the minor characters in his cycle were drawn from life, as far as he could get at it from Charleston records and legends. One family in particular, the Waltons, are the center of the series, taking the place of an individual hero.

The Partisan illustrates the great attention its author was giving to the historical basis of his story; in several places the romance passes from fiction to a bare historical record. Its astonishing virtue is the great spirit with which the adventurous moments are recounted. Singleton, the hero, who at the end of the series marries Katharine Walton, is somewhat too heroic to be interesting as a character, and Colonel Walton is at best a substantial lay-figure. But Singleton's adventures, especially his daring rescue of Walton at the close of the first novel, are self-sufficient even without character analysis.   Colonel Walton, too, is made interesting by the danger he undergoes. His escape from hanging makes him in a way the hero of the last novel in the series, for the fortunes of the other characters depend upon his, and he challenges attention actively as a leader of the partisan troop.

Yet it must be confessed frankly that Simms is no master of portraiture; still less does he depict character. The women who appear in these and other stories are generally paler to the imagination than Cooper's worst—and nothing harsher need be said. Like Cooper, Simms delights in a formal pattern of social behavior, which when garbed in a blue gown or a red, is intended to become to the reader's imagination a personality, distinct from another pattern in white. It is chiefly by their geographical location and their external appearance that the female characters are told one from the other; and as Simms is generally careless in the external description, often they cannot be told apart at all. Perhaps if any woman in the three novels would be recognizable when met in real life, it would be Moll Harvey, Katharine Walton's rival, yet it is only by careful inference that the reader is able to detect the color of her eyes and hair. He is discouraged in the effort by this sort of dithyramb,—serviceable, if ever, only to keep the Harpers' type-setter busy: "Moll Harvey was of middle size and most symmetrical figure. Ease and grace were natural to her as life itself; but her motion was not simply that of ease and grace. There was a free, joyous impulse in her movements, an exquisite elasticity, which displayed itself in a thousand caprices of gesture, and seemed to carry her forward buoyantly as a thing possessing the infinite support and treasure of the air. As song to ordinary speech, such was the relation which her action bore to the common movements of her sex. A fairy property in her nature seemed to bring with her the spring and all its flowers where she came; and the loveliness which appeared to ray out from her person, as she walked or danced, compelled the involuntary homage of the eye, making the thought forgetful of all search or inquiry except through that single medium."

In some of these books the conversation occasionally sparkles, to the great encouragement of the reader. But these bright spots are due to the insertion of clever bits of repartee current in Charleston tradition. They rarely come very naturally from the lips into which Simms inserts them, and the author makes the illusion more difficult by stating in a scrupulous foot-note where the witticism was first uttered. Of course it is useless to take a romancer to task for his dialogue, if his genius is solely in adventure; but Simms' hasty methods of writing cannot be defended, and to them largely may be laid his failure to cover his tracks or build up his characters. What he lost by not revising his work may be illustrated again from Moll Harvey. When she has cheated Balfour of his hope to win Katharine Walton, it apparently occurs to Simms that a girl would need a strong motive to become the murderess of Colonel Walton; the love story as told so far does not justify her. Simms therefore hints that Moll Harvey had been Balfour's mistress. "There was a story and relations between them," he says, "of which we have not heard." It is a pity we have not heard; for if she had lived through a tragic past her mad jealousy would have been interesting, not wooden from the start, and Balfour's devilish character would have seemed less a thing of merely theatrical terror.

Two characters only remain notable, from the three novels —Lieutenant Porgy, whose career continued through the Revolutionary romances, and Whitherspoon, the faithful scout in *Mellichampe*. To describe chivalry, personal loyalty and integrity, comes easy to a man like Simms—the danger usually being that such a character lends itself to maudlin exaggeration. In Whitherspoon Simms manages to keep within artistic bounds, and the scout is easily thought of with Cooper's men. Porgy has been called a prose Falstaff; his rotundity, his boastfulness, and his general fatness physical and mental, encourage the notion. But it seems the author meant him as a burlesque of himself in certain moods. The likeness is not now recognizable. Porgy's boastfulness and his love of good eating might well be set up as claims to further kinship with Parolles and Friar Tuck; in the method by which his humor is developed—monologue assisted by timely questions—he might derive from, or anticipate, negro minstrelsy.

" 'Here I am at home,' he says. 'The Santee did well enough; but there's a sweetness, a softness, a plumpness, a beauty about bird and beast along the Ashley, that you find in the same animals nowhere else. God bless my mother!'
" 'For what in particular, Lieutenant?'
" 'That she chose it for my birthplace. I shouldn't have been half the man I am born anywhere else; shouldn't have had such discriminating tastes, such a fine appetite, such a sense of the beautiful in nature.' "

Simms' feeling for history was at its strongest in *Katharine Walton,*—which explains why that story is somewhat less interesting than *The Partisan.* From the earlier book the incidents of the light-horse bands are continued, and Marion's men, breaking cover at unexpected places, give the story its movement and charm. But undoubtedly Simms in this volume cared more about the portraits of Charleston society, the traditions he had heard all his life in his native city. If Charleston at the end of the eighteenth century had been as rich in notable people as London, Simms might have given us as important a gallery as we view in *Henry Esmond* or *The Virginians;* but alas for local pride! None of the portraits he labored at bear remembered names; only a passing reference to the home of Cotesworth Pinckney stirs the reader with a little thrill of recognition. Simms' own account of the book on the whole is just, and we may well leave it with his comment: "a large proportion of the work, and much of the interest, will be found to consist in the delineation of the social world of Charleston, during the Revolutionary period. These delineations are so many different studies, pursued during a series of many years, and under the guidance of the most various and the best authorities. The matter, in fact, is mostly historical, even when merely social. The portraits are mostly of real persons. The descriptions of life, manners, customs, movements, the social aspects in general, have all been drawn from sources as unquestionable as abundant. The social reunions, in many instances, as described in the story, were real occurrences. The anecdotes, the very repartees, though never before in print, are gathered from tradition and authority." A story so pieced together may fail of the highest success in romance, but the method was not a lazy one; the reader thinks kindly of *Katharine Walton*, as an honorable document in its author's character.

V

Immediately after the publication of *Mellichampe* Simms married his second wife, Miss Chevillette Roach, of Barnwell, South Carolina. Miss Roach lived with her father, Mr. Nash Roach, at Woodlands, their plantation, which soon became known as the home of the novelist. Even before the estate came into his control through the death of his father-in-law, in 1858, Simms was to all purposes owner of Woodlands and dispenser of its hospitalities. Mr. Roach was a chronic sufferer from the gout; perhaps he had brought with him from England those pleasant eighteenth-century habits of conviviality that are supposed to usher in gouty old age. It is certain that his son-in-law fell in naturally with any such household customs, and under his régime the entertaining at Woodlands became famous. Bryant and other Northern friends came here and felt the charm of the place; Simms' Southern friends of course visited him more often. The summers he spent at Charleston or in the North, but in the cool months he was busy writing in the fine library at Woodlands, or managing the estate,—no light task.

These were the happiest years Simms was to know. His wife seems to have been a woman of character and charm; his own fortunes were fairly established, his reputation gave him an honored position, and the dignified plantation home afforded all the leisure and luxury a writer needed. It is clear he made good use of his prosperity. Although his hospitalities consumed much time, he held himself rigorously to a large amount of literary work every day,—none but a genius of his perseverance could have accomplished so much. In these years his resemblance to Scott appeared in many ways— in the variety of his human interests, in his industry, and in his turn for medieval hospitality. His social gifts were great; in contrast with Cooper, he maintained all his life that high standard of lovable charm that is proverbial of the Southern gentleman. Vehement as his opinions were, he lacked no charity towards other men, and his trying losses never embittered him. If he failed of the highest accomplishment in literature, at least his life is something for Americans to be proud of, for no other of our great writers of fiction save Irving was so lovable and so gifted among his fellow-men.

He was a voluble talker on all subjects, on some of which his discourse must have been thin, yet from all accounts very interesting. If he monopolized the conversation, making himself the arbiter of every question and winning among his friends a certain comparison to Dr. Johnson, perhaps it was the Celt in him more than the Southerner; his father bequeathed him that vehemence, and enriched his talk also with a kind of wit, a turn for epigrams and little verses. One suspects that the scenes in Charleston ball-rooms, in *Katharine*

Walton, may be reliable clues to the sort of conversation Simms was master of—a trifle elaborate and premeditated here and there, but intellectually alert.

It is easy to recall him as he appeared then—strongly built, inclined to stoutness, of a noble bearing. His face was not a literary one; the keen eye and the firm set of the mouth suggests the man of action. But something intellectual, if massive, is read in the high forehead and in the total expression of the features. Looking on his portrait, one is aware of largeness and heroism.

Altogether Simms at Woodland must have represented a fine type of the Southerner before the war,—a slaveholder, treating his slaves with thoughtful affection, himself enjoying the leisure and culture of an old world aristocrat. There is something curious in the fate that made him thus typical; undoubtedly he would have espoused the Southern cause with the same conviction and ardor even if he had not been in position to know from experience the best arguments for its social system; but being the man he was, in the position he had come to occupy, he became a sort of exponent of his people, justifying their cause if that had been possible, and suffering the full weight of their tragedy. No Southerner was probably ever more thoroughly convinced than he of the righteousness of slavery, and in equal measure, of the master's duty to the slave. The sixty or seventy negroes on his place found in him their best friend. He would send a slave to Charleston to consult a physician, paying the man's expenses as well as giving him this practical liberty. Each slave family was permitted to raise chickens and vegetables, which Simms bought from them—thus recognizing their right to the profit of their labor. He was considered, by those who saw no other side to the question, to be an argument for the beneficence of slavery as an institution, and he himself, like many Southerners of refinement and goodness, apparently believed that all other slaveholders were equally philanthropical.

For a while the problem did not bother him greatly; he was busy and happy with his writing. That *Katharine Walton* did not immediately follow *Mellichampe* must be explained by the officious criticism of some friends, who persuaded him that his native state was not the rich soil needed for producing romantic plots. He listened to their argument, laid aside the last member of his trilogy, and wrote *Pelayo; a Story of the Goth*, which was something of a failure, though in 1838, the year of its appearance, its author's prestige would carry for at least a respectable distance anything he wrote. He knew his mistake, and in the introduction to *Katharine Walton* he speaks with some pride of the possibilities in South Carolina's history for an indefinite number of romances. An interesting suggestion has been made that perhaps he tried to write romances on foreign subjects just because his greater rival Cooper had failed in the attempt. That may well be so; but if it be, Simms deserved failure for transgressing his own principles. He always knew the advantage to be got from developing native material. Cooper in his excursions had a clear conscience, because it was necessary to depict foreign scenes in order to illustrate his thesis—the superiority of democratic over feudal institutions. But one may easily become too subtle over such points; a good story carries with it its own ethics,—a poor story has none. *Pelayo* and its sequel seven years later, *Count Julian, or The Last Days of The Goth*, are forgotten books, whereas *The Bravo* and *The Headsman* still have admiring readers.

In this year, 1838, Simms collected some short tales, his faith in which has not been justified—*Carl Werner; an Imaginative Story; with other Tales of Imagination*. This collection with the novel called *The Damsel of Darien*, may be passed over charitably, as examples of their author's worst.

It is not to be expected that a man of his temperament, committed to hasty methods of writing, should have a critical knowledge of himself; Simms loved all the children of his pen without distinction, and was happy in editing and republishing several volumes that should have not been printed a first time.

No strong suspicion of the general poorness of his work in these two or three years troubled him, but he got as near to the truth as to wonder whether his books were not selling on the strength of his name. Accordingly he published anonymously *Richard Hurdis, or The Avenger of Blood*, in 1838. In this story he reverted to the type of border romance in which he had first won his public; it was his natural material. But he did not learn much from the experiment; when this anonymous book succeeded he seems to have proved to himself that all his other writings had succeeded on their merits. He continued to work this old vein in a sequel, *Border Beagles; a Tale of Mississippi*, 1840, and in *Beauchampe, or the Kentucky Tragedy*, 1842.

The first and the second of these stories are tales of desperate adventure, founded on the exploits of the Murrell gang of robbers in the Southwest. The facts for these tales Simms got personally from Virgil A. Stewart, who had captured Murrell, and from Stewart's own account of his experiences. The books are purely sensational; they deal with criminal rather than patriotic warfare and accordingly are reduced to the level of the dime novel, but they are well told so far as the interest is concerned. *Beauchampe* is of another type; one wonders how Simms could bring himself to write it. The plot is a careful narrative of a murder case that attracted attention in Kentucky in 1828. One Kentucky Colonel discovered that his wife before her marriage had been seduced by another Kentucky Colonel, and the enraged husband promptly killed the villain. For this murder he was executed, after he and his wife had attempted suicide. Dealing with this sensation of the moment, the novel had a large sale in Kentucky. Fourteen years later Simms returned to the subject in *Charlemont, or The Pride of The Village*, which also had a large sale in the district of the murder. Much as one must deplore the bad taste that permitted Simms to dabble in such a wretched mire, one must admit his sincerity; he apparently thought, after faulty standards not uncommon in his time, that he was serving the cause of domestic virtue by advertising this sorry tragedy, and from his contemporaries he received praise for consigning "the seducer and slanderer of female innocence" to that "immortality of infamy which he so richly deserved."

It must be confessed that happy as his home life was in these years, and industrious as he was, Simms was turning out little that deserves permanent record. Almost all that he wrote then has been totally forgotten; the only purpose in mentioning it here is to give a just picture of his application and perseverance. Two novels were produced in 1841, neither of which was worthy of its author. *The Kinsmen, or the Black Riders of The Congaree*, now known as *The Scout*, is a tale of two half-brothers on opposite sides in the Revolutionary struggles in South Carolina. The story adds nothing to the pictures Simms had drawn in *The Partisan* and *Mellichampe*, though the character of the scout, John Bannister, is fine. For the most part the sensationalism in which his pen had recently dipped gave the tale an ignoble cast. The second novel of the year, *Confession; or The Blind Heart*, is compounded of the sediment of the Kentucky tragedy plus some bad Shaksperian criticism. Convinced that Othello was not jealous, and that there was room in literature for a truly jealous Othello, he worked out his theory relentlessly in an unlovely story.

From 1842 to 1850 Simms wrote no memorable book. His

pen was perhaps busier than ever, but the clouds of the coming war were gathering and he had other work in hand than romance. Though he had taken the Union side in the nullification days, he was altogether a states' rights man in the question of slavery, and he threw himself vehemently into the great quarrel. In his latest novels where he allowed his characters at times to speak his views as to the future of the United States, it is made clear that he expected and welcomed a separation of North and South. To a Northerner it often seems that every Southerner had a different reason for seceding, and some notable leaders, like Lee, are figures of sorrowful doom because they fought with regret, and from complex motives. Simms is not at all of this class. Whatever the great Virginians might find in the issue, of inevitable loyalty to their state or defense of their invaded homes, Simms was an aggressive advocate of slavery, and saw in that institution the one cause and justification of the coming war. He is therefore typical of the Northerner's notion of the Southerner; what he stood for was what Mrs. Stowe attacked in her portrait of Uncle Tom's first master and Eva's father.

To lend his pen to the cause, Simms turned from his fiction to magazine work, editing for a while the *Southron*, the *Southern Quarterly Review*, a small Georgia magazine called *Orion*, and a formidably named venture of his own, the *Southern and Western Monthly Magazine and Review*, usually spoken of as *Simms' Magazine*. Like other publications of the kind in the South, these magazines found in their sprouting a mere point of departure from which to decay. Simms understood their doom better than most Southerners, but he was satisfied with the dozen or less expiring numbers of each that gave him an opportunity to speak out. For example, he would print this challenge to the abolitionists: "We beg, once for all, to say to our Northern readers, writers and publishers, that, in the South, we hold slavery to be an especially and wisely devised institution of heaven; devised for the benefit, the improvement, and safety, morally, socially, and physically, of a barbarous and inferior race, who would otherwise perish by famine or by filth, by the sword, by disease, by waste, and destinies forever gnawing, consuming, and finally destroying."

These vague horrors of the negro's threatening fate suggest the stump orator's rhetoric, but Simms could state the issue simply enough. At a later time he writes: "If it be admitted that the institution of slavery is a wrong done to the negro, the question is at an end. No people can be justified for continuance in error and injustice. Once admit that there is a wrong and a crime, and it must be followed by expiation and atonement. In the South we think otherwise. We hold the African under moral and just titles, founded upon his characteristics, his nature, his necessities and our own; and our accountability is to the God of both races. We, alone, are in possession of the facts of the case, and our consciences are in no way troubled in relation to our rights to hold the negro in bondage. Perhaps our consciences are a thought too easy; but we believe ourselves quite equal to the argument whenever we appear before the proper tribunal. But we are a people, a nation, with arms in our hands, and in sufficient numbers to compel the respect of other nations; and we shall never submit the case to the judgment of another people, until they show themselves of a superior virtue and intellect."

Here was plain talk, but be it said to Simms' credit, it was probably more enlightened and more diplomatic than anything he heard from his associates. There was nothing frigid just then in South Carolinian speech. What Simms did not say in print he could say in his public orations, of which he delivered a good many, and from 1844 to 1846 he represented his county in the state legislature. His success as the champion of the ideas of his section got him finally the nomination for lieutenant-governor of South Carolina, in 1846, but he lost the election by one vote.

His journalistic work had led him into some pleasant by-paths. He took to writing criticism, partly because he wanted to, and partly because his magazines needed filling. His best work in that direction is collected in the volume called *Views and Reviews in American Literature, History, and Fiction*, 1846,—a volume made notable by the admirable essay on Cooper. More scholarly in intention, but less happy, was the *Supplement to the Plays of William Shakspeare*, 1848, an edition of seven apocryphal plays, which exposed but too plainly the inadequate training of the editor. More satisfactory were the biographies of some of his favorite heroes,— Marion, 1844; Captain John Smith, 1846; the Chevalier Bayard, 1848; and General Greene, 1849—this last a work which he pretended only to edit, but which is probably his own. The four lives do credit to the author's heart; they illustrate his hero-worship, undimmed in trying days.

During these years of general writing Simms was coming to his own in England. Several of his novels had been printed there and had no mean measure of popularity. In Germany, too, his best romances were following Cooper's in translation. These facts must have given Simms a just self-respect which explains much of his optimism. His home life continued prosperous and happy, though sorrow shared the house when three of his children died in infancy. Three others, born before 1848, grew up—a son named after him, and two daughters, Mary Lawson and Chevillette Eliza.

VI

By 1852 Simms had made some excursions into the drama; indeed, he had written everything but an epic. In this year, however, he fortunately returned to his best vein with the romance called at first *The Sword and The Distaff, or Fair, Fat, and Forty*, republished two years later as *Woodcraft*. This book concludes the adventures of Lieutenant Porgy and the other surviving characters of the Revolutionary trilogy; in many aspects it is the best of the distended series, full of spirited characters and remarkable scenes. No other of Simms' novels gives perhaps a stronger taste of his quality, the distinction of his subject and manner from Cooper's. Doubtless many a boy, attracted by the title, has made Simms' acquaintance first in this story; and he can still recall that stirring panorama of the embarking British army, and the kidnapping of Bostwick and his reappearance before McKewn, and clearest of all, the examination and murder of the outlaw Norris. These are such scenes as Stevenson delighted in, ganglions of romance, which embody character and emotion in an act or attitude remarkably striking to the mind's eye.

No matter how undisciplined his genius, Simms could not drive a pen over so many thousand pages without learning something of his craft, and this romance is swifter, closer knit and simpler than anything that had gone before. The plot is built of few elements. Porgy, returning from the war to his estate, finds himself heavily in debt to an unscrupulous spy named McKewn, who by pretending to serve both British and Americans has got his clutches upon much valuable property, including Porgy's. The lieutenant is in love with Mrs. Eveleigh, a rich widow whose comfortable estate adjoins his; yet his attentions are free from mercenary calculations. McKewn hires several ruffians, led by Bostwick, to steal some slaves from Mrs. Eveleigh; the gang overdo their part, attack the lady herself, and get into a most sanguinary fight with her son and her overseer, Fordham. Porgy and his troopers come to the rescue; the remainder of the story is taken up with the actual warfare between Bostwick and Porgy, and the legal warfare between Porgy and McKewn.

Mrs. Eveleigh is a remarkable character, drawn with such

individual traits that she suggests no counterpart in Simms or Cooper. She is a woman of great dignity, yet with that capacity for "managing" which is usually ascribed to New England heroines. She has both humor and common sense; there is never the slightest danger that she will marry the valiant Porgy, much as she likes him; and her initial success in recovering her slaves from the British is an augury of her fitness to cope with McKewn. Her character does not belong to romance at all; the charm of it is its rounded truth to life. Even in the excitement of the robber attack she is unheroic, though brave; Simms describes her mingled indignation and fright with a tactful art that saves her both to reality and to sympathy.

Fordham, her overseer—the trained backwoodsman and fighter, is one of Simms' scouts, far different from Cooper's type. He too is in no way superhuman; in the story he begins his adventures by being knocked senseless and bound hand and foot by the robbers, and he is released by the negro girl, Jenny. But he gives the impression of force and skill, and his loyalty is as great as Leatherstocking's. He is in no respect a philosopher; perhaps that makes his chief distinction from the Northern scout; he is simply a man of action and he rarely talks. His relation to his employer, Mrs. Eveleigh, illustrates more truly than Simms perhaps realized the democratic ideals that would follow such a struggle as the Revolution, where men must learn to reckon with each other in terms of intrinsic manhood.

This unconscious record of democracy is of course most clear in the description of Porgy and his band. The fat lieutenant would be a poor encourager of class feeling under any conditions, and in the guerilla warfare he and his men had become sworn brothers. Yet in this last account of him Porgy is less fat to the imagination, more nearly a romantic hero, than in the other stories. For one thing, he appears as a

leader, instead of a mere follower in Marion's camp or Singleton's; and his private troubles give occasion for more dignified forbearance than he had been credited with. He is
still, however, the center of the humor of the story. The scene
in which the sheriff comes to attach his property and finds the
covered dishes at table to contain convenient pistols, is one of
the best comedy episodes in our literature, funny of itself, and
true to the characters that act it. And Porgy's twofold attempt at matrimony, which results in his rejection by Mrs.
Eveleigh and Mrs. Griffin almost at the same time, is from
an artistic point of view a most successful solution of his
career; he remains unheroic and ludicrous, and the reader is
satisfied that he is not heartbroken, since he could transfer
his suit so quickly.

The power Simms had developed earlier in portraying low
villains and murderers gives to this story some of its most striking scenes. Bostwick, the hired ruffian, is at first simply a
stock figure from the rogue's gallery, but as the story pro-
gresses he becomes a most interesting individual. Nothing
like him had appeared before in the American novel. When
he is drugged and carried off to sea, he gains vastly in the
reader's sympathy; at the close of the story he is ennobled
into an incarnation of nemesis. But the transformation is
logical,—he loses none of his original villainy, and his whole
course, from end to end, is seen to have been ordered by his
own perverted moral sense. He is at his worst when with his
neglected family. To speak truth, Mrs. Bostwick, ill-treated
creature that she is, and little Dory, her saint-like daughter,
are the chief disappointments of the book. How tiresomely
good they can be may be seen at the end of the fifty-fifth chapter, where little Dory tells Arthur Eveleigh to go home and
ask his mother's forgiveness for making her angry. The irrev-
erent reader, keyed up to the healthy tone of adventure everywhere else in the book, finds these soft spots in the road rather

slow going, and feels unwarranted sympathy with the father
who stays away from that home.   Yet the fact remains that
Bostwick treats his sickly wife cruelly, and he is least interesting in her presence.   His character is most powerfully brought
out in the great episode of the book, the trial of Norris, where
he feels justified in killing the tortured comrade who is about
to confess.

That Simms could have written so stirring a romance in the
midst of fierce distractions is simply another proof that he was
a born story-teller.   He was in the thick of political controversy these days, contributing to the slavery propaganda and
carrying on a heated warfare with Lorenzo Sabine, the
Northern historian, who had cast some discredit on South
Carolina's share in the Revolution.   At another season
Simms' acquaintance with the history of his state might have
brought him through the debate with honor, but he lost his
temper and indulged in general compliments at the expense of
Northern patriots.

In 1854 he gave some successful lectures in Virginia and
published under a pseudonym a very ambitious story, *Vas-
conselos: a Romance of the New World*.   The fortunes of De
Soto presented admirable material for the romancer, and
Simms had kept the theme in mind since the days when he
had visited his father and found the forgotten grave.   The
book fails because of the author's lack of taste—that want of
artistic sense that distinguishes between morbidly interesting
and really charming incident.   The story has plot and character and fine descriptions, and its subject is great, but the
glamor of romance is rubbed off it in so many places that it
cuts a sorry figure.   Simms had allowed his thoughts to dwell
too long on murder stories and ruffianly scenes; his imagination now filled his books with a tiresomely long list of undesirable citizens.

During this same year appeared *Southward Ho!*—the

collection of stories already referred to, and in the two following years he completed *The Forayers* and its sequel, *Eutaw*,
intended to form the connecting links between *Katharine
Walton* and *Woodcraft*. In the rapid interest of the adventure
and the general atmosphere of guerilla warfare these volumes
hold the reader almost as well as the other members of the
series. If they seem to fall short at all, it is because the other
stories have preceded them and the reader has supped a bit
too full of horrors. Porgy and Marion's men, the English
troopers and the villainous robber gangs that made the war
their own occasion, still pour from the swamps and thickets,
butcher each other and on retiring leave a corpse or two swing-
ing in the breeze. A very little of that sort of literature goes a
long way, and Simms imagined far too much of it. There is
no excuse in a book designed to give pleasure for such an
episode as that in *Eutaw*, where Hurricane Nell arrives just
in time to see her brother hanged, whom she had tried so hard
to rescue.

In this character of Hurricane Nell Simms gave expression
to his interest in a popular kind of metaphysics; and whatever the scientific weaknesses might be in his knowledge of
psychology, he makes an impressive artistic use of it in this
strange creature, gifted with second sight. Her eccentric ap-
parel, her horsemanship, and the immunity she enjoys among
the harmful wild creatures of the swamps give her outwardly
a weird distinction, and her astonishing divinations are reported with such tact that the reader as well as her wretched
brother is impressed, if not convinced. In the handling of
abnormal character Simms often shows unexpected shrewdness. It would have been tempting to most romancers to
create in this unusual individuality a motive center for the
plot; so much supernatural wisdom at first sight ought not to
go to waste. At least Nell could have a controlling influence
in the events, like Norna of the Fitful Head. But in real life

the gift of second sight is never put to use,—indeed, it is distinguished from ordinary foresight only when it has come to nothing; and Simms follows his historical material closely, leaving Nell as a tragic figure on the outskirts of his story.

Hell-Fire Dick and Hurricane Nell give *Eutaw* an advantage in interest over *The Forayers*. Dick's chance acquaintance with *Pilgrim's Progress* and the services the great allegory renders him, are things to remember with affection; little that Simms wrote is more charming. Perhaps it is a touch of sentimentality that associates with Bunyan's book Henry Travis's reluctance to murder a defenseless man, and Dick in his repentant mood is a curiously warped specimen of morality, but in his soldier interest in Christian's warfare he is delightful. The secret of the charm is Simms' own love of Bunyan, a lifelong passion; by ascribing to Dick the naïve interest a child would take in the book, he recorded his own memories and came at the true character of the border ruffian.

VII

These volumes completed the series of historical romances of the Revolution. They mark also the end of whatever good fortune Simms was to enjoy. From the moment of their publication the great war closed in upon him, in one way or another, and he began to feel the edge of the disaster to which he and his nearest friends were blindly urging their state. In his trips to the North, which he had made through all these years whenever a book was to be published, he did what missionary work he could for the cause of slavery, and got something of a reputation for his vehement haranguing on the subject. In the winter of 1856 a Northern lecture tour was arranged for him, which ought to have benefited both himself and the country. Unfortunately he began the tour, at a lecture in New York on November 18, with a reply to his old adversary, Sabine, and a passing attack upon Charles Sumner. His audience listened in courteous silence for an hour and a half, and when he ended they gave him a round of applause, but at his next lecture, three nights later, only seventeen people appeared. Simms abandoned the tour, much hurt at the treatment, while the Northern papers congratulated him on getting off so easily. His own disappointment was probably no greater than that of his Northern friends, Bancroft, Bryant, Duyckinck and others, who had planned the tour.

On his return to the South his adventures in the enemy's country reflected a certain credit upon him,—at least his friends thought so, and they arranged for him other less ambitious tours. He was becoming also something of a dictator among the younger Southern writers, most of whom must have met him in his innumerable magazine editings. They formed a club in his honor, where he played Dr. Johnson in a broad style to their admiration, rejoicing much in their generous loyalty, and proud of his nickname among them, "Father Abbott." In their youthful idolizing of the veteran writer only a few of them perceived that his social ways belonged to a departing order, nor did they consider it other than a tribute to his style of conversation that neighbors two blocks off were aware of it. So much for his evenings with the club; he often had their companionship less formally, in bookshops or in their offices, where his presence, however welcome, probably made sad havoc with their routine duties. The inevitable blossom of all this enthusiastic soil was another periodical, *Russell's Magazine*, edited by Paul Hayne and W. B. Carlisle. Simms was a contributor, and the venture had the look of prosperity until the war killed it in 1860.

But there were some of the literary youth of South Carolina who resented Simms' leadership and managed to wound his large heart. And in 1858 the yellow fever invaded Charleston and two of his sons died in the same day. This was the sort of blow from which not even a heroic nature could recover. A month later, recalling his dead father's advice not to stay in Charleston, Simms wrote, "Thirty odd years have passed, and I can now mournfully say the old man was right. All that I have done has been poured to waste in Charleston, which has never smiled on any of my labors, which has steadily ignored my claims, which has disparaged me to the last, has been the last place to give me its adhesion, to which I owe no favor, having never received an office, or a compliment, or a dollar at her hands; and, with the exception of some dozen of her citizens, who have been kind to me, and some scores of her young men, who have honored me with a loving sympathy and something like reverence, which has always treated me rather as a public enemy, to be sneered at, than as a dutiful son doing her honor. *And I, too, know it as a place of tombs.* I have buried six dear children within its soil! Great God! What is the sort of slavery which brings me hither!"

His friends tried to cheer him, and he did what he could for himself by writing at a new romance, *The Cassique of Kiawah*, published in 1859. The book showed that Simms still had the mastery of such incidents as raids and chases, and in the part of the story that is on the sea his imagination is a sufficient substitute for the experience he lacked. It was probably to his advantage that the period in which the story is placed is earlier than his minute knowledge reached, for the tale is freer of bald historical passages than many of his romances. The flutter of approval which the novel stirred among his friends and perhaps among a more public audience did not presage any immortality for it, but the praise must have been grateful to Simms, and therefore it is pleasant to remember.

How little the South in general appreciated his services was painfully illustrated by the omission of his name from the list of editors invited in 1856 to prepare a "series of books in every department of study, from the earliest primer to the highest grade of literature and science"—the series to be for the general improvement of the Southern youth through books not tainted with Northern notions of civilization and freedom. The natural protest against this ignoring of the South's only important man of letters came from a New York journal, and Simms' unappreciative state was roused to take notice of his existence by appointing him to educational boards and conventions; but Simms was not deceived, and continued to grieve over his rejection by his own people.

But personal regrets and sorrows, lack of appreciation, or the loss of his Charleston house by fire, in 1860, were not allowed to overshadow Simms' great concern in the coming Presidential election. He hoped for a break between the North and South, though if possible not a bloody one, and the election of Lincoln was to him a signal for the new Confederacy which should be founded upon slavery. However other Southerners might prefer to phrase the issue, Simms still frankly advocated slavery. When it was clearly a matter of fighting for his principles, his main regret was that he himself, on account of age and ill-health, could not go to the front. But he could write voluminous letters to his friends suggesting defenses for Charleston harbor with an amateur's assurance,—with a soundness of judgment, too, that was later demonstrated in the practice of his theories; he could also have his say, time and again, on the main theme of slavery. One who reads his life pauses often at this period of it—if one is a Northerner—to wonder at his frankness, and to compare much of his reasoning with Lincoln's in spite of the difference in their conclusions. We almost hear the echoes of the Cooper Institute speech, strangely transformed, in such words as these,—"Either negro slavery is a beneficent, merciful, God-chartered institution, or it is not. If beneficent, why limit it? Is it better for the negro to be a barbarian and savage in his own country, than to work out his deliverance in this? If better, why be at the pains to cast censure on the morals of the institution?" Be it said for the credit of Simms' logic in this passage that he takes for granted the beneficence of slavery because he is writing to another Southerner.

In 1861 two more of his children died of fever, and a year later Woodlands was burned down. The cause of the fire was not discovered, nor could it have made much difference; everything was lost except a new wing of the building, into which most of his library was carried and saved. His manuscripts had been packed a few days before, in readiness for flight from the Yankees; their preservation was his brightest comfort. He wrote to a friend, with a flash of his old courage, that he did not despair nor despond, but added that it took all his strength to endure such repeated strokes of fortune.

The desperate sorrow of these years is written plainest in those letters in which he cherishes his hopes in the face of undisguisable ruin. How pathetic is his faith! "It cannot be that God will deliver us into the hands of these atrocious heathens. As between us and the Deity, there is no doubt a sad reckoning to make; but as between us and these accursed Yankees, no reproach lies at our doors, unless that single one of having too long slept within the coils of the serpent. I have faith in God, my friend. He may punish us, and we must suffer, for this is the meed of our desert; but he will not let us sink. I have faith in his promise, in his mercy, and I know that after this tribulation, our peace shall return once more, our prosperity, our friends; and the 'song of the turtle shall be heard in the land.' "

It is not necessary to dwell on the long series of disasters that fell on Simms during the war. His wife died on September 10, 1863; after that sorrow he felt that no suffering in comparison could seem great. He was in Columbia during the sack of the city by Sherman's troops, but was protected by a young officer who had the bright good fortune to know and appreciate his stories. But the young officer's desire to do honor to literature in Simms' person could not save the remnant of Woodlands nor the library it contained; after an examination by the Northern soldiers, the place was left to the mercy of stragglers or incendiaries or negroes,—who ever did it, the place was burned to the ground. When a friend offered his condolence, Simms exclaimed, "Talk not to me about my losses, when the State is lost."

Nor is it necessary to speak at length of the years immediately following the war—years almost as tragic for the Southerner as the war itself. Simms bore the change with the utmost courage. His chief support financially he earned by his connection with newspapers, editing the *Daily South Carolinian* with Timrod, and writing for other journals. Woodlands was practically worthless as a source of income, for the freed negroes would not work, and Gilmore Simms, the eldest son, found he could get nothing out of the place. Economic conditions in Charleston were so wretched that all who could go elsewhere did so; Simms himself thought of coming North, if for no other reason, to escape the horde of unfortunates who tried to earn money by writing and appealed to him to place their work. He did actually go North for a few months, but the trip was largely a business visit to his publishers; he was not the man to be content at such a moment away from his people. On his return he began a serial story, *Joscelyn*, for a magazine, and prepared for the press a volume of war poems by various authors,—a collection that on the whole did more credit to his patriotic impulses than to his critical faculty.

The younger writers in his club still looked up to him for guidance, and he continued to exercise his unselfish faculty of cheering and inspiring other men. He was sorely needed; perhaps if we could judge men's lives correctly we should find that his noblest achievement was in the leadership of those years. Timrod was practically starving; Hayne was as poor, if not as helpless. How miserable his own situation was

Simms does not let us see, though we can guess from the fact that in the house where he stayed there were practically three families, sixteen persons in all, and their total income was thirty dollars a week. He could write bravely, however, even of such conditions: "Fortunately my daughters have all been taught to do their own work, fit their own dresses, and they go to work cheerfully, and sing merrily while they toil; and their elasticity helps to encourage and strengthen me in my labor. The picture of Irving, etc., will help to cover the bomb-shell holes still in our walls. The room in which I sleep is still excoriated with those missiles." From this room, which he shared with two sons, he managed to collect from Northern and masonic friends money for the relief of destitute families, and between his literary labors he distributed these funds, all too little, among the Charleston poor.

In 1867 he and his daughter Mary paid a visit to New York, and their Northern friends, learning of their presence, entertained them royally. His reputation in that part of the country had grown even outside of the large circle of his friends; his entertainment was in fact so incessantly hospitable that he fell ill. His return to the South in September was made sad by the death of Timrod, whose illness had added to Simms' burdens of sympathy. He took the remaining copies of Timrod's poems off the hands of the Northern publishers and sold them in the South for the benefit of Timrod's family.

In the next year Simms started to build a small frame house on the site of Woodlands, for he had definitely given up the thought of living in any other section of the country. Modest as his plans were, the building proved costly and troublesome, so much so that he was in desperate straits by the time it was finished. He paid a flying visit to the North to make contracts for stories, and he says he was writing at the time two romances at once. His historical collection, material bearing upon the history of South Carolina, he had been forced to sell; now he sent to a Northern friend all the autographs in his possession which he thought worth saving. The Southern journals for which he wrote failed to pay him. At the end of the year he was living at Woodlands again in four rooms—all he could afford to build.

Simms practically ended his life by overwork. For nine months he worked at his desk without walking a mile a week; by this sacrifice of all wholesome exercise he managed to complete two romances, but broke down before he could finish the third. The quality of these last stories is what might be expected from the circumstances of their creation. Simms was no longer writing for fame nor for art, but for bread. He was too old to recover from such a debauch of toil. By June, 1870, he and his friends realized his alarming condition, but the end was sooner perhaps than any expected. His magnificent physique was completely broken down, and he died at Charleston on June 11.

VIII

One who makes the acquaintance of the writings or the life of Simms is easily persuaded of the verdict long ago pronounced upon him, that he was far nobler than his books. Even with such an opinion one can find room to call his books noble too; their faults were the result of the time and place in which they were written, but their excellencies make them kin to all high romance. Like Cooper, Simms is remembered chiefly for a series of books—the Revolutionary romances— and one or two other masterpieces standing alone. In the border strife of *Guy Rivers* he discovered his great knack of portraying the outlaw in the South and Southwest; in the Revolutionary romances he combined this outlaw interest with historical portraiture, thus linking the two strains of his genius. As his career advanced he became more realistic, not always to the advantage of his art. *The Yemassee*, coming early, was his purest romance and the best expression of the poetry in him. Though it does not belong to his great cycle of stories, it is near them all by virtue of that love of his state out of which sprang everything worthy that Simms wrote.

If one considers the Revolutionary tales, from *The Partisan* to *Woodcraft*, taking the order in which they should be read, one is aware of Simms' two chief faults. Though a prolific writer, he is not creative in the highest sense; by comparison Cooper's range seems enormous. From book to book, crowded with incident though they are, Simms repeats his situations and characters, working almost by a formula. The outlaws must be hanged, the young officers must fall in love with the daughters of the enemy, the heroine must be held in duress by the cruel rival, or must bestow her hand as the price of her father's life. These melodramatic situations Simms can vary with astounding power; if one were to read any single romance, the impression of forceful genius would be absolute, but with each additional volume of the series the impression lessens.

The second weakness in almost all of Simms' work is one of art, a fault that could have been remedied by better methods of work. Few of his stories have unity of tone, or "blend." They seem to have been written in unrelated moods. No one atmosphere envelopes them. In this respect the contrast with Cooper's best work is striking. It might be said that the cause of this fault was poverty of imagination; but it is more reasonable to think that if Simms had written with fewer distractions and had revised his work, he could have attained that unity of effect that art demands. In some of his shorter works, such as *The Maroon*, he did succeed in giving to the poetic story absolute keeping, and if he could do it in a short story he might have done it in a long one.

But matters of art are somewhat beside the point in his work. He was a story-teller, and when all is said, his best stories were well worth telling and are still worth reading. We should count him precious in our literature if we did not have Cooper, for they two alone tell us on the grand scale a story for its own sake. Both came of romancing blood. The myth-making faculty that slept in Cooper's Northland inheritance was matched by the Celtic fire of legend and loyalty in Simms. Though he was typical of the South,—and of the North too in his historical conscience,—he was Celtic in his love of purely unmoral incident. Cooper makes the successes of his scouts a matter of skill and character; Simms in his most stirring moments makes them matters of happy circumstances, irresistible as Cuchullain's luck.

Yet in one literary way Simms will always be more than anything else a type of the South. From the beginning to the end of his work he dwelt lovingly upon his country's past, with a sad sense of faded glory. The young Southerner now thinks of the days before the war as the happy prime of his state, and is melancholy over her lost battle-fields, but in that very prime Simms was thinking as sadly of the bright days of Revolutionary honor. Perhaps there was something Celtic, too, in this habitual retrospect. But it is probably fair to say that the Southern social system, doomed from the beginning, preyed upon the imagination of this man, and of many others, with a subtle consciousness of retrogression. Cooper had showed America the road to the frontier of its dreams; progress was his great theme. Simms looked backward like the immortal Spanish Don,—almost as lovable and almost as forlorn.

NATHANIEL HAWTHORNE

I

HAWTHORNE and Poe are the artists of American literature. Poe's claims to the leading place can be made strong by including all his varied achievements, in prose and verse. But as a novelist Hawthorne has no rival in his own country for literary skill,—for sustained excellence on a large scale, for the management of plot, and for the magic of language that denotes the master of style. And the rivalry with Poe ceases entirely when we leave these more external matters and turn to the content of Hawthorne's work; for his genius expressed so completely a remarkable phase of human experience, that his name stands more for his subject than for his treatment of it. He is the novelist, as Emerson is the poet, of New England. The Puritan character which Cooper failed to sympathize with, is the very subject of Hawthorne's work; so that if he has limitations in comparison with the universal story-tellers, like Scott or Balzac, the deficiency is not so much in the small amount of his product as in his inability to see life except as a Puritan world, from a Puritan standpoint; and the limitation is more clearly defined by his temperamental preoccupation with one aspect of the Puritan nature.

New England's contribution to the American novel is represented chiefly in Hawthorne and Mrs. Stowe. The two writers are complementary, exhibiting to an almost exaggerated degree the paradox of Puritanism. The devotion to a cause in action, the yearning to achieve the kingdom of God in a practical way on earth, and the great efficiency of the at-

tempt,—these Puritan traits make up the genius of the author
of *Uncle Tom's Cabin*. But the Puritan had more subtle
experiences than these, especially as he drew away from his
definite religion. When he desired to build the kingdom of
God, he looked for the pattern of it, not in history nor in the
fortunes of those about him, but in his own heart. The
prime requisite of his way of life was that he should be free to
know himself,—to learn his dreams as a first step toward
bringing them forth; therefore he was a solitary, preoccupied
figure, even among others of his kind, and the outer world
had most value to him as a molding influence upon his vision. Such a temperament as is here indicated was perilous
to art, finding little joy in the natural senses, and holding
but weakly to the reality of matter-of-fact things. From its
peril Spenser and Milton were saved by the enormous flood of
Renaissance tradition and by the imperative call to practical
duties, which redeemed in both the thinness of their ascetic
natures. But to many a Puritan the spectacle of life became
less real than his thoughts, since his dream of the world was
more fixed than the world itself; he approached all experience
with a mental reservation, with the scientist's experimental
mood, as though the moment might prove a touchstone of
truth and falsehood, to lighten or leave darkened his soul.
This subjective habit of Puritanism, almost to the exclusion of
other aspects, is the secret of Hawthorne's character and
writings.

The solitude of his life is sometimes attributed to the custom of his boyhood, when he dwelt in extreme seclusion with
his lonely family. But his mother's preference for a hermit
way of living was itself the expression of the brooding, philosophizing mind the son inherited. To her temperament as
to his, it was desirable to be alone.

> That each should in his house abide,
> Therefore was the world so wide,

sings Emerson; and when Hawthorne in his maturity visited Shakspere's birthplace, he wondered how the poet's genius could unfold in a house that permitted so little solitude. The remark illustrates both his difficulty in comprehending the nature of Shakspere's genius, and the peculiar quality of his own. His life seems one long attempt to get away by himself, where the world could not take hold on him. Had he been a complete Puritan, some zeal for realizing his dream would have gone with the dream itself. But all action was foreign to his temper; no reform, no battle, not even the pleasant duties of daily life, ever wholly engaged his interest. And in his stories he portrayed men from the point of view his own habit involved,—as undergoing life and watching the effect, rather than living it and causing it to be. His interest is never in action, in the sense that applies to Scott or Cooper; in few of his books is the active side of Puritanism represented, and in fewer still is there record of any achievement, of the kind that ordinarily makes life and books satisfactory; it is little to him whether his characters, judged by tangible results, succeed or fail. The actions that condition the story frequently occur before it begins, and are left untold. He has eyes only for the effect of life upon character as it follows from the character's own will, or from the actions of others.

Evidently so great a genius as Hawthorne's, occupied with a unique expression of humanity, should not be quarreled with if what he says and the way he says it are quite unlike anything else found in novels. To all readers—and they are the majority—who prefer the picture of life that is vital and reproduces without apparent reflection the flood of common or romantic incident, Hawthorne makes to some extent an ineffectual appeal; and if to think be contrary to man's nature as it is to his habit, they are right who would place his genius in an inferior rank. But it is obviously unjust to pass sentence upon him, as recent and able criticism has done, because his stories present no strong sense of outward reality, and his very characters often seem to themselves as it were creatures of a trance. To condemn his work on such grounds is simply to complain that instead of being a realist, he is a psychologist and a poet. The Puritan vision in him is his only reality, and by comparison the outside world seems to him a thing of phantom and allegory. He is the child of the author of the *Faerie Queene*.

II

William Hawthorne, or Hathorne, the novelist's ancestor who transplanted a branch of the family line from Wiltshire to New England, seems not to have been an ineffectual Puritan. Whatever visionary traits he may have had are swallowed up by time, while the record of his energy is still distinct. He came over with Winthrop to Boston, in 1630, and settling in Dorchester, promptly became a leader among his fellows,— in the legislature, where he was Speaker for seven or eight years; in the practical improvement of the settlement, clearing the forests and planting the fields; in warfare against the Indians and in explorations, even until he was seventy years old; in rigid enforcement of the laws, condemning murderers or Quakers to the scaffold or the whipping-post; in business ventures, in which he succeeded; and finally in preaching, which he seems to have done with vigor and effect. That he had the finer qualities of the spirit is suggested by a copy of Sidney's *Arcadia*, in his possession, and his ability to write with the dignity of his age and with much personal adroitness is proved by his letter to Secretary Morrice, in 1666, declining to obey the order of Charles II summoning Governor Bellingham and himself to England. The old Puritan puts the case of the Colonies with sound reasoning and much picturesqueness; the flame of liberty burning in him is concealed more or less by wise policy, but it breaks out finely in a prophetic hint as to where the Colonies may arrive if they fail of their rights: "What extremity may force them to, that God only knows, who is wonderful in counsel and mighty in working, whose thoughts are not as man's, and his counsel only shall stand."

In the next generation John Hawthorne became the chief person of the family, a narrower Puritan than his father, but only less able. As Judge he presided at several witchcraft trials, and a curse was laid on him and his blood by one he condemned to die. During his life the family lost the title-deed to the land in Maine where afterwards the town of Raymond grew up, and the papers were recovered only when the claim had become valueless. Both incidents the novelist used in *The House of the Seven Gables*. The other Hawthornes of that generation took to the sea, and like their father were active, efficient men.

Of a different temper was Joseph Hawthorne, the next of the line. He was a quiet-loving person with a bent toward agriculture; the family genius skipped a generation and left him undisturbed. His son Daniel, however, had both ambition and capacity, and was a lover of the sea. In the Revolution he commanded a privateer, *Fair America*, whose adventures were chronicled in an old ballad, and he got himself the popular title of "Bold Daniel." He wooed the Muse too, in a practical short-hand sort of way; a girl named Mary Rondel won his heart, and he used to underline amatory portions of the *Arcadia* in his great-grandfather's precious copy, wherein Mary evidently read and found love-confessions ready-made. But the courtship proved a failure, the lovers apparently quarreled, and Mary died. Daniel laid aside the *Arcadia* and won the hand of Rachel Phelps by more direct methods. His son Nathaniel, born in 1775, was a sea-captain of reserved, melancholy manner, but of considerable ability. He married Elizabeth Clarke Manning, a woman of beauty and character, whose ancestry was as honorable and sturdy as his own.   When he died in 1808 he left her with two daughters, Elizabeth and Louise, and a son, Nathaniel, the future novelist.

Heredity and family history seems to count even more with Hawthorne than with most writers.   A nature as sensitive as his to all noble influences would find much fascination in the past, and he allowed it to affect him in other ways than through the inheritance of blood and temperament. The tradition of strong characters made gentler and perhaps weaker by time, such as the memory of his house handed down, from the immigrant ancestor to his thoughtful father and secluded mother, came to be almost his habitual conception of life.   In the shorter stories as well as in *The House of the Seven Gables* and *The Marble Faun*, the plot is often rooted in just such a transformation of a family, and in the other tales, with hardly an exception, the effect of time and its changes upon character is a constant theme, so that the attention is fixed on the past.   To reproduce early environment or local or family traditions is of course nothing unusual among writers; Cooper used his boyhood and his home for his best material, and Scott far more conspicuously immortalized a traditional world.   But Hawthorne's uniqueness is best felt by contrast with these very novelists.   They reproduce the past as it occurred, with the panorama of events and circumstances.   Hawthorne reproduces its effects upon men's character, with the minimum attention to the outward fact. It is impossible for him to write any story whose interest is entirely in the present; the story of the effect of life, his typical theme, logically involves an interest in the previous cause, so that the mind usually takes possession of his writings more by exploring the past he suggests, than by living in the phantom present he tries to describe.

The home in which Hawthorne grew up was peculiarly calculated to develop the poet and dreamer in him.   From his birth, July 4, 1804, until his father's death four years later, the old Salem house probably differed little from many another sea captain's dwelling, but from the beginning of her widowhood his mother cherished her sorrow in an extraordinary seclusion, eating her meals apart from the children, and estranging them from natural social interests. The older sister, Elizabeth, shared her mother's temperament, as did Hawthorne himself, and their way of life simply developed abnormally their meditative bent. The other sister, Louise, younger than the novelist, had a more usual zest in the world about her, and with opportunity would have taken the average young girl's part in society. Only the strong Puritan strain in all three children could have made so gloomy a childhood lovable. They lived in their own thoughts, but were affectionate, and their reverence for their remarkable mother was very great. It is easy, however, to imagine that Hawthorne's home life was more an experience of ideas than of the heart; to his mother in her seclusion he could hardly be bound by intimate daily ties, and his attitude toward her and toward this aspect of his boyhood seems best indicated by his self-analytical record of her death-bed, years later:—

"About five o'clock I went to my mother's chamber, and was shocked to see such an alteration since my last visit. I love my mother; but there has been, ever since boyhood, a sort of coldness of intercourse between us, such as is apt to come between persons of strong feelings if they are not managed rightly. I did not expect to be much moved at the time,—that is to say, not to feel any overpowering emotion struggling just then,—though I knew I should deeply remember and regret her. Mrs. Dike was in the chamber; Louisa pointed to a chair near the bed, but I was moved to kneel down close by my mother, and take her hand. She knew me, but could only murmur a few indistinct words; among which I understood an injunction to take care of my sisters. Mrs. Dike left the chamber, and then I found the tears slowly gathering in my eyes. I tried to keep them down, but it would not be; I kept filling up, till, for a few moments, I shook with sobs. For a long time I knelt there, holding her hand; and surely it is the darkest hour I ever lived. Afterwards I stood by the open window and looked through the crevice of the curtain. The shouts, laughter, and cries of the two children had come up into the chamber from the open air, making a strange contrast with the death-bed scene. And now, through the crevice of the curtain, I saw my little Una of the golden locks, looking very beautiful, and so full of spirits and life that she was life itself. And then I looked at my poor dying mother, and seemed to see the whole of human existence at once, standing in the dusky midst of it."

In his first years Hawthorne was an active boy, but from his tenth year until he was twelve, an accident in an outdoor game lamed him, and he was thrown upon mental resources for occupation and amusement. His school-teacher, Dr. Joseph Worcester of dictionary fame, gave Hawthorne his lessons at home, and the boy found himself early in the great poets, especially Shakspere, Milton, and Spenser. The first book he ever bought was *The Faerie Queene*. Besides these books and *The Pilgrim's Progress*, he read history and fiction; so that literature at its best was as much the foundation of his art, as nature was the inspiration of Cooper's.

But strangely enough, Hawthorne's boyhood was completed by an acquaintance with the wild forest not unlike Cooper's. In 1818 his mother removed for a year to Raymond, Maine, where her brother Robert, who interested himself in his nephew, had built a large house for himself and another for her. In the wilderness that inclosed the settlement many of the conditions of the Otsego colony must have been repeated—the solitude, the frontier society, the waters on which it was situated, Sebago Lake. Here Hawthorne spent what he considered his happiest days, leading a pleasant adventurous life, boy-fashion. To this period belongs the First Diary, which may or may not be genuine. If it is, the picture of his year in Raymond shows a more normal, thought-free character than we associate with him later.

In 1819 he was back in Salem with his uncles, Richard and Robert Manning, his mother and sisters remaining in Raymond. The next two years were devoted to preparation for college, with much literary activity besides. He wrote verses and prose, and issued a short-lived paper, *The Spectator*, which for four numbers circulated in the family. His reading in general literature was continued and broadened, and in his letters he ventured critical opinions on what he had read. Scott's novels were his favorites, with *Caleb Williams* next in order. Yet in the very letter in which his literary enthusiasm is outpoured, he shows a trace of that irresolution in his attitude toward his art which was to appear often in his later life, and which went with his contemplative nature. "I have almost given up writing poetry," he says. "No man can be a poet and a bookkeeper at the same time." It was not the last time that he found himself ready to "give up" writing, or was discouraged by the conflict of his inward vision and outward circumstance. In a later letter to his mother he discussed the choice of a profession in a mood which in spite of some playfulness shows his temperamental reluctance to commit any ideal to practice: "I have not yet concluded what profession I shall have. The being a minister is of course out of the question. I should not think that even you would desire me to choose so dull a way of life. Oh, no, mother, I was not born to vegetate forever in one place, and to live and die as calm and as tranquil as a puddle of water. As to lawyers, there are so many of them already that one-half of them (upon a moderate calculation) are in a state of actual starvation. A physician, then, seems to be 'Hobson's choice'; but yet I should not like to live by the diseases and infirmities of my fellow-creatures. And it would weigh very heavily on my conscience, in the course of my practice, if I should chance to

send any unlucky patient 'ad infernum,' which being inter-
preted is, 'to the realms below.' Oʰ that I was rich enough
to live without a profession! What do you think of my becoming an author, and relying for support on my pen? Indeed, I think the illegibility of my handwriting is very author-
like.''

In 1821 Hawthorne entered Bowdoin College, at Brunswick, Maine, in the class with Longfellow, and one year below Franklin Pierce, his close friend, who afterward became
President of the United States. The four years that followed
were happy and not wholly unprofitable, though Hawthorne
was no student, and his comparative poverty kept him from
much social activity. His expenses were paid by his uncle
Robert, and the fact that he was to that degree dependent
weighed somewhat on his New England pride, of which he
always had a good share. Though quiet and reserved, he
made friends and took part in the general college life—perhaps more than an average part in the card-playing and
gambling that went on. At least he was singled out for mild
punishment in a crusade the authorities made against the
college card-players in the Spring of 1822, as a frank and self-
possessed letter to his mother announced; and his companions
were among the more convivial, less studious fellows, at the
other end of the class from the scholarly Longfellow. Yet at
his graduation he stood eighteenth in the class of thirty-eight,
and was entitled to a Commencement part, which he for-
feited, however, because of his unwillingness to speak in public. Pierce and others were his firm friends when he left, and
Horatio Bridge was his intimate companion. The impression he made on the college was of self-respecting goodfellow-
ship; to the few discerning ones he seemed to promise great
things, and they kept their faith in him. Bridge especially
encouraged him by his confidence, and Hawthorne later
wrote that his friend was more responsible than any one else

for his being a writer. The complete acknowledgment of
his indebtedness is in the dedicatory letter prefixed to *The
Snow Image*, and it illustrates Hawthorne's college days,
besides expressing his friendly gratitude:

"On you, if on no other person, I am entitled to rely, to
sustain the position of my Dedicatee. If anybody is responsible for my being at this day an author, it is yourself. I know
not whence your faith came; but while we were lads together
at a country college,—gathering blueberries, in study-hours,
under those tall academic pines; or watching the great logs, as
they tumbled along the current of the Androscoggin; or shooting pigeons and gray squirrels in the woods; or bat-fowling in
the summer twilight; or catching trouts in that shadowy little
stream which, I suppose, is still wandering riverward through
the forest,—though you and I will never cast a line in it
again,—two idle lads, in short (as we need not fear to acknowledge now), doing a hundred things that the Faculty
never heard of, or else it had been the worse for us,—still it
was your prognostic of your friend's destiny, that he was to
be a writer of fiction.

"And a fiction-monger, in due season, he became. But
was there ever such a weary delay in obtaining the slightest
recognition from the public, as in my case? I sat down by the
wayside of life, like a man under enchantment, and a shrub-
bery sprang up around me, and the bushes grew to be saplings, and the saplings became trees, until no exit appeared
possible, through the entangling depths of my obscurity. And
there, perhaps, I should be sitting at this moment, with the
moss on the imprisoning tree trunks, and the yellow leaves of
more than a score of Autumns piled above me, if it had not
been for you. For it was through your intervention—and
that, moreover, unknown to himself—that your early friend
was brought before the public, somewhat more prominently
than theretofore, in the first volume of *Twice Told Tales*."

III

The patient solitude that Hawthorne here refers to figura-
tively, was spent in the old house in Salem during practically

the next twelve years. His mother had returned thither in 1822, somewhat against his wish, for he thought the seclusion of Raymond better suited to her comfort. Now at the close of his college course he rejoined the little family, and took up with them a life of curious isolation. His mother's habits of solitary mourning had not changed, and as his sisters grew up, they also had formed separate habits, and lived each in her own world. When Hawthorne took his place again in the household it was with the determination to become a writer; the necessary meditation of his art reinforced his temperamental shyness and the home tradition, and it is no wonder that he became perhaps the greatest recluse of the group. The family rarely met, even at meals, and Hawthorne seldom went out of his room, except for a walk in the morning or evening. The mornings he spent in study, the afternoons in writing, the evenings in reading. Later he seems to have made some brief journeys in Connecticut, Vermont, New York and New Hampshire, probably through the generosity of his uncles, but the twelve years he spent in the old Salem house remained in his memory as a single unbroken solitude. Not twenty people in Salem knew of his existence, he thought, nor did his family share his ambition beyond the necessary faith to allow him to attempt a living by writing. He never read his stories and sketches to them; less than any other author, perhaps, he was encouraged by the proverbial audience of admiring relatives. If he gave in his later writings the effect of low vitality, of a certain lack of ambition, his long and silent devotion to his craft should correct that impression, for the years in the lonely house are a record of faithful work in discouraging conditions that the most energetic writer might be proud of.

Nor were they, on the whole, unhappy years; they were too busy for that. A passage in the preface to the complete edition of *Twice Told Tales*, in 1851, relates the discouragements

of his devoted apprenticeship with a cheerfulness probably
not assumed with the good fortune of delayed success:

"Throughout the time above specified, he had no incitement
to literary effort in a reasonable prospect of reputation or
profit, nothing but the pleasure itself of composition—an enjoyment not at all amiss in its way, and perhaps essential to
the merit of the work in hand, but which, in the long run, will
hardly keep the chill out of a writer's heart, or the numbness
out of his fingers. To this total lack of sympathy, at the age
when his mind would naturally have been most effervescent,
the public owe it (and it is certainly an effect not to be regretted on either part) that the author can show nothing for
the thought and industry of that portion of his life, save the
forty sketches, or thereabouts, included in these volumes.

"Much more, indeed, he wrote; and some very small part
of it might yet be rummaged out (but it would not be worth
the trouble) among the dingy pages of fifteen-or-twenty-year
old periodicals, or within the shabby morocco covers of faded
souvenirs. The remainder of the works alluded to had a very
brief existence, but, on the score of brilliancy, enjoyed a fate
vastly superior to that of their brotherhood, which succeeded
in getting through the press. In a word, the Author burned
them without mercy or remorse, and, moreover, without any
subsequent regret, and had more than one occasion to marvel
that such very dull stuff, as he knew his condemned manuscripts to be, should yet have possessed inflammability enough
to set the chimney on fire!"

The first product of these days was *Fanshawe*, published
in 1828 in Boston. Hawthorne paid the cost of this book, one
hundred dollars, and as it proved a complete failure, he was
later at some pains to destroy all the copies he could get his
hands on, making his sister and his intimate friends surrender
their copies for another chimney blaze. After his death, however, the story was reprinted from one volume that had escaped his critical rigor.

Hawthorne's judgment in suppressing his inferior work was
always excellent; there never was, perhaps, a better self-

critic. The stories and sketches he would have been glad to
let go undelayed to oblivion are not only clearly below his
quality, but sometimes they are different in kind, and seem
not to have been written by him at all. In *Fanshawe* there is
little to suggest his typical genius. There is no subtlety in the
well-defined characters, there is no brooding or meditating
upon life; the action is brisk, and the incident counts for more
than the persons. Hawthorne apparently was trying to write
in the Scott vein,—that is, attempting the one thing he could
not accomplish, a romantic story of adventure. With no
knowledge of the stir of life to draw on for realistic incident,
he was hopelessly handicapped. That he turned to the college world he had recently left, and used it for the setting of
his story as the only society in his experience, shows perhaps
that he knew the need of facts in this kind of novel, but the
result has not the desirable illusion of actuality. The only
part of the story that has quality occurs before the action begins; it is the description of the little college, of the kindly
president and his formidable spouse,—a quiet picture in
which Hawthorne's magic realism is at least promised, and
much of his humor also. The paragraph summing up the
student body is still on the whole true of the small New England college; it is easy to recognize the country boy, in his
Freshman rusticity, and in the increased dignity and more
precise tailoring of Sophomore year, or the town-bred youths,
the "models of fashion to their rustic companions, over whom
they asserted a superiority in external accomplishments, which
the fresh though unpolished intellect of the sons of the forest
denied them in their literary competitions." And equally true,
though more striking in discernment, considering his youth,
and marking already his distrust of the practical application
of ideals, is his description of the few young descendants of
the aborigines, "to whom an impracticable philanthropy was
endeavoring to impart the benefits of civilization."

The character of Dr. Welmoth, the college President, is the only attractive one in the story; it is well described, but loses dignity as soon as it is launched upon the impossible incidents of the plot. Fanshawe, the hero, wins attention by the devoted solitude of his life, and by his mental isolation even when the plot compels him to mingle among others. When he rejects the heroine's love and returns to the fatal studies which are his doom, no matter how unreal the tale seems it has this much of Hawthorne in it, that the character is kept true to that curious isolation which was so much the fate of himself and the chief persons in his books.

Though *Fanshawe* was in every sense a failure, it was a long time before Hawthorne produced another story as ambitious, or perhaps as promising. Like Cooper and Longfellow, he was interested in native themes, and projected a series to be called *Provincial Tales*, but the material for these stories was either discarded or worked up in other forms. Perhaps the anonymous tale, *The Young Provincial*, an account of adventures in the battle of Bunker Hill, which appeared in *The Token* of 1830, is one of this series. Much of Hawthorne's publishing for the next years was in this annual, edited by S. G. Goodrich, of "Peter Parley" fame, or in other similar gift books. In *The Token* appeared *Roger Malvin's Burial*, *The Gentle Boy*—for which thirty-five dollars were paid—and others of the well-known tales. Goodrich also attempted to find a publisher for the *Provincial Tales*, and in general was a good friend to the young writer, introducing him to the editor of *The New England Magazine*, in which his work afterward appeared.

It was always Hawthorne's habit to use his own experience for the material of his writings, so that though little is said specifically of these 'prentice years, a probably correct notion of his industry and his discouragements can be gained from *The Devil In Manuscript*, in which the speaker visits his friend, an author named "Oberon"—one of Hawthorne's pen-names—and assists at the burning of unsuccessful manuscripts. Many of Hawthorne's moods are in the sketch—his humor as well as his self-analysis.

"You cannot conceive," says Oberon, "what an effect the composition of these tales has had on me. I have become ambitious of a bubble, and careless of solid reputation. I am surrounding myself with shadows, which bewilder me, by aping the realities of life. They have drawn me aside from the beaten path of the world, and led me into a strange sort of solitude,—a solitude in the midst of men,—where nobody wishes for what I do, nor thinks nor feels as I do. The tales have done all this.

"They have been offered to some seventeen booksellers. It would make you stare to read their answers. . . . One man publishes nothing but school-books; another has five novels already under examination. . . . Another gentleman is just giving up business on purpose, I verily believe, to escape publishing my book. Several, however, would not absolutely decline the agency, on my advancing half the cost of an edition, and giving bonds for the remainder, besides a high percentage to themselves, whether the book sells or not.

"And then the various moods in which I wrote! Sometimes my ideas were like precious stones under the earth, requiring toil to dig them up, and care to polish and brighten them; but often a delicious stream of thought would gush out before the page at once, like water sparkling up suddenly in the desert; and when it had passed I gnawed my pen hopelessly, or blundered on with cold and miserable toil, as if there were a wall of ice between me and my subject.

"I find no traces of the golden pen with which I wrote in characters of fire. My treasure of fairy coin is changed to worthless dross. My picture, painted in what seemed the loveliest hues, presents nothing but a faded and indistinguishable surface. I have been eloquent and poetical and humorous in a dream,—and behold! it is all nonsense, now that I am awake."

The sketch concludes with the setting fire of the chimney,

in the process of burning the manuscripts,—the incident already referred to. The manuscript that Hawthorne actually burned was the *Seven Tales of My Native Land*, a series of stories for which he could find no publisher. But in spite of his shadowy life and his plentiful discouragements, his stories were slowly making their way in the gift-book annuals and magazines, and what is more important, he was developing his remarkable style. What the Hawthorne-lover feels most sharply in *Fanshawe* is the total absence of that mellow charm of language which now seems but a natural echo of his own name; the first book was written correctly, but with a tedious flatness, unrelieved by any lift of phrase or sentence. And this improvement of style seems not to have been won by outward craft or calculation, as Poe would have us believe he wrote, but rather by a more faithful transference of his own moods into words,—as though by long self-study he more effectively grasped the subtler reliefs and contrasts of his exquisite nature, and with increased skill became more sincere. His art is the same in any form of writing at any given time. His letters and private journals have the same witchery, the same finality, as his published work; so closely is the effect bound up in his personality, that in his mature days his style seems rather a portion of what he expressed, than a means of expressing it.

An increasing mastery of so rare a gift could not fail, even in Hawthorne's obscurity, to win some praise from readers of finer judgment. Park Benjamin, reviewing *The Token* for 1836, singled out Hawthorne, as an English critic in the same year also did, for special praise. The American editor spoke of him as the "most pleasing writer of fanciful prose, except Irving, in the country." Perhaps it was meager praise, after five or six years of faithful work, but it had the accent of authority; evidently where he made his mark, he would make it indelibly.

In 1836 Goodrich got for him the editorship of *The American Magazine of Useful and Entertaining Knowledge*, an unimportant journal published in Boston. His salary was to be five hundred dollars, which in view of his small earnings as a story-writer seemed to him and his friends an assuring sum. It turned out, however, that he had to write practically all of the magazine, with some help from his older sister, and in June the company failed, owing him part of his salary. He blamed Goodrich at first, but fortunately did not quarrel with so useful a friend; he and Elizabeth Hawthorne shortly afterward wrote one of the *Peter Parley* books, the *Universal History on the Basis of Geography*, the money for which he gave to his sister,—one hundred dollars. His name did not appear on the title-page of this book, and though it had a large circulation, it brought him no fame, nor was the money he received in any proportion to its success.

His scattered stories continued to attract the attention of a few discerning minds, but their anonymity seriously prevented him from making a reputation. It has been explained that this secrecy was not entirely due to his modesty. It would have injured the circulation of any annual to have several of its articles obviously by the same writer, and for this reason Hawthorne naturally fell into the habit of letting his work go unclaimed, or signing it by pen-names, such as "Oberon," and "Ashley Allen Roger." By 1836, however, his stories were beginning to connect themselves with his real name, which was announced with shrewd praise, probably by Park Benjamin, in *The American Monthly Magazine* for October of that year:—

"The author of 'Sights from a Steeple,' of 'The Gentle Boy,' and of 'The Wedding Knell,' we believe to be one and the same individual. The assertion may sound bold, yet we hesitate not to call this author second to no man in this country, except Washington Irving. . . . Yes, to us the style of

Nathaniel Hawthorne is more pleasing, more fascinating, than any one's except their dear Geoffry Crayon! This mention of the real name of our author may be reprobated by him. His modesty is the best proof of his true excellence. How different does such a man appear to us from one who anxiously writes his name on every public post! We have read a sufficient number of his pieces to make the reputation of a dozen of our Yankee scribblers; and yet how few have heard the name above written! He does not even cover himself with the same anonymous shield at all times; but liberally gives the praise, which, concentrated on one, would be great, to several unknowns. If Mr. Hawthorne would but collect his various tales and essays into one volume, we can assure him that their success would be brilliant—certainly in England, perhaps in this country."

That Hawthorne did finally collect into a volume the fruits of his twelve years of seclusion, was due, though he did not know it at the time, to his friend Bridge, whose service, as we have seen, he afterwards acknowledged in the dedication of *The Snow Image*. Bridge had kept in intimate touch with his college friend, and was convinced that one reasonable success would probably draw him out of his seclusion into fame and the wholesome companionship of his fellows. He therefore consulted with Goodrich, who undertook to get an edition of a thousand copies published, if two hundred and fifty dollars were guaranteed against the cost. Bridge guaranteed that sum, without Hawthorne's knowledge, and under the title of *Twice Told Tales*, a collection of previously issued stories was published in Boston in 1837. A second edition, with another volume of stories added, appeared in 1842; it was the first edition, however, that fairly started his fame, and ended his long and curious apprenticeship.

At first the volume made little headway, but its hold on the public extended without interruption. *The American Monthly Magazine* praised the author again, with some journalistic self-congratulation at having praised him before.

Another criticism hailed the book as typically American, a true expression of New England. But the most generous and intelligent praise came from Longfellow, whom Hawthorne had known little in college and less since then, but who recognized in the new author an old classmate, and hastened to say a characteristically kind word for his genius. Longfellow already had his Harvard professorship, and his praise, in the pages of the *North American Review*, carried as much weight as any criticism. Hawthorne had sent him the book with a modest reintroduction of himself to the poet's memory,—

"We were not, it is true, so well acquainted at college that I can plead an absolute right to inflict my twice-told tediousness upon you; but I have often regretted that we were not better known to each other, and have been glad of your success in literature and in more important matters. . . . The present volumes contain such articles as seemed best worth offering to a public a second time; and I should like to flatter myself that they would repay you some part of the pleasure which I have derived from your own 'Outre-Mer.'"

Longfellow's review, after pointing out in a somewhat exuberant style the poetic attributes he finds in the newly-risen star, especially the quality of the past in romance, proceeds to the cardinal merits of the stories, their truth to the New England past, and the exquisite style in which they are written. His praise of the native themes was to be expected, since the tide of Americanism was strong in his verse, but it is interesting to see that his bright spirit caught nothing of the dark shadows of Hawthorne's Puritanism, although recognizing with delight its picturesque charm for literary purposes:

"Who would not like to have been present at the court of the worshipful Thomas Gorges, in those palmy days of the law when Tom Heard was fined five shillings for being drunk, and John Payne the same, 'for swearing one oath'? Who would not like to have seen Thomas Taylor presented to the

grand jury 'for abusing Captain Raynes, being in authority, by thee-ing and thou-ing him'; and John Wardell likewise,
for denying Cambridge College to be an ordinance of God;
and people fined for winking at comely damsels in church;
and others for being common sleepers there on the Lord's
Day? Truly, many quaint and quiet customs, many comic
scenes and strange adventures, many wild and wondrous
things, fit for humorous tale and soft, pathetic story, lie all
about us here in New England."

The gratitude of Hawthorne's letter acknowledging this
praise has in it something pathetic; there were at least five
persons, he said,—his mother, his two sisters, his aunt and
himself, who would thereafter believe Longfellow to be the
most sagacious critic on earth. Beneath the playful tone is the
consciousness of his isolation, which perhaps he felt most
keenly when this first applause called him into the general
world. The same consciousness is plainly expressed in a later
letter to Longfellow, giving an account of his life since graduation, and laying a naturally exaggerated emphasis on the in-
effectiveness of the twelve quiet years. His self-distrust and
his modesty count in the description: "By some witchcraft or
other—for I really cannot assign any reasonable why and
wherefore—I have been carried apart from the main current
of life, and find it impossible to get back again. Since we last
met, which you remember was in Sawtell's room, where you
read a farewell poem to the relics of the class,—ever since
then I have secluded myself from society; and yet I never
meant any such thing, nor dreamed what sort of life I was
going to lead. I have made a captive of myself, and put me
into a dungeon, and now I cannot find the key to let myself
out,—and if the door were open, I should be almost afraid to
come out. You tell me that you have met with trouble and
changes. I know not what these may have been, but I can
assure you that trouble is the next best thing to enjoyment,
and that there is no fate in this world so horrible as to have no

share in either its joys or sorrows. For the last ten years, I have not lived, but only dreamed of living."

This letter marks probably the lowest depths of Hawthorne's seclusion and depression. While he was writing it his fortune had changed, and though the brooding self-analysis was to remain the chief trait of his nature, the record of his later life shows that he took a busy, if a quiet, part in daily affairs, and was a far less shadowy personage than he himself and some of his critics have said.

IV

The *Twice Told Tales*, in the later complete edition, sum up practically all sides of Hawthorne's genius, and in a way supply the key to his longer works. One hesitates to call them "short stories," lest the term should imply a definite form or a limited subject; for they range from dramatic scenes of almost tragic intensity to cheerful essays in the vein of conversation, suggesting usually a larger movement of thought, especially in the tragic scenes, than the brief form can include, and reproducing in the essays the apparent fugitive moods and fancies of a dreamer, without any form at all. This is not to deny for a moment the perfect grasp of theme and economy of effect that result in the unity and purpose of a work of art; it is only saying that these tales of Hawthorne's are nearer to Irving's than to Poe's, belonging with the eighteenth century essay rather than with the sharply focused, well-economized short stories of the modern French artists. The resemblance to the eighteenth century essay is stronger because these tales, like Addison's papers, often seem to feel their way out of the philosophizing mood into straightforward narrative; they prophesy on the one side a development, which Hawthorne reached in *The Scarlet Letter*, and on the other hand they show the preponderance in his nature of the analyzing, meditative faculty, for which the essay is the readiest medium, and which was to assert itself overwhelmingly in his later romances.

The dramatic scene is represented in the collection chiefly by the stories of colonial legend, such as *The Gray Champion*, which Hawthorne wisely placed first, *Endicott and the Red Cross*, and *Howe's Masquerade*. In the first of these, as Hawthorne's best critic has pointed out, he found a type of story suited to his gifts, and by repeated use of it he brought it to a peculiar perfection; so far as outward setting is concerned, it is the literary method in *The Scarlet Letter*. It is an appeal to the eye, a brief and carefully prepared action, and a final tableau. The mechanical setting, however, counts with the reader far less than the sense of mystery conveyed in most of the examples of this type; even when the source of the mystery is explained away, as in *Edward Randolph's Portrait*, the effect on the reader is unimpaired. The reason discloses the deep moral strain in Hawthorne's art; the mystery he is interested in is never a thing of morbid nerves, of uncanny atmosphere, nor of mechanical device, as in the romantic novelists from whom Brockden Brown derived, or in Poe; it is always in normal life itself, as the story teaches the reader to reflect upon it and weigh its significance. Whether the Gray Champion is or is not one of the regicides, coming opportunely from his hiding-place, is of less moment than the mystery of truth driving tyranny back upon itself, of which he is the parable, and which is emphasized by the linking of the fights at Lexington and Bunker Hill with his spirit; whether Edward Randolph's portrait of itself became visible to warn Thomas Hutchinson of his soul's peril, or whether Alice Vane renewed the old picture for a time by an Italian painter's trick, is as nothing compared with the mysterious curse that fell on Randolph, as he came to believe, for the blood shed by his betrayal of a free country.

In some of the historical tales, however,—particularly in

Endicott and the Red Cross, Hawthorne presents what is for him a rare theme, the Puritan as a man of action. When he puts aside for a moment the meditative character he is so fitted to portray, and attempts the militant New Englander of the first days, the effective portrait that results is probably an exaggeration of fanaticism,—a character, as has been noticed, nearer the Covenanter than the New England Puritan, and perhaps derived from Scott. In his defiance of a tyrannical church and king Endicott is clothed in an ideal of courageous patriotism, and he has the reader's approval as well as Hawthorne's in the closing words: "Forever honored be the name of Endicott! We look back through the mist of ages, and recognize in the rending of the Red Cross from New England's banner the first omen of that deliverance which our fathers consummated after the bones of the stern Puritan had lain more than a century in the dust." But Endicott's real sternness, the Covenanter quality that Hawthorne is inclined to ascribe to his Puritan men of action, is displayed more effectively, with little to justify its force, in *The Maypole of Merry Mount.* Few of Hawthorne's tableaux hold a place longer in the memory than the picture of the hard captain face to face with the Lord and Lady of the May,—types of two ideals of life, which in their irreconcilable conflict had haunted the English imagination for centuries. The meeting is too momentous for even Endicott to escape its influence; the narrowness of his imagination is emphasized by the very pity he can hardly conceal:

"The youth, in the peril of the moment, had dropped his gilded staff, and thrown his arm about the Lady of the May, who leaned against his breast, too lightly to burden him, but with weight enough to express that their destinies were linked together, for good or evil. They looked first at each other, and then into the grim captain's face. There they stood, in the first hour of wedlock, while the idle pleasures, of which their companions were the emblems, had given place to the

sternest cares of life, personified by the dark Puritans. But
never had their youthful beauty seemed so pure and high as
when its glow was chastened by adversity.

" 'Youth,' said Endicott, 'ye stand in an evil case, thou
and thy maiden wife. Make ready presently, for I am minded
that ye shall both have a token to remember your wedding
day!'

" 'Stern man,' cried the May Lord, 'how can I move thee?
Were the means at hand, I would resist to the death. Being
powerless, I entreat. Do with me as thou wilt, but let Edith
go untouched!'

" 'Not so,' replied the immitigable zealot, 'We are not
wont to show an idle courtesy to that sex which requireth the
stricter discipline. What sayest thou, maid? Shall thy silken
bridegroom suffer thy share of the penalty, besides his own?'

" 'Be it death,' said Edith, 'and lay it all on me!'

"Truly, as Endicott had said, the poor lovers stood in a
woeful case. Their foes were triumphant, their friends captive and abased, their home desolate, the benighted wilderness around them, and a rigorous destiny, in the shape of the
Puritan leader, their only guide. Yet the deepening twilight
could not altogether conceal that the iron man was softened;
he smiled at the fair spectacle of early love; he almost sighed
for the inevitable blight of early hopes.

" 'The troubles of life have come hastily upon this young
couple,' observed Endicott. 'We will see how they comfort
themselves under their present trials ere we burden them with
greater.' "

In all the dramatic scenes dealing with history Hawthorne
selects for treatment a critical moment of change, when a new
era asserts itself perceptibly over an enfeebled past. He has
no interest in action, beyond such economical limits as may
show forth character, and for history as an evolution he cares
little; he sees life in its instant of fatal choice, much as Brown-
ing sees it, and the choice is usually strongly influenced by the
past, so that it appears the work of destiny. But Hawthorne
also clothes the past with a peculiar moral value; he frequently personifies it, so that it enters the scene, at the dra-

matic crises, to establish long-delayed justice or to point a warning. This is the mission of the Gray Champion, of Edward Randolph's portrait, and of the phantom procession in *Howe's Masquerade*. The vitality of the past in this type of story is as significant as the promise of the new age, and bears the peculiar mark of Hawthorne's reflective temperament.

In none of his stories does Hawthorne seem so committed in his sympathies as in these historical scenes. Yet even in the most vigorous of them some part of his nature remains stubbornly and critically aloof, observing with exact justice the flaws in what he admires. Unlike Mrs. Stowe, Hawthorne could advocate nothing; he holds no brief for any man nor any life, nor altogether for any single deed; nor even for human nature at large. The many aspects of truth, weighed in his careful thought, induce humor or irony, but lead to no final judgment. While he honors Endicott for asserting human liberty, he is scrupulous to portray those elements in the scene that indicate the Puritan use of freedom,—the whipping-post, the pillory and the stock; the Episcopalian and the suspected Catholic confined by the head, and the man who had drunk a health to the king, confined by the legs; the "Wanton Gospeller," who had dared to put an original interpretation upon Holy Writ, and the woman with a cleft stick on her tongue, who had wagged that unruly member against the elders of the church. The irony of Hawthorne's picture is admirable, yet for fear his humor may seem to make a distinction between the inconsistencies of one age and another, he makes haste to insert the characteristic warning:

"Let not the reader argue, from any of these evidences of iniquity, that the times of the Puritans were more vicious than our own, when, as we pass along the very street of this sketch, we discern no badge of infamy on man or woman. It was the policy of our ancestors to search out even the most secret sins, and expose them to shame, without fear or favor, in the broadest light of the noonday sun. Were such the custom now, perchance we might find materials for a no less piquant sketch than the above."

This, it should be remembered, is in the story that records Endicott's heroic blow for liberty. The ironical paradox of the scene is clear enough. If we needed further proof of Hawthorne's unwillingness to take sides or pass judgment,— what seems his most un-Puritan trait,—we might find it in these other words, evidently his own, from the *Journal of an African Cruiser*, which he edited for his friend Bridge in 1845: "It is remarkable that Defoe, a man of the most severe and delicate conscience, should have made his hero a slave-dealer, and should display a perfect insensibility to anything culpable in the traffic. Morality has taken a great step in advance since that day, or, at least, it has thrown a strong light upon one spot, with perhaps a corresponding shadow upon some other. The next age may shift the illumination, and show us sins as great as that of the slave trade, but which now enter into the daily practice of men claiming to be just and wise."

In strong contrast to the dramatic scenes in *Twice Told Tales* are the sketches of the essay type, full of gentle wisdom and keen observation, of which *A Rill from the Town Pump* is perhaps the best-known example. In this kind of writing Hawthorne uses the most meager materials; all he needs is some one place or object for his meditations to center about, and with this simple unity he can dispense with any other structure. None of his work seems more natural than these essay-sketches, probably because they represent with little change the way his mind took hold of life. The commonest object would suggest to him the experiences it was open to, and his speculations would explore its history or its use in search of simple parables. *David Swan, The Toll-Gatherer's*

Day, Sights from a Steeple and *Sunday at Home*, all are variations of the type; from a fixed point the reader is made to feel the normal movement of life as it touches that point, and to discern its humble lessons.   It is characteristic of Hawthorne that the attitude assumed is always passive; life as it molds the soul is his theme, and the element of fate is as strong in the various accidents here reckoned with, as is the sense of the past in the dramatic sketches.   It is equally characteristic of Hawthorne, however, and it should not be forgotten, that in these essays the temper is beautifully sane and cheerful. They have nothing of the morbid shadow which attaches itself, in other portions of his work, to his preoccupation with the problem of sin, and which too often is remembered as the sole atmosphere of his art.   These quiet, happy essays, full of village wisdom, rich though limited, and slightly elevated, if at all, above the pitch of thoughtful conversation, are in prose the counterpart of Longfellow's more popular poems, and appeal to the same taste.   If it has been the custom in our time to think lightly of Longfellow's transparent melodies, it is not surprising that these equally obvious prose meditations should seem somewhat infantile.   But the appreciative reader knows the rarity of this clear atmosphere, in both prose and verse; it has never been duplicated in its original purity of thought and word; it seems a blossoming in art of the more delicate celestial strains of the Puritan temper, with neither its overdeveloped conscience nor its will to be accomplishing.   With all the strong moral contrasts with which these essay-tales abound, Hawthorne troubles himself little in them to arrive at any conclusion; sometimes he sees several conclusions, all contradictory.   Whether David Swan would have been better or worse off had be waked to meet any of the intruders upon his nap, is not determined in Hawthorne's mind; if the reader passes at first a hasty judgment, in his sympathy with the pretty girl and his dislike of the thieves, he may catch some of the author's prudence, and reconsider; and if he makes any final deduction, it will be a cheerful reverence for fate. "Sleeping or waking, we hear not the airy footsteps of the strange things that almost happen. Does it not argue a superintending Providence that, while viewless and unexpected events thrust themselves continually athwart our path, there should still be regularity enough in mortal life to render foresight even partially available?"

Hawthorne's genius takes a third form in these tales in the studies of psychological experience, or homely allegory, such as *Wakefield* or *Dr. Heidegger's Experiment*. Perhaps stories in many ways so different should hardly be classed together; they have a common trait, however, in the deep philosophical interest which they seem to play upon and half express. In the more psychological sketches Hawthorne is apparently fascinated by the power of a chance resolve, or what seems a chance resolve, to shape a man's life; so Wakefield in the spirit of his strange joke takes up his residence in the street next his home, and finding it daily more difficult to go back, becomes almost permanently exiled. The moral is plain enough, and Hawthorne states it more plainly still in several places: "Amid the seeming confusion," he says, "of our mysterious world, individuals are so nicely adjusted to a system, and systems to one another and to a whole, that, by stepping aside for a moment, a man exposes himself to a fearful risk of losing his place forever." This is simply to say, what Hawthorne was destined to say many times again, with varied emphasis but unchanged conviction, that a man's life is compelled in one direction or another by an increasingly absolute fate, made up of his own acts. "Would that I had a folio to write, instead of an article of a dozen pages! Then might I exemplify how an influence beyond our control lays its strong hand on every deed which we do, and weaves its consequences into an iron tissue of necessity."

This fatalistic bent belongs to Hawthorne's nature; it belongs also to the scientific temper, and it shows chiefly in those stories which are semi-scientific in their psychological subject-matter or treatment.   It has been thought by most of Hawthorne's biographers that his theory of the fatality of acts was founded largely upon a tragic experience of his own life. In the belief that a young lady, whom he knew well, had been insulted, he challenged the supposed offender to a duel, but was prevented from carrying out his purpose by his friends Pierce and Cilley, who showed him that the supposed insult was entirely mythical.   A few years later Cilley was himself challenged by a political enemy, and the fact that Hawthorne had been willing to fight a duel is said to have persuaded him not to decline; and his opponent killed him.   But whether or not this account be true, and whether Hawthorne brooded over his share in his friend's death, *Wakefield* was published before Cilley was killed, and the fatalism there expressed came from the author's temperament, not from his experience.

The same sense of fate is in the homely allegories, and their moral vein is no less strong, but Hawthorne uses them chiefly to point the significant coincidences and contrasts of daily life. *Dr. Heidegger's Experiment* teaches as a general moral the uselessness of avoiding the natural lot; to be young again after many years proves no advantage to the Widow Wycherly.   But Hawthorne interests us also in the incongruous mirth that comes with artificial youth to the old people; "They laughed loudly at their old-fashioned attire, the wide-skirted coats and flapped waistcoats of the young men, and the ancient cap and gown of the blooming girl.   One limped across the floor like a gouty grandfather; one set a pair of spectacles astride of his nose, and pretended to pore over the black-letter pages of the book of magic; a third seated himself in an armchair, and strove to imitate the venerable dignity of Dr. Heidegger. Then all shouted mirthfully, and leaped about the room." As a kind of parallel to this uncanny restoration, Hawthorne describes the recovered beauty of the dried rose the Doctor has cherished for half a century; it reinforces the sense of fate, for its fading comes without any fault of its own; unlike the human characters, it has not brought age upon itself a second time by thoughtless or undignified conduct.

These first stories of Hawthorne's, with their threefold interest in the dramatic side of history, in the reflective wisdom of every-day life, such as makes the material of the familiar essay, and in the psychological or allegorical situation,—give in outline the qualities and limitations of his genius, which his later books simply expand and illustrate. In these brief tales and sketches he comes directly into comparison with Irving and Poe, the other masters of the short story in American literature. The Addisonian influence in both Irving and Hawthorne makes certain resemblances between them quite natural; Poe, in his essay on Hawthorne's *Tales*, repeatedly marks the likeness; "*The Spectator*, Mr. Irving, and Hawthorne have in common," he says, "that tranquil and subdued manner which I have chosen to denominate *repose;*" and in another place, "the natural" in composition, he says, "is best exemplified, among English writers, in Addison, Irving, and Hawthorne." In the essay type of sketch, where he deals with a limited life, illuminating it by wise reflection and humor, Hawthorne is nearest the New York writer; they are alike, also, in a certain lack of energy in their grip of the story—a tendency to play with it—for which Hawthorne has been severely criticized. The emotional appeal that has made *Rip Van Winkle* beloved of American playgoers, is largely due to the familiar stage-version and to Mr. Jefferson's acting; Irving's story is pale and slight in comparison. And the *Legend of Sleepy Hollow*, though more

richly varied in human character and stronger in plot, is yet a
fanciful tale, and belongs among the most fragile creations of
poetry. The humorous interest in character as it shows itself in homely encounters, the parochial curiosity, delight-
fully caught in the episode of The Stout Gentleman, in *Brace-
bridge Hall*, is of the very fabric of Hawthorne's genius in
its lighter moments. Yet the resemblances between the two
stylistic masters of American prose need not seem to weigh
heavily against their large differences. In the very lightness
of touch, the trifling moment in which they seem to find
common ground, they are totally unlike, as one hardly needs
to point out; Irving's manner suggests great riches of experience and a wide culture, borne without consciousness, and
enjoyed without more reflection than is needed for storing
away such comfortable wisdom; Hawthorne's lightness inevitably suggests shadows withdrawn for the moment only—
his nature, for once relaxed into playfulness, is at once narrower and deeper than Irving's, and sunlight in it is a surprise. More than any other of our prose writers, Irving is
simply a man of letters; his interest is in life as it lends itself to
happy memories and literary record; he is neither a political
theorist like Cooper, nor a propounder and experimenter of
esthetic theory, like Poe, nor a moral psychologist like Hawthorne. In a sense he is even more occupied with the past
than Hawthorne, for out of the past his temper rescues no
light for the future, no destiny for the race, but only the charm
and flavor of age, of ancient cheerful customs and old wine.
His genius lent itself to no exploring, except backwards into
the golden world of books and bookish tradition; though he
made the attempt, he could not grapple with the new frontier
world of Cooper, nor would he even attempt the spiritual ex-
ploration in which Hawthorne is most himself. For that reason, perhaps, Irving's great gifts and beautiful nature seem to
have been left behind in the movement of American literature;

he is still beloved, but he takes his place in the memory among English writers, as though he belonged to the old country, so much of whose charm as a literary shrine he discovered for the English-speaking race.

It is with Edgar Allan Poe, however, that Hawthorne is most often and most naturally compared. They two have practised the writing of the short story in America with a mastery still unapproached; and both are notable, in the popular opinion, for a dark strain in their art, a morbid temperament which singularly joins their fame. In mere technic, the management of incident, the description of scene, and most of all in a perfect unity of tone, which gives to their masterpieces a remarkable effect of completeness, they readily stand comparison with each other, and in deeper ways they suggest similarities. Most obvious of their common traits is their preoccupation with wickedness and death,—with that sort of concealed sin especially that produces mental horror in the reader; to the uncritical reader *The Black Cat, William Wilson, The Cask of Amontillado*, and *Ligeia*, the first titles that come to mind, have a strong affinity to *The Minister's Black Veil, The Wedding Knell*, or, to anticipate in Hawthorne's work, *Rappaccini's Daughter* and *Ethan Brand*. In only one respect, however, are these writers alike; they are both masters of artistic "keeping"; they both have control of the single mood or color or plot at will, so that *The Fall of the House of Usher* is a unit of atmosphere, *The Masque of the Red Death* a unit of color, *Rappaccini's Daughter* a unit of idea. But this is only to say that both writers are masters of the short story. In other respects they are strikingly individual. Poe is unapproached in the intellectual vigor of many of his plots; Hawthorne is as unique in American literature for style, in the deepest sense. With Poe the motive of his art is essentially intellectual, and therefore he appears to work from without; Hawthorne's genius is the flowering of New England char-

acter, and character is always his subject, and therefore his
art appears to work from within. He studies the experiences
of the soul for their effect upon the soul's destiny; Poe studies
all incidents in their own world, for their own sake, with regard to their scientific or artistic relation to each other, not
to the soul, and his highest interest is not spiritual but psychological.

It is doubtless unwise to believe Poe's account of his own
mental processes. No poet, probably, could have accomplished by purely intellectual methods so emotional a masterpiece as *The Raven*. The intuition of the artist, which gets
so little credit in Poe's self-analysis, must have been his in
superb measure. Yet it must be conceded that his main preoccupation, outside of the poems and the few great romances
already mentioned, is with reason rather than emotion or
character, and his criticisms of other writing than his own are
founded on purely intellectual appreciations. His essential
separation from Hawthorne's spirit is written in every line of
the essay on his great contemporary's *Tales*. The management of allegory, the successful keeping of tone, the finely
restrained manner, and the ordinary working up of plot—
these engaged Poe's attention; but with the deeper meaning,—
what he calls the "mysticism,"—he is curiously out of tune.
He digresses characteristically to show that Hawthorne had
plagiarized from *William Wilson* in *Howe's Masquerade*.
Considering the different temperaments of the writers, we
are not surprised that Poe overlooks the distinction between
his own conception of a haunting double, and Hawthorne's
phantom pageant, with its twofold mystery of the past and the
future. Yet it is certainly remarkable that Poe should attempt
to establish the supposed plagiarism, not in the likeness of
plot or situation, but in fancied resemblances of language,
which must be italicized to be noticed. The whole essay, and
particularly this passage, significant for all it is blind to, or

intentionally fails to mention, in Hawthorne's work, serves as an easy measure of difference in the nature and art of the two men.

Most characteristically, however, Hawthorne and Poe differ in the treatment of evil. The readiest way to a distinction is to say that Hawthorne deals with sin, and Poe with crime. The actual deed monopolizes Poe's attention; or if he studies its consequences, as in *The Black Cat*, it is only so far as they lead to other outward deeds, all linked together in a logical fate, but apart from the soul. Whatever horror belongs with such tales Poe depicts with great power, as in this story or in *The Cask of Amontillado;* but the horror is treated as an artistic effect, studied lovingly for its own sake; it is physical, and springs from no fundamental sense of right or wrong. The victim in *The Cask of Amontillado* does not deserve his fate; the murderer in *The Black Cat* does deserve his; yet the horror of the first story is without pity, and in the second it is without approval of the doomed man's fate. Poe's art is in the highest sense literary. It derives from the Gothic tales of terror, and is nourished by esthetic and nervous rather than by moral experiences. On the other hand, it need hardly be stated again that Hawthorne's art is a natural expression of a deep nature brooding upon the enigma of character and its relation to evil—the fit problem for a son of the Puritans; and his art takes on beauty, not by forethought, but out of the sources of his own loving nature. How far he departed temperamentally from Poe's unmoral interest in crime as a literary asset, is witnessed by Poe's ignoring of the theme in Hawthorne's work, as though unaware that their paths even appeared to cross in the study of evil. He pronounced rashly that Hawthorne's genius lay entirely in the bright, Addisonian sketches of cheerful village life, and shut his eyes to the strange power that was to create *The Scarlet Letter* and *The Marble Faun.*

V

After the publication of *Twice Told Tales* Hawthorne's life continued for a while unchanged. He wrote more stories and lived quietly at home, though his friends cast about to find occupation for him that would bring more immediate fame and profit. It belonged to the charm of his character to arouse such loyal interest in those who penetrated his seclusion, and few artists have been served by their friends with more kindness and wisdom than Hawthorne. His life changed decisively, however, not through their efforts, but through his acquaintance with Sophia Peabody, with whom he fell in love, and who became his wife. The Peabodys, once neighbors of the Hawthornes in his childhood, had lost sight of the family during Mrs. Hawthorne's residence in Maine. After the appearance of *Twice Told Tales*, Elizabeth Peabody recognized in the author a childhood acquaintance, and reopened the intercourse of the two households. She herself was a woman of intellect and character, still remembered for her work in education; her sister Mary was to be the wife of Horace Mann; Sophia, the youngest, was an artist, a person of strong enthusiasms and delicate sensitiveness, altogether as rare a being as Hawthorne ever conceived in his stories, and the severe headaches that had made her practically an invalid for twenty years, though they left her fragile, had diminished nothing of the sweetness of her character.

It was in 1838 that Hawthorne and his sisters first called on the neighboring family. The meeting of Hawthorne and his future wife has been described by Elizabeth Peabody.

"I was alone in the drawing-room; but Sophia, who was still an invalid, was in her chamber. As soon as I could, I ran upstairs to her and said, 'O Sophia, you must get up and dress and come down! The Hawthornes are here, and you never saw anything so splendid as he is—he is handsomer

than Lord Byron!' She laughed, but refused to come, remarking that since he had called once, he would call again.

"He did call again, as Sophia had predicted, not long afterwards; and this time she came down, in her simple white
wrapper, and sat on the sofa. As I said 'My sister, Sophia,'
he rose and looked at her intently,—he did not realize how
intently. As we went on talking, she would frequently inter-
pose a remark, in her low, sweet voice. Every time she did
so, he would look at her again, with the same piercing, in-
drawing gaze. I was struck with it, and thought, 'What if he
should fall in love with her!' and the thought troubled me;
for she had often told me that nothing would ever tempt her
to marry, and inflict on a husband the care of an invalid."

In the course of the friendship that sprang up between the
Peabodys and the Hawthornes much characteristic light is
thrown upon both families. Hawthorne for some time was
far more the friend than the lover, and in spite of Elizabeth
Peabody's premonition no one seems to have suspected the
attachment that was gathering force—unless it was Elizabeth
Hawthorne, who perhaps showed her interest in the matter
when she appropriated the flowers Elizabeth Peabody had
sent to her brother, saying that they would be unworthily
bestowed upon him, "who professes to regard the love of
flowers as a feminine taste. So I permitted him to look at
them, but considered them a gift to myself."

Hawthorne showed his realization of his love by a determined effort to make an immediate place for himself in the
world. The dream-life that had been his, suddenly paled,
and he was ready to do anything practical that might give
him the prospect he now needed. He was secretly engaged to
Sophia Peabody, his own mother not being told, for fear the
shock of the news might prove disastrous to her. The marriage must have seemed far away to both the lovers, for
Sophia had engaged herself on condition that she recovered
from her invalidism—a condition that bade fair to be insur-

mountable; and of course Hawthorne had to find means to support her. Such means seemed at hand, however, in the appointment as weigher and gauger in the Boston Custom-house, where George Bancroft, the historian, was collector of the port. So Hawthorne left the little room in the old house, in which he had won his first share of fame, and took up his new and comparatively humble duties in January, 1839.

The entries in his journal give a clear record of those duties, all of which he performed conscientiously; they also give evidence that these rough experiences were stored in his memory as precious points of contact with real life. In a letter to Longfellow soon after the appointment Hawthorne wrote jocularly of the literary use to which he might turn his new career, and the journal is a more serious witness to the minute attention he gave to every human interest in the routine of his work. While he was literally toiling, getting down to the wharf each day before the workmen, so that their working hours, by which they were paid, might be as long as possible, he was also, as he realized, disciplining his dreamer's soul to actual things—the best unconscious preparation for such writing as *The Scarlet Letter*. Just what his life was, or a large daily part of it, is told in the entry for February 7, 1839.—

"Yesterday and day before, measuring a load of coal from the schooner Thomas Lowder, of St. John's, N. B. A little, black, dirty vessel. The coal stowed in the hold, so as to fill the schooner full, and make her a solid mass of black material. The master, Best, a likely young man; his mate a fellow jabbering in some strange gibberish, English I believe—or nearer that than anything else—but gushing out all together—whole sentences confounded into one long, unintelligible word. Irishmen shovelling the coal into the two Custom-house tubs, to be craned out of the hold, and others wheeling it away in barrows, to be laden into wagons. The first day, I walked the wharf, suffering not a little from cold; yesterday, I sat in the cabin, whence I could look through the interstices of the bulkhead, or whatever they call it, into the hold. My eyes, what a cabin! Three paces would more than measure it in any direction, and it was filled with barrels, not clean and new, but black, and containing probably the provender of the vessel; jugs, firkins, the cook's utensils and kitchen furniture—everything grimy and sable with coal dust. There were two or three tiers of berths; and the blankets, etc., are not to be thought of. A cooking stove, wherein was burning some of the coal—excellent fuel, burning as freely as wood, and without the bituminous melting of Newcastle coal. The cook of the vessel, a grimy, unshaven, middle-aged man, trimming the fire at need, and sometimes washing his dishes in water that seemed to have cleansed the whole world beforehand—the draining of gutters, or caught at sink-spouts. In the cessations of labor, the Irishmen in the hold would poke their heads through the open space into the cabin and call 'Cook!'—for a drink of water or a pipe—whereupon Cook would fill a short black pipe, put a coal into it, and stick it into the Irishman's mouth. Here sat I on a bench before the fire, the other guests of the cabin being the stevedore, who takes the job of getting the coal ashore, and the owner of the horse that raised the tackle—the horse being driven by a boy. The cabin was lined with slabs—the rudest and dirtiest hole imaginable, yet the passengers had been accommodated here in the trip from New Brunswick. The bitter zero atmosphere came down the companion-way, and threw its chill over me sometimes, but I was pretty comfortable, though, on reaching home, I found that I had swaggered through several thronged streets with coal streaks on my visage.

"The wharfinger's office is a general resort and refuge for people who have business to do on the wharf, in the spaces before work is commenced, between the hours of one and two, etc. A salamander stove—a table of the signals, wharves, and agent of packets plying to and from Boston—a snuff-box—a few chairs, etc., constituting the furniture. A news-paper."

For a while Hawthorne's genius gathered strength, Antæuslike, from this sordid contact; then the severe restraint became irksome. Throughout his life all attempts to deal closely with actual, routine things ended in a discontent of the spirit which had no relation to indolence, but simply proved to what realm he was native. His own words, from which the best accounts of the next years must be taken, show the stages of this discontent. The first note is sounded on July 3, 1839.

"I do not mean to imply that I am unhappy or discontented, for this is not the case. My life is only a burden in the same way that it is to every toilsome man; and mine is a healthy weariness, such as needs only a night's sleep to remove it. But from henceforth forever I shall be entitled to call the sons of toil my brothers, and shall know how to sympathize with them, seeing that I likewise have risen at the dawn, and borne the fervor of the midday sun, nor turned my heavy footsteps homeward till eventide. Years hence, perhaps, the experience that my heart is acquiring now will flow out in truth and wisdom."

By the following February the discontent becomes more apparent.

"All day long again have I been engaged in a very black business,—as black as a coal; and, though my face and hands have undergone a thorough purification, I feel not altogether fit to hold communion with doves. Methinks my profession is somewhat akin to that of a chimney-sweeper; but the latter has the advantage over me, because, after climbing up through the darksome flue of the chimney, he merges into the midst of the golden air, and sings out his melodies far over the heads of the whole tribe of weary earth-plodders."

A month later Hawthorne speaks for a moment of the compensation for his weary toil.

"It is good for me, on many accounts, that my life has had this passage in it. I know much more than I did a year ago. I have a stronger sense of power to act as a man among men. I have gained worldly wisdom, and wisdom also that is not altogether of this world. And, when I quit this earthly cavern where I am now buried, nothing will cling to me that ought to be left behind. Men will not perceive, I trust, by my look, or the tenor of my thoughts and feelings, that I have been a custom-house officer."

And still later, when his duties took him to the cleaner work of inspecting the salt vessels, he writes,—

"Rejoice with me, for I am free from a load of coal which has been pressing upon my shoulders throughout all the hot weather. I am convinced that Christian's burden consisted of coal; and no wonder he felt so relieved, when it fell off and rolled into the sepulchre. His load, however, at the utmost, could not have been more than a few bushels, whereas mine was exactly one hundred and thirty-five chaldrons and seven tubs."

Hawthorne's work in the Boston Custom-house ended in April, 1841, with a change of political administration. In 1840, after the death of their brother George, for some time an invalid, the Peabodys had moved to Boston, and the lovers saw much of each other; however impatient he must have been and wearied of his office, Hawthorne could not have been unhappy during this period. Apparently he had expected to save some leisure each day for writing, but the routine of his tasks left him inspiration for little besides the notes and sketches in his journal. Had he stayed longer in this environment, perhaps he would have found his voice again; as it was, his genius was chiefly occupied in absorbing and assimilating the materials of his novel experiences. Exception must be made, however, of three books for children, published between November, 1840, and February, 1841, and written— it has been suggested—under the influence of Elizabeth Peabody, who had started a book-store. The three volumes,— *Grandfather's Chair*, *Famous Old People* and *Liberty Tree*, are a series of historical tales of early New England, admirably written, with an obvious educational purpose. Hawthorne's long acquaintance with the New England past must have made this writing a simple task, but its purpose naturally prevented him from developing the material in characteristically subtle ways. Yet if little of his genius finds important expression here, it should be remembered that these books, like the later reworking of the Greek myths, expressed his interest in children,—no negligible part of his nature.

Upon losing his position in the Custom-house, Hawthorne joined the Brook Farm movement, apparently with the hope that it might provide a home eventually for himself and his betrothed. It has never been thought that he entered the community through any deep sympathy with its aims; his spirit never kindled in any social cause, nor any reform. The community idea had, indeed, long appealed to him, he had been interested in the Shakers, had half whimsically thought of joining them, and had used the community as a theme in his writing. But there is little doubt that he joined the movement now as a practical, and in that sense selfish, experiment. From his salary in the Custom-house he had saved a thousand dollars; he invested the whole sum in the new transcendental enterprise, and took his place in the Brook Farm circle early in April, 1841.

"The Brook Farm Institute of Agriculture and Education," at Roxbury, Massachusetts, had its origin in the circle of the Boston Transcendentalists. George Ripley and W. H. Channing were apparently the prime movers in the scheme to establish an ideal society, where the earthly distractions of life should be reduced to their proper minimum, and the soul left free to expand in the new philosophy. Emerson and the older Transcendentalists discouraged the attempt, but Ripley persisted, and early in 1841 bought a milk farm in West Roxbury, and organized the proposed community into a stock company. At first fifty thousand dollars was the capitalization spoken of; then thirty thousand; and finally twenty-four shares, of five hundred dollars each, were taken. The farm, one hundred and seventy acres in extent, cost ten thousand five hundred dollars, and it was immediately mortgaged for six thousand dollars. The financing of the enterprise was somewhat elaborate, and when considered in all its details, appears perplexingly impractical. The humor of the community's history begins with the first election of officers, when Hawthorne, who had invested his savings in two shares, was made a member of the "Direction of Finance"; perhaps the humor began earlier, in the selection, for agricultural purposes, of land obviously worn out and fit only for pasture.

The Transcendentalists rarely understated their ideals. The aim of Brook Farm was "to insure a more natural union between intellectual and manual labor than now exists; to combine the thinker and the worker, as far as possible, in the same individual; to guarantee the highest mental freedom, by providing all with labor adapted to their tastes and talents, and securing to them the fruits of their industry; to do away with the necessity of menial services by opening the benefits of education and the profits of labor to all; and thus to prepare a society of liberal, intelligent, and cultivated persons, whose relations with each other would permit a more wholesome and simple life than can be led amidst the pressure of our competitive institutions." But smile as one will, this strange experiment is remembered as an incident in enough famous lives, here meeting in "The House of the Interpreter," "The Pilgrim House," and the other simple buildings with fine names, to insure the immortality of Brook Farm in American history. Hither came Margaret Fuller, and Charles Dana, founder of the New York *Sun*, and George William Curtis— perhaps the most lovable of the community; and less enthusiastic, but destined to higher fame, came Hawthorne.

One turns to his note-books, as usual, for the indelible sketches of his daily life.

"Here I am," he writes, "in a polar Paradise! I know not how to interpret this aspect of nature,—whether it be of good or evil omen to our enterprise. But I reflect that the Plymouth pilgrims arrived in the midst of storm, and stepped ashore upon mountain snow-drifts; and, nevertheless, they prospered, and became a great people,—and doubtless it will be the same with us. I laud my stars, however, that you will not have your first impressions of (perhaps) our future home from such a day as this. . . . Through faith, I persist in believing that Spring and Summer will come in their due season; but the unregenerated man shivers within me, and suggests a doubt whether I may not have wandered within the precincts of the Arctic Circle, and chosen my heritage among everlasting snows. . . . I have not yet taken my first lesson in agriculture, except that I went to see our cows foddered, yesterday afternoon. We have eight of our own; and the number is now increased by a transcendental heifer belonging to Miss Margaret Fuller. She is very fractious, I believe, and apt to kick over the milk-pail. . . . I intend to convert myself into a milk-maid this evening, but I pray Heaven that Mr. Ripley may be moved to assign me the kindliest cow in the herd, otherwise I shall perform my duty with fear and trembling.

"Before breakfast I went out to the barn and began to chop hay for the cattle, and with such 'righteous vehemence,' as Mr. Ripley says, did I labor, that in the space of ten minutes I broke the machine. Then I brought wood and replenished the fires; and finally went down to breakfast, and ate up a huge mound of buckwheat cakes. After breakfast, Mr. Ripley put a four-pronged instrument into my hands, which he gave me to understand was a pitchfork; and he and Mr. Farley being armed with similar weapons, we all three commenced a gallant attack upon a heap of manure. This office being concluded, and I having purified myself, I sit down to finish this letter.

"What an abominable hand do I scribble! but I have been chopping wood and turning a grindstone all the forenoon; and such occupations are likely to disturb the equilibrium of the muscles and sinews. It is an endless surprise to me how much work there is to be done in the world; but, thank God, I am able to do my share of it,—and my ability increases daily. . . . I milked two cows this morning, and would send you some of the milk, only that it is mingled with that which was drawn forth by Mr. Dismal View and the rest of my brethren."

There is something strangely amusing in the faith Hawthorne had in this new work of his hands; perhaps no American, not even Emerson, was less adapted for a routine of toil. Hawthorne's reflective, brooding nature, his inheritance from one part of the Puritan temper, led him in the very midst of his barnyard duties to wander in his dream world, and to feel the unreality of actual things. Not a day went by, he said, that did not teach him how facts are changed in their passage through the human mind, until truth seems a fantasy, never to be grasped. He found amusement in the comrade who quoted Latin and made classical allusions while turning over the manure-pile; his whole residence at Brook Farm suggests the same incongruity. Some pathos also belongs to the picture, if we remember how often in his career Hawthorne yearned for an actual, hand-to-hand grapple with life, and how all his attempts disappointed him with a sense that his most rugged experiences—in the Custom-house, at Brook Farm, in the Liverpool Consulate—were turned into phantoms by the magic of his self-analysis. Even had the Brook Farm enterprise succeeded in its general purpose, it would have failed for Hawthorne; for as soon as he had stored up the ideas and sensations any way of life could contribute, that way of life began to pall upon him, and he longed for freedom. Early in May, 1841, he records the first glimmering of discontent, when he writes that he would not be so patient if he were not engaged in a righteous and heavenly-blessed way of life. But a slight acquaintance with his nature is enough to convince us that he would not long be patient with any convention for such purely moral reasons; the fact that he mentions no others shows that the experience was already unproductive in spiritual ways. By another month his discontent finds clear expression. "In the midst of toil, or after a hard day's work in the gold-mine, my soul obstinately refuses to be poured out on paper. That abominable gold-mine! Thank God, we anticipate getting rid of its treasures in the course of two or three days! Of all hateful places that is the worst, and I shall never comfort myself for having spent so many days of blessed sunshine there. It is my opinion that a man's soul may be buried and perish under a dung-heap, or in a furrow of the field, just as well as under a pile of money."

By August Hawthorne's frame of mind was in direct contrast with all his first hopes of the Farm,—both for himself and for the community. "In a little more than a fortnight," he wrote, "I shall be free from my bondage,—free to enjoy Nature,—free to think and feel. . . . Even my Customhouse experience was not such a thralldom and weariness; my mind and heart were free. Oh, labor is the curse of the world, and nobody can meddle with it without becoming proportionably brutified! Is it a praiseworthy matter that I have spent five golden months in providing food for cows and horses? It is not so." Later in the same month he writes Sophia Peabody that they must no longer depend upon the Farm for their hope of a home; it was extremely doubtful whether the community could be permanent. During a visit to his home in Salem in September he writes of the past months as though they were already part of antiquity, and describes characteristically the illusion they had become. The words might be applied to most of the "practical" passages in his life:

"I should judge it to be twenty years since I left Brook Farm; and this I take to be one proof that my life there was an unnatural and unsuitable, and therefore an unreal, one. It already looks like a dream behind me. The real Me was never an associate of the community; there has been a spectral Appearance there, sounding the horn at day break, and milking the cows, and hoeing potatoes, and raking hay, toiling in the sun, and doing me the honor to assume my name. But this spectre was not myself. Nevertheless, it is somewhat remarkable that my hands have, during the past summer, grown very brown and rough, insomuch that many people persist in believing that I, after all, was the aforesaid spectral horn-sounder, cow-milker, potato-hoer, and hay-raker. But such people do not know a reality from a shadow."

Hawthorne returned to Brook Farm, but as a resident rather than worker, and with the conviction that this second stay was only temporary. He intended to use his new leisure for writing, but even his release from the farm labor did not give him the solitude his genius needed. His residence at the Farm produced at the time only one book, *Biographical Stories for Children*, 1842,—simply told lives of Benjamin West, Isaac Newton, Samuel Johnson, Oliver Cromwell, Benjamin Franklin, and Queen Christina; one story, *A Virtuoso's Collection*, in *The Boston Miscellany*, May, 1842; and the enlarged edition of *Twice Told Tales*, in the same year. The best that Brook Farm had done for his genius was to give it material, to be used later; at the moment, Hawthorne very naturally felt that his time there had been wasted.

In so far as he had hoped to win a home in the community, Hawthorne had worse than failed; he had lost even the few savings with which he began. Having practically nothing left but his slight literary prospects, he and Sophia now made a poet's choice, and determined, since poor they were, to be poor together. They found a home that promised suitable privacy in the Old Manse, at Concord, and they were accordingly married on July 9, 1842, at Boston.

VI

Hawthorne has described the Old Manse in the introductory sketch in the *Mosses*, and his journal gives a more detailed record of his life in the house. The home, so secluded, so steeped in the past, suited his genius peculiarly; perhaps none of his later homes accommodated themselves so fully to the way of life his temperament desired. Yet for that very reason the residence in the Old Manse, ideally happy in his love and in the birth of his first child Una, on March 3, 1844, was not very profitable to Hawthorne for any advance in his profession. The image under which he most often represented his new joys, the original Paradise, was true in this sense also, that so far as his own account can be trusted he did very little work. "A rainy day,—a rainy day," he writes. "I am commanded to take my pen in hand, and I am therefore banished to the little ten-foot-square apartment misnamed my study; but perhaps the dismalness of the day and the dulness of my solitude will be the prominent characteristics of what I write. And what is there to write about? Happiness has no succession of events, because it is a part of eternity; and we have been living in eternity ever since we came to this old manse." It is no cause for wonder that this sense of Eden should have colored Hawthorne's thought of his young home, or should have chained his energies for a time; quiet as the life was, so that the unusual caller was a matter for humorous comment in the journal, these were rare spirits in the neighborhood, rare enough to reduce an appreciative mind to a state of inactive wonder. A sense of these privileges is in all that Hawthorne writes of that time, and he generously includes the few less important in the glamor he sets around the great ones. George Prescott came daily "to bring three pints of milk from some ambrosial cow," and sometimes to make an offering of mortal flowers; Emerson came and feasted on the household's "nectar and ambrosia, and Thoreau came to hear the Hawthorne's musical box,—or that was his fate, if not his purpose." How should one toil at writing, if one could walk out of an August afternoon and find Margaret Fuller reading a strange book under the trees, where presently Emerson also would appear, wise and quaintly humorous, to say that there were Muses in the woods that day, and whispers in the breeze!

Even a social community so select and vague as that which the Hawthornes may be said to have made their own, presented at times embarrassing problems. At the very beginning of their residence in the Old Manse Margaret Fuller determined that her sister and brother-in-law, Mr. and Mrs. Ellery Channing, should board in the novelist's household. Hawthorne's letter declining the proposal is a model of tactful self-assertion, and leaves the only impression of energy, however quiet, that one can rescue from this period of his life. Other problems, not recorded, must have been met with similar adroitness and effect, for the remembrance of him in the neighborhood was entirely pleasant—almost affectionate.

During the years at the Old Manse Hawthorne published many of the stories later gathered in the *Mosses*, and edited Bridge's *Journal of an African Cruiser*. Practically all this writing was done between 1843 and 1845; the first year in Concord had been quite unfruitful. As the time went on, Hawthorne may have been stirred to increasing effort by the poverty that began to threaten him and more than threaten. It was characteristic of him that he should work under pressure, and the failing pocket-book now gave pressure enough to rouse even a more lethargic nature. It is not entirely apparent, in the family correspondence, how poor the Hawthornes were at the end of their stay in the Old Manse, for Sophia, like her husband, wrote of their life with playful cheerfulness. But much should be read between the lines of her account of

their Christmas housekeeping, when the cook was in Boston
and Hawthorne did the work. "He rose betimes in the mornings, and kindled fires in the kitchen and breakfastroom, and
by the time I came down, the tea-kettle boiled, and potatoes
were baked and rice cooked, and my lord sat with a book,
superintending. Just imagine that superb head peeping at
the rice or examining the potatoes with the air and port of a
monarch! And that *angelico riso* on his face, lifting him clean
out of culinary scenes into the arc of the gods. . . . On
Christmas day we had a truly Paradisaical dinner of preserved quince and apple, dates, and bread and cheese, and
milk."

It was Hawthorne's good fortune, or more properly, it was
the just reward of his genius and nature, to be appreciated
and loyally served by a few capable friends. Through them
he had been called to Bancroft's attention, with the result of
the appointment in the Boston Custom-house. Now one
May day in 1845, Horatio Bridge, affectionately known as the
"Admiral," and Franklin Pierce made a visit to Hawthorne,
and gave him, as his wife said, solid hope. They found Hawthorne in the shed, hewing wood, and brought him out in a
triumphant gale of boyish spirits, Pierce with his arm encir-
cling the novelist's workman's frock, and Bridge dancing and
gesticulating and opening his round eyes "like an owl."

In the following summer Bridge organized a "sailor house-
party" at his quarters at Portsmouth Navy Yard, for the purpose of introducing Hawthorne to other friends influential in
politics. Pierce was there, and Senator Atherton of New
Hampshire, and Senator Fairfield of Maine. These were the
important guests, and Hawthorne's charm fell upon them all.
One has a sense of something not quite noble in Hawthorne's
willingness to apply thus for government positions,—for he
must have understood the intention of his friends. But love
of country, strongly as he felt it in his own way, never took the

form of jealous scruple with him, as it did with Cooper; he never felt called upon to defend his country with anything like Cooper's enthusiasm, nor indeed, to defend it at all; he accepted politics simply as a natural condition, and criticized politicians like ordinary human beings, impartially, without reference to the system that made them as they were. This attitude, clearly defined in the foreign note-books and in the introduction to *The Scarlet Letter*, adds materially to the popular conception of the bloodlessness of Hawthorne's character; his passive acceptance of public conditions appears to be cynical, or at least very far from the attitude his countrymen expect in their best men. But the explanation lies again in that inwardness of his nature, that fixed contemplation of the effects of life, which left him small interest in life itself. Hawthorne is habitually jealous of the power of his office-holding upon his soul; when he sees ignoble symptoms there, he is immediately strenuous in his wish to be free; until his soul is so touched, he is indifferent to the possibilities of outward things. However one-sided this frame of mind may be, it is capable of defense on its own grounds; certainly Hawthorne's genius justified itself, and a critical method that would seek to hold him to the standards that would measure Cooper, will give only vague and unsatisfactory results.

On March 23, 1846, Hawthorne was made surveyor of the Salem Custom-house, at a salary of twelve hundred dollars, and he returned to his boyhood home. So confident was he of the appointment, that he had in fact returned to the old house the previous October. During the four years that he now spent in Salem, he lived first in the Herbert Street home, with his mother and sisters, and then as the larger family proved too many, he removed to a house in Chestnut Street, and still later, to a house in Mall Street, where his mother and sisters afterward rejoined him, and where his mother died. In 1846 part of the summer and autumn were spent in Boston, in Carver Street, and there the son, Julian, was born. In a letter a year later Sophia Hawthorne describes the new Mall Street home; the account indicates the change in the environment of Hawthorne's genius since he first left the somber dwelling of his youth:

"My husband's study will be high from all noise, and it will be to me a Paradise of Peace to think of him alone and still, yet within my reach. He has now lived in the nursery a year without a chance for one hour's uninterrupted musing, and without his desk being once opened! He—the heaven-gifted Seer—to spend his life between the Custom-house and the nursery! I want him to be with me, not because he *must* be, but only when he is just in the mood for all the scenes of Babydom. In the evening he is always mine, for then he never wishes to write. . . . It will be very pleasant to have Madame Hawthorne in the house. Her suite of rooms is wholly distinct from ours, so that we shall only meet when we choose to do so. There are very few people in the world whom I should like or would consent to have in the house even in this way; but Madame Hawthorne is so uninterfering, of so much delicacy, that I shall never know she is near excepting when I wish it; and she has so much kindness and sense and spirit that she will be a great resource in emergencies. . . . I am so glad to win her out of that Castle Dismal, and from the mysterious chamber into which no mortal ever peeped, till Una was born, and Julian,—for they alone have entered the *penetralia*. Into that chamber the sun never shines. Into these rooms in Mall Street it blazes without stint."

Hawthorne took up his duties in the Custom-house with more than the pride he usually felt in each new attempt toward practical service. There was here, in addition, a family tradition to inspire him; he imagined his ancestors, sturdy and efficient as they were, beholding with satisfaction their dreamer descendant as he took his place in their line. We have his feelings in his own words in the sketch of the Custom-house which so incongruously prefaces *The Scarlet Letter*. Certainly, those of his ghostly great-grandsires who questioned his story-writing, as he fancied, and judged him a degenerate, no more serviceable to mankind in his day and generation than a fiddler,—must have approved the vigor with which he seems to have discharged his duties. He had more leisure than at the Boston Custom-house,—only three or four hours of the day had to be given to business; but in that time he made a solid impression upon his comrades of his ability, and sometimes, too, of his strong temper. He is said to have been "tempestuous" when aroused; "What in God's name have you sent on board my ship as an inspector?" asked one captain who had fled up the wharf and taken refuge in the office. Much humor and some ill-nature is in the introduction to *The Scarlet Letter;* it is easy to think back to the causes of that sharp portrait of indolent, official life, with the emphasis on its meanness; the firm hand of his ancestors and the brooding aloofness of his own nature made his environment hardly attractive, for all his temporary pride in practical work.

His leisure gave Hawthorne opportunity to come out of himself and mingle more with the society that experience and his wife's good influence had taught him to like. But it gave him no inspiration to write. His duties each day prevented the creative mood. It was not long before he realized again the disgust with actual things, taken simply as facts, which had made Brook Farm a failure for him spiritually as well as financially, and which earlier had made Brook Farm seem a land of promise to which he could escape from the Boston Custom-house. After he had extracted by the alchemy of his genius, the inner meaning of any experience, the experience was for him empty and lifeless, and his nature struggled to be unchained from it as from a corpse. But for a while, at least, his new existence in Salem was smooth enough.

Early in 1846 the *Mosses from an Old Manse* had been published in New York. The volume is naturally associated with the *Twice Told Tales*, and in many respects it represents the same stage of Hawthorne's art. The contents consist of stories and sketches, the latter bordering always upon the essay, and the former rich in speculation upon the chances and possibilities of life. In these later stories, too, Hawthorne's imagination, as his critics have pointed out, busies itself usually with a physical symbol, very clearly defined and treated allegorically. The ready examples are found in *The Birthmark*, where the one flaw in perfect beauty is made the necessary condition of human life, and in *Egotism; Or the Bosom Serpent*, the title of which tells the story, except that the bosom serpent is killed or driven out by the entrance of love into Roderick's heart. In the essays, such as the genial *Fire Worship*, there is the pleasant cheerfulness of the earlier volume, hardly more mature or in any way altered, and certainly no less delightful. Some indication of the happiness of the past few years might be suspected in this essay, so full of the hearth, or in *The New Adam and Eve*, with its echo of the Hawthornes' Concord sentiment, and its picture of perfect love; but this allegory was conceived, and its title practically assigned to it, in 1836. Almost all the *Mosses* are entered in their germ around that year in Hawthorne's note-book.

Though these stories belong to the same general inspiration as the *Twice Told Tales*, they give on the whole a different impression. Most obviously, they differ in a greater emphasis upon allegory, and a slighter—indeed negligible—interest in history, or in the past in any form. *Roger Malvin's Burial* is the only story that draws even remotely upon that source of romance. And in the allegorical tendency of the majority of the pieces—*The Birthmark, Rappaccini's Daughter, Feathertop*—the interest is rather experimental than didactic; Hawthorne throws life into certain strange combinations, to see what will come of them; and this curiosity, most often deeply philosophical, is spent at times upon mere fancies of juxtaposition, as in *The Virtuoso's Collection*, in which, to use his own note for the story, he pictures "an imaginary museum, containing such articles as Aaron's rod, the petticoat of General Harrison, the pistol with which Benton shot Jackson—and then a diorama, consisting of political or other scenes, or done in wax-work." Whatever else Hawthorne's art might become, *The Mosses from an Old Manse* indicated that he was to be a kind of experimenter with life, caring less for the outward established order of experience than for the new significances and possibilities of the soul. At the same time, the reserve which keeps his personality so distant from his work, takes from it also that impression of passionate ideal search which can ennoble the experiments of philosopher or scientist; the absence of emotion from Hawthorne's curiosity is the main excuse for judging him, as his recent critics have judged, ineffectual and cold; and that absence of emotion is most felt in this volume. At best, the curiosity to experiment with life is pitiful, in *The Birthmark;* at the other extreme, in *Feathertop*, it is trifling.

Since these allegorical stories are devoted so largely to spiritual experiment, it is not surprising that their genesis is usually in an idea, rather than in a plot. It is usually considered the mark of a true story-teller that he thinks in terms of plot; whether or not we must infer that Hawthorne was no true story-teller, it is clear from entries in his note-book that the experiment was the thing which occurred to him, and the story was worked out to convey the idea. Some illustration of this habit of mind has been casually given already; it can hardly be made too clear. "A hint of a story,—some incident which should bring on a general war; and the chief actor in the incident to have something corresponding to the mischief he had caused;" "A well-concerted train of events to be thrown into confusion by some misplaced circumstance, unsuspected till the catastrophe, yet exerting its influence from beginning

to end;" "Cannon transformed to church-bells;" "Follow
out the fantasy of a man taking his life by instalments, instead of at one payment,—say ten years of life alternately
with ten years of suspended animation"—these are typical
notes. More familiar, because of their later form, are these:
"A snake taken into a man's stomach and nourished there
from fifteen years to thirty-five, tormenting him most horribly.
A type of envy or some evil passion." "The semblance of a
human face to be formed on the side of a mountain, or in the
fracture of a small stone, by a *lusus naturæ*. The face is an
object of curiosity for years or centuries, and by and by a boy
is born, whose features gradually assume the aspect of that
portrait. At some critical juncture, the resemblance is found
to be perfect. A prophecy may be connected." "A person
to be the death of his beloved in trying to raise her to more
than mortal perfection; yet this should be a comfort to him
for having aimed so highly and holily." Among these notes
is the brief anecdote of the lovers of Acadia, which in Longfellow's hands became *Evangeline;* and one final illustration,
with a richness of suggestion that elaboration could hardly
have increased, deserves to be remembered among Hawthorne's most typical work,—"A person to be writing a tale,
and to find that it shapes itself against his intentions; that the
characters act otherwise than he thought; that unforeseen
events occur; and a catastrophe comes which he strives in
vain to avert. It might shadow forth his own fate,—he having made himself one of the personages."

To whatever degree Hawthorne's predisposition toward
allegory may have injured his longer romances, when combined with other narrative elements, certainly in the *Mosses*
he attains to almost unique skill in this kind of writing. Perhaps no other modern writer has managed to indicate so
much of the soul's deeper experiences through this medium,
which still is strange and artificial to the race, for all its fa-

miliarity with sacred parables. Hawthorne's matchless sense
of "keeping," the gift that distinguishes all of his tales, serves
to make his allegory understandable by rejecting every note
that is foreign to the spirit of the combined fable and inner
meaning. This praise, however, can be given only to his short
allegories; in the longer romances his parable is at times
pressed far, and confused. And his undoubted gift for pure
story-telling aids the allegory immensely, as a similar gift
aided Bunyan, by finding for the germ idea a dress always of
quaint interest, and often of surprising ingenuity. The relation between *The Birthmark*, complete and inevitable as it
seems in the fitness of its plot, and the original note for it,
when the outward circumstances of that plot were unthought
of, is a matter for study and wonder. Surely that acquaintance with the actual must have been amazingly large, from
which Hawthorne could take a series of incidents inevitably
in such a high state of selection.

In only two pieces is the allegorical content submerged to
the point where the narrative becomes truly a story, but in
Roger Malvin's Burial and *Rappaccini's Daughter* Hawthorne's genius in story-telling has supreme examples. The
first is set in the early frontier history of New England, and
belongs to the class of tales of which the *Gray Champion*
came first. The allegorical method is laid aside for once, and
the theme of fate is substituted. The youth who promises to
return to bury his dead father-in-law, and fails to keep his
word, at last expiates his neglect by the unintentional murder
of his own child on that very spot. This fatalistic avenging
of sin is as much in the web of Hawthorne's mind as the allegorical method is in his art; but the reader finds a main interest in the change of Reuben's character, as his consciousness of guilt pursues him. Hawthorne comes to his own in
the theme of the secret sin that was to pursue the young warrior
to a ghastly expiation; the story is among the most powerful

he wrote, since it was such a hard choice to leave Roger Malvin to a lonely death, or to throw away youth and life in a useless effort to comfort him; once the wrong choice is made, the theme of fate shadows the story irresistibly. Here is the very heart of the gloom which Hawthorne finds characteristic in human nature—wrong judgment, turning into secret sin.

"There was now in the breast of Reuben Bourne an incommunicable thought—something he was to conceal most heedfully from her whom he most loved and trusted. He regretted, deeply and bitterly, the moral cowardice that had restrained his words when he was about to disclose the truth to Dorcas; but pride, the fear of losing her affection, the dread of universal scorn, forbade him to rectify this falsehood. He felt that for leaving Roger Malvin he deserved no censure. His presence, the gratuitous sacrifice of his own life, would have added only another and a needless agony to the last moments of the dying man; but concealment had imparted to a justifiable act much of the secret effect of guilt; and Reuben, while reason told him that he had done right, experienced in no small degree the mental horrors which punish the perpetrator of undiscovered crime. By a certain association of ideas, he at times almost imagined himself a murderer. For years, also, a thought would occasionally recur, which, though he perceived all its folly and extravagance, he had not the power to banish from his mind. It was a haunting and torturing fancy that his father-in-law was yet sitting at the foot of the rock, on the withered forest leaves, alive, and awaiting his pledged assistance."

Roger Malvin's Burial is the most powerful story, morally, of the *Mosses from an Old Manse*, but *Rappaccini's Daughter* is more characteristic of the volume, and perhaps of Hawthorne's genius. The plot is subtly allegorical, and deals with one of those experiments with strange possibilities of life which have been considered before. The story is remarkable chiefly, perhaps, because of the perfect skill necessary to make such a fanciful adventure seem real. Hawthorne had transcribed in his note-book from Burton's *Anatomy of Melancholy* the account of the woman, fed on poisons, who had been sent to Alexander for the purpose of destroying him. The story is removed into that cold realm of thought in which Hawthorne's allegories so often flourish, by the change of the motive from passion for revenge upon a usurping conqueror, to mere scientific curiosity; Rappaccini feeds his daughter on poisons simply to watch the result. And the allegorical bent is given to the tale by the fatal effect of the antidote; Beatrice has fed on poisons so long that the wholesome drug kills her. If we add that the antidote, and consequently the death of Beatrice, is procured by Doctor Baglioni out of professional jealousy, we have enumerated the simple elements of the story. But its power is in the subtle skill that paints the poisonous influence as a thing of tropical, if baneful, beauty,—that makes Beatrice seem the natural kindred of the terrible flower, fed with no grosser nourishment than its fragrance; the same skill keeps before us the sinister, intellectual face of Rappaccini among the passionate flowers, incarnate evil betraying the impulses of life. To set Beatrice in her garden, where the poison flower explains and prepares for the disclosure of her nature, is the device of genius.

What, more than anything else, gives all the stories in the volume their weight, whether they are allegorical or not, is Hawthorne's insistence upon the two themes of fate and sin. How sin enters a life unawares, or how the mere sight of it contaminates, or, in the lighter sketches, how untruth in some form masquerades and gives impress to the lives it crosses— one of these subjects is almost sure to enter each tale; and in each, the inexorable consequence of sin or error is portrayed with a depth that makes even the most fanciful allegory grip the attention. The darkest version of this fate is in *Young Goodman Brown*, where the dream of the devil's orgies blights every waking moment thereafter, making Goodman Brown a sad, a darkly meditative, a distrustful, if not a desperate man. But it is in the other stories too, as the passing illustrations will have shown, and it is near the center of Hawthorne's philosophy. Few readers will not follow such a theme with human interest, whether or not they regret its gloom; and this human interest justifies the allegorical fabric of the tales, which otherwise might easily be fanciful and ineffective. With the *Mosses* Hawthorne had finished his apprenticeship; he had mastered a few great themes, and acquired practically flawless skill in treating them, and through theme and technic both, he had learned to express his own character. The apparently unproductive years in the Salem Custom-house were to prove but a resting spell before the creation of his masterpiece.

VII

Hawthorne wrote practically nothing during this residence at Salem until November, 1847, when he began to write every day. The results of this industry were a few more short stories, in the general vein of the *Tales* and the *Mosses*,—*The Snow Image*, the *Great Stone Face*, *Main Street*, and perhaps *Ethan Brand*, if a reference in a letter from Sophia Hawthorne, in 1848, may be taken to describe this tragic study. The stories were gathered in a volume entitled *The Snow Image and Other Twice Told Tales*, and published in Boston in 1852. But this was all Hawthorne wrote till 1849.

In June of that year, with a change of administration, he was naturally dismissed from office. His disappointment— for he had apparently hoped to remain—was increased by a charge that he had used his position for political partisanship. His indifference to all politics ought to have acquitted him rather easily, but a useless controversy followed, with the effect of making him thoroughly detest his native city. For that feeling it has been shown he was much to blame. Salem would doubtless have honored him if he had allowed it the privilege; but though he had come out of himself more than in his youth, he had managed to keep his character and temperament largely unknown.

To other causes of annoyance was now added the practical question of supporting his family. The salary at the Customhouse had been sufficient to clear him of old debts, but he had saved nothing. If it had not been for this poverty, he would have received his new freedom with unmixed joy, for his spirit was weary enough of bread-and-butter routine. He wrote to a friend, asking for literary employment; evidently he hoped once more to support himself with his pen. The manner, however, in which his wife received the news of his dismissal, gave a definite direction to his plans. He came home earlier than usual, the day he lost his office, and Mrs. Hawthorne, on learning the cause, exclaimed, "Oh, then you can write your book!" Hawthorne felt quite unable to share her pleasure in the opportune leisure, not knowing how he could support his family till the book was done; but his wife, without his knowledge, had saved up a considerable sum out of her household money, and now brought forth this faery hoard from the drawer of her desk. That afternoon Hawthorne began *The Scarlet Letter*.

The romance was written in circumstances of extreme sorrow. In July, 1849, Madam Hawthorne, who was then living with her son, began to fail rapidly, and it was soon apparent that her end was near. The care of nursing her, for some reason, fell not upon her daughters, but upon Sophia Hawthorne, and Hawthorne himself was distracted from his book by many simple household cares. What was in his mind at the time is recorded in the journal, to which he had recourse as an outlet of personal feelings not to be expressed in a less intimate way. His account of his mother's death-bed has been quoted; the journal pictures in still greater detail the travesty on that solemn scene, played by Una and Julian in their childish game: "Julian is now lying on his couch in the character of sick grandmamma, while Una waits on him as Mrs. Dike. She prompts him in the performance, showing a quite perfect knowledge of how it should all be: 'Now, stretch out your hands to be held.' 'Will you have some of this jelly?' Julian starts up to take the imaginary jelly. 'No; grandmamma lies still.' He smacks his lips. 'You must not move your lips so hard.' 'Do you think Una had better come up?' 'No.' 'You feel so, don't you?' His round curly head and rosy face, with a twinkling smile upon it, do not look the character very well. Now Una is transformed into grandmamma, and Julian is mamma, taking care of her. She groans, and speaks with difficulty, and moves herself feebly and wearisomely; then lies perfectly still, as if in an insensible state; then rouses herself and calls for wine; then lies down on her back with clasped hands; then puts them to her head. It recalls the scene of yesterday with frightful distinctness; and out of the midst of it little Una looks at me with a smile of glee."

Hawthorne's mother died on the last day of July. As the care of his two sisters devolved upon Hawthorne, he and his wife began to plan immediately to leave Salem for a more economical and less sad-memoried home. The change was not made, however, until the next year. Hawthorne worked industriously at his romance,—nine hours a day, if we may take seriously a remark in one of his wife's letters; and his wife took to her painting again, evidently with an idea of adding to their diminishing funds. But it was quite impossible to make up in any such way the heavy expenses of the summer, and Hawthorne was in a situation of very real embarrassment, when in January, 1850, a tactful letter from his friend Hillard brought a check for a most convenient amount, contributed by anonymous friends. "I know the sensitive edge of your temperament," wrote Hillard, "but do not speak or think of obligation. It is only paying, in a very imperfect measure, the debt we owe you for what you have done for American Literature." Hawthorne's reply is not that of a dreamer; but of a proud man deeply humiliated by misfortune, yet sincerely grateful. It was a dark moment when he wrote, "It is something else besides pride that teaches me that ill-success in life is really and justly a matter of shame. I am ashamed of it, and I ought to be. The fault of a failure is attributable—in a great degree at least—to the man who fails. I should apply this truth in judging of other men; and it behooves me not to shun its point or edge in taking it home to my *own* heart. Nobody has a right to live in the world unless he be strong and able, and applies his ability to good purpose." A little less than three years later Hawthorne was able to return the money to Hillard with interest; it is easy to imagine the satisfaction with which the second letter was written, after so short an interval, but with the consciousness that his family were secure from risk of poverty. "This act of kindness," he writes, "did me an unspeakable amount of good; for it came when I most needed to be assured that anybody thought it worth while to keep me from sinking. And it did me even greater good than this, in making me sensible of the need of sterner efforts than my former ones, in order to establish a right for myself to live and be comfortable."

Four days after the receipt of Hillard's gift, *The Scarlet Letter* was finished. So much has been recorded of the circumstances in which the book was written and found its way to publication, that its history can best be told in quotation. Hawthorne himself tells how he read the last pages to his wife, the day he wrote them, and how he broke down, through sheer nervous excitement after the severe task of composition. As to his wife, "It broke her heart, and sent her to bed with a grievous headache, which I look upon as a tremendous success." The most striking memory of the book, however, is the account given by James T. Fields, telling how he came, in a way that seems curiously fated, to be its publisher.

"In the winter of 1849, after he had been ejected from the Custom-house, I went down to Salem to see him and inquire after his health, for we heard he had been suffering from illness. He was then living in a modest wooden house in Mall Street, if I remember rightly the location. I found him alone in a chamber over the sitting-room of the dwelling; and as the day was cold, he was hovering near a stove. We fell into talk about his future prospects, and he was, as I feared I should find him, in a very desponding mood. 'Now,' said I, 'is the time for you to publish, for I know during these years in Salem you must have got something ready for the press.' 'Nonsense,' said he; 'what heart had I to write anything, when my publishers (M. & Company) have been so many years trying to sell a small edition of the *Twice Told Tales* ?' I still pressed upon him the good chances he would have now with something new. 'Who would risk publishing a book for *me*, the most unpopular writer in America ?' 'I would,' said I, 'and would start with an edition of two thousand copies of anything you write.' 'What madness!' he exclaimed; 'your friendship for me gets the better of your judgment. No, no,' he continued; 'I have no money to indemnify a publisher's losses on my account.' I looked at my watch and found that the train would soon be starting for Boston, and I knew there was not much time to lose in trying to discover what had been his literary work during these last few years at Salem. I remember that I pressed him to reveal to me what he had been writing. He shook his head and gave me to understand he had produced nothing. At that moment I caught sight of a bureau or set of drawers near where we were sitting; and immediately it occurred to me that hidden away somewhere in that article of furniture was a story or stories by the author of *Twice Told Tales*, and I became so positive of it that I charged him vehemently with the fact. He seemed surprised, I thought, but shook his head again; and I rose to take my leave, begging him not to come into the cold entry, saying I would come back and see him again in a few days. I was hurrying down the stairs when he called after me from the chamber, asking me to stop a moment. Then quickly stepping into the entry with a roll of manuscript in his hands, he said: 'How in Heaven's name did you know this thing was there? As you have found me out, take what I have written, and tell me, after you get home and have time to read it, if it is good for anything. It is either very good or very bad,—I don't know which.' On my way up to Boston I read the germ of *The Scarlet Letter;* before I slept that night I wrote him a note all aglow with admiration of the marvelous story he had put into my hands, and told him that I would come again to Salem the next day and arrange for its publication."

Hawthorne had intended to include in the volume with his not very lengthy romance several other stories, which he afterward published in *The Snow Image.* By itself *The Scarlet Letter*, he thought, was too somber, and he feared to stake the book entirely on that one chance. But his publisher's keen judgment was for putting out the great story on its own merits, and so complete was his confidence that he made the first edition five thousand instead of two. It was put on sale in April, 1850, and a second edition was at once called for.

Much of the material and the method of *The Scarlet Letter* is but developed from the *Twice Told Tales.* The main idea, which gives the book its title, had in fact been sketched in the description of the public square in *Endicott and The Red Cross.* Among the other citizens in that picture Hawthorne had described a young woman "whose doom it was to wear the letter A on the breast of her gown, in the eyes of all the world and her own children. And even her own children knew what that initial signified. Sporting with her infamy, the lost and desperate creature had embroidered the fatal token in scarlet cloth, with golden thread, and the nicest art of needlework; so that the capital A might have been thought to mean Admirable, or anything rather than Adulteress." In using a symbol as the starting point of his theme, as a physical design to be developed and played with by his imagination, Hawthorne simply continued the method of the earlier story, or of *The Birthmark*, or of *Lady Eleanor's Mantle*. So in portraying the social conditions of early New England he continued that interest in history which was a prime motive with him. Just as the *Twice Told Tales* contain the solidest material of his shorter work, so *The Scarlet Letter* has in every sense a basis in reality that none other of his longer romances approached. Both the environment, the setting of the story, and the allegorical symbol, are felt to be historical, and the truths which the book teaches effectively are not allegorized on the surface of the tale, but are implicit in its heart, as in life itself. For this reason the one artistic blemish of the book has been located in the scene where the meteoric lights frame a scarlet A in the heavens. So absolute is the reality of the book, that this fanciful symbolizing of the minister's conscience is resented; in one of Hawthorne's lighter studies it would have passed unnoticed.

The greatness of the story lies in its universal theme, its elevated tone, and the extreme simplicity of its treatment. The theme is the effect of sin upon the soul that commits it— especially of secret sin, since Dimmesdale's experience makes the tale. All the characters are noble, as in a Greek story— strongly developed in themselves, and holding high position in the community, so that their experiences are large and important, as many critics have remarked, like the heroic adventure of Attic tragedy. This resemblance of tone is increased by the sense of destiny and retribution in the romance, dark and inexorable as ever the will of the gods was imagined by ancient poets. And in construction the story is the simplest and most closely knit that Hawthorne, or perhaps American literature, produced. The plot needs for its strictest purposes but three characters—the lover, the wife, and the injured husband who determines to find the lover and force him to confess his guilt. Pearl gives meaning to the story; she serves, as Hawthorne is careful to tell us, to embody the scarlet letter, all its torture and mercy; she serves also to represent Hester's own youth, and so explains the mother's history by repeating the character in that first passionate form which otherwise we should not see. We take it for granted that she inherits her mother rather than her father, except for the faery daintiness of appearance and manner, which might have belonged to the minister when he was a boy. And these three main characters are studied with a single intensity that excludes any other interests; the tale indeed "keeps close to its point," as Hawthorne said.

From *The Scarlet Letter* Hawthorne's cold experimental mood is completely absent, and in its place is an interest in life, which, though outwardly restrained, is truly passionate. It is usual, perhaps, to attribute the study of sin to the Puritan temperament, but it takes only a little perception to see that the attitude in this romance cannot easily be matched in Spenser or Milton or Bunyan, nor in what we know of the New England Puritans. The issue of sin, here represented, is so absolute and so dark, so far from the hope of forgiveness, that the Puritan himself rejects its harsh fatality; and on the other hand, the value placed upon life is here so strong, and the sympathy with human desires is so overwhelming, that much which the Puritan would condemn as sin gets away from rigid categories, and stands in a troublesome compromise between right and wrong. Both of these variations from the Puritan ideal are, of course, the gift of Hawthorne's own personality. He was a fatalist at heart, and the power of evil to breed evil had occupied his thoughts. He was naturally impressed, also, by the difficulty of judging sin by conventional standards; he knew, as he had written of the slave-trade, that what one age thought evil, the next might pass by, if not approve, and for those sins which spring from the best impulses of the heart, he had a leniency that could not be found even in Mrs. Stowe's work, cheerful Puritan as she was. The sin in *The Scarlet Letter* is Dimmesdale's cowardice in refusing to acknowledge the child, and Chillingworth's revengeful determination, first to discover Pearl's father, and then—as he grows more fiend-like—to kill that father's soul. The sin for which Hester is punished is hardly presented as sin at all. The wrong of it is balanced in the story by the cruel, loveless marriage Chillingworth had imposed upon her youth, in comparison with which her love for Dimmesdale seems heaven-sent. If that love is sin, the story, true to life, presents the difficult paradox of sin ennobling a soul, for through her love of Pearl and her self-forgetting pity for Dimmesdale Hester's soul is unquestionably ennobled. But in the critical moment when the minister learns that his tormenting physician is the man he wronged, both he and Hester, after all their suffering, see their love as a holy thing, not to be regretted; and Chillingworth himself, at the very beginning of the story, admits to Hester that her unfaithfulness was no worse than the wrong he had done her. "Mine was the first wrong," he said, "when I betrayed thy budding youth into a false and unnatural relation with my decay. . . . Between thee and me, the scale hangs fairly balanced."

Upon the original sin, then, Hawthorne passes no judgment. The community, however, following a conservative and literal ideal of morality, do pass judgment upon Hester. The punishment they bestow illustrates, as has well been said, the clumsy failure of law to reach the soul. But Hawthorne makes another, equally subtle, use of the Puritan community and their stern law to emphasize, against that somber background, the natural force of generous youth. Radical enough in the Old Country, the Puritans stand in the New World for a very rigid conventionality; their ideas seem already stultified, inelastic, out of sympathy with the expanse of nature into which they have penetrated. Hester and Dimmesdale, whether Hawthorne intended it so or not, are creatures of a new life, a larger world and larger ideas. Their fit place of meeting is in the forest, whither the conventional community do not come. In no real way are they an integral part of that community; they are opposed to it, and to the age-long untenderness for which it stands, less picturesquely but as truly as the Lord and Lady of the May were opposed to Endicott and his men, in the tale of Merry Mount. Indeed, the theme of the individual rising above the community's ideal appears under many guises in *The Scarlet Letter*,—in the single kind word for Hester from the curious crowd around the pillory; in the generous impulses of Dr. Wilson and the Governor, when they let themselves be persuaded not to take Hester's child from her; and most in Hester herself, the largest mind and the largest nature in the book,—for whom the world's law was no law. "It was an age in which the human intellect, newly emancipated, had taken a more active and a wider range than for many centuries before. Men of the sword had overthrown nobles and kings. Men bolder than these had overthrown and rearranged—not actually, but within the sphere of theory, which was their most real abode—the whole system of ancient prejudice, wherewith was linked much of ancient principle. Hester Prynne imbibed this spirit. She assumed a freedom of speculation, then common enough on the other side of the Atlantic, but which our forefathers, had they known it, would have held to be a deadlier crime than that stigmatized by the scarlet letter. In her lonesome cottage by the sea-shore, thoughts visited her, such as dared to enter no other dwelling in New England—shadowy guests, that would have been as perilous as demons to their entertainer, could they have been seen so much as knocking at her door."

Since Hawthorne's interest is always in the effect of life on the soul, and here in the effect of sin, he leaves untold the story of Dimmesdale's love for Hester, and begins the romance so long after the episodes which condition it, that curiosity itself is baffled in the effort to imagine the story of Hester's fall. When we first see her and her lover, the sin has already had a changing effect upon both; Hester has been strengthened by her very resistance to persecution, and ennobled by her resolve not to betray her lover, and the cowardice of the minister has already weakened his nature to a degree that renders it hard to conceive of him as the passionate lover. Such an arrangement of the plot doubtless came naturally from Hawthorne's lack of interest in the first sin, but it serves also to raise the story to a lofty tone, by showing Hester, not as receiving love, but as giving it,—becoming through her pity as much the protector of Dimmesdale as of Pearl. Her bosom pillows the broken-hearted minister not as a lover but as a son; even her plan to flee with him is an act of generous rescue, not at all of passion. That Hester was a different woman when Dimmesdale first won her is plainly intimated, but her old nature has been purified, and when she comes to Dimmesdale's rescue at last, her love is without dross.

The effect of sin unconfessed is the theme of the minister's story, and it needs no comment; Dimmesdale's character, examined outside this allegorical intention, is hard to understand. This weakness seems inbred and habitual; one questions how he could have won the love of such a woman as Hester, except as he wins it at the end, through pity. This apparent difficulty is in the fact that Dimmesdale's nature, when we first see it, is more changed from what it was, than Hester's; on him the sin still lays its full weight, but her public expiation, little as she knows it, has relieved her from the full evil of the inward curse. And Dimmesdale's sin was the act of impulse, as his confession is at last. We see him in his normal mood, and in that state the sin would have been im-

possible for him. Nothing could show a more complete misunderstanding of Hawthorne's romance than the charge, actually made at the time, that the story pandered to base
thoughts, and ushered in an era of "French" literature. The
interest is so far removed, at the very beginning of the story,
from any episode of passion, that the reader almost forgets,
as he is meant to do, the nature of the sin for which Hester is
punished and Dimmesdale persecuted.

In Chillingworth Hawthorne shows the working out of
private revenge—as ineffectual for its purpose as the public
retribution of the law. The wronged physician, who for all
the latent evil in his nature yet begins his revenge with a
sense of justice, passes gradually from a dark ambition to discover the father of Pearl, to a fiendish determination to ruin
the minister's soul. No one recognizes better than Chillingworth, at the conclusion of the tale, that for Dimmesdale to
confess his sin would be to regain his lost manhood, though
such a confession was what the physician first desired as his
revenge. The terrible revolution in his own character is
shown by his frantic effort at last to keep the secret, lest the
minister escape. That evil breeds evil, is the moral he
teaches,—a theme peculiarly Hawthorne's. It is reflected
from many passages in this book, and elsewhere throughout
his work. The principle is at work in Hester's heart, when at
first her self-consciousness of sin begets sight all too keen into
the sinfulness of others she had thought pure. Like young
Goodman Brown, she sees uncovered the blackness of secret
sins; the honored matron, the young maiden, are revealed by
the light of the scarlet letter to be of her fallen sisterhood.
That Hester was not altogether lost, is shown by her determined resistance to this fearful loss of faith in her kind. This,
however, is but one aspect of the evil principle. Even accidental sin, the wrong come at through ignorant impulse, fascinated Hawthorne's mind with its power over conduct. In

the Introduction to the *Mosses* he had dwelt on the story
Lowell told him, of a youth who chanced on the scene of the
Concord fight, with an axe in his hand, immediately after
the battle; a wounded British soldier raised himself from the
ground before him and stared into his face,—whereupon the
boy, by a nervous impulse, brained the wretch with a single
blow. "The story comes home to me like truth," says Hawthorne. "Oftentimes, as an intellectual and moral exercise,
I have sought to follow that poor youth through his subsequent career, and observe how his soul was tortured by the
bloodstain, contracted as it had been before the long custom
of war had robbed human life of its sanctity, and while it
still seemed murderous to slay a brother man. This one circumstance has borne more fruit for me than all that history
tells us of the fight." Some of the fruit of the incident is to be
found in these stricken characters of *The Scarlet Letter*, especially in Chillingworth. He is impelled to his diabolical
revenge by the sin of Hester, which in turn he himself admits
was conditioned by his own loveless marriage with her,—and
that initial wrong was error, not sin. The worst of his purpose is accomplished when he bids Hester tell Dimmesdale
who the physician is, and gives as his reason for the permission, his belief that all three persons are in the grip of fate.
"By thy first step awry," he tells Hester, "thou didst plant
the germ of evil; but since that moment, it has all been a dark
necessity. You that have wronged me are not sinful, save in
a kind of typical illusion; neither am I fiend-like, who have
snatched a fiend's office from his hands. It is our fate. Let
the black flower blossom as it may."

In these words and elsewhere in the story Chillingworth
makes some appeal to our sympathy; but the infrequent moment is soon forgotten in the general malevolence of his
career, and he is the one utterly lost person in the book. Dimmesdale's pitiful heroism at the last justifies Hester's love;

Hester herself rises far above her sin into a glorified womanhood; Chillingworth almost if not quite repeats the history
of Rappaccini's daughter, and having fed his soul exclusively on moral poisons, perishes when that ill fare is taken
away.

Much of the problem of the story and most of the hope in
it comes through the character of Pearl. She creates the problem, to Hester's mind, not only because her rebellious mood
makes her the incarnation of her mother's wilfulness, but also
because, though the child of sin, she is lovable and lovely;
"How strange, indeed! Man had marked this woman's sin
by a scarlet letter, which had such potent and disastrous efficacy that no human sympathy could reach her, save it were
sinful like herself. God, as a direct consequence of the sin
which man thus punished, had given her a lovely child, whose
place was on that same dishonored bosom, to connect her
parents forever with the race and descent of mortals, and to be
finally a blessed soul in heaven!" Whatever comfort could
be had from the paradox, Hester at first put aside, not daring
to make it hers. Yet as Pearl is the incarnation of Hester's
sin, so in mastering the evil in the child's nature, and direct-
ing its strong impulses, the mother conquers her own wilfulness and saves her own soul. Dimmesdale's keen instinct,
sharpened by envy of Hester's misery, so nobler than his,
sees the truth and phrases it for the Governor and Mr. Wilson,—that the child was the salvation as well as the torture of
the mother, teaching her, "as it were by the Creator's sacred
pledge, that, if she bring the child to heaven, the child also
will bring its parent thither. Herein is the sinful mother
happier," he said, "than the sinful father." Before the story
is finished, Pearl's elfish heart has been softened and humanized. At her father's death her soul is saved beyond even
Hester's fear; "As her tears fell upon her father's cheek, they
were the pledge that she would grow up amid human joy and

sorrow, nor forever do battle with the world, but be a woman in it."

It is a kind of impertinence to speak of the technical greatness of such a masterpiece as *The Scarlet Letter*. Yet the reader would be indeed thankless who failed to note how much of his pleasure is in the solemn, musical cadence with which the story moves. The lofty manner extends even to the dialogue, so that the varied characters speak alike in a somber eloquence permissible in romance. Like Cooper, Hawthorne does not excel in the naturalness of his dialogue; the passages in which Hester faces the physician, or Governor Bellingham, or Mr. Wilson, have their power from their deep emotion rather than from the verisimilitude of the speeches they contain. And it is noteworthy that the largest and most powerful sections of the story,—the chapters dealing with the changes of Hester's character, and Dimmesdale's, and Pearl's and Chillingworth's—those subtle analyses which are the heart of the book,—all represent the story indirectly, with no conversation, no action, and no person on the stage. This striking trait marks the book's near kinship with the essay type—with the germs of the novel rather than with its developed modern form; and it indicates further, by his choice of method, how much more deeply Hawthorne was concerned with the lessons and philosophies of life—natural essay material, than with the presentation of life itself.

VIII

Late in the spring of 1850 the Hawthornes removed to a little red house, since burned down, in Lenox, where for a year and a half they were to enjoy a simple home, quite as happy as the Old Manse. The fame that came from *The Scarlet Letter* would have made a greater difference to another man; to Hawthorne it meant little beyond the comfortable future it promised. He never had the slightest wish to be

lionized at any time in his life, and now he retired to a solitude
almost as complete as though he were indeed the most obscure of American writers, instead of one of the most noted.
A few friends in the neighborhood visited the household,—
Herman Melville, the novelist, Fields, Holmes, and others;
Fanny Kemble would ride up on her strong black horse and
converse, "in heroic phrases," with the inmates, and once at
least delighted the small boy of the family by giving him a
spirited gallop astride the saddle before her. But it was in the
inner happiness of his home that Hawthorne found the recreation he much needed. How happy that household was is seen
in the family letters of the time; it is enough here to state the
fact, for the Hawthorne home remained proverbial for its
ideal sweetness, even among the characteristically happy domestic histories of American literary men.

In August Hawthorne began his second novel, *The House
of the Seven Gables*, and finished it on January 26, 1851. The
record of its composition comes from both the writer and his
wife. In October Hawthorne wrote to his publisher that he
should not be doing his best work until after the first frost,
which always colored his imagination as it did the foliage. A
month later he shows more clearly that he is troubled by what
he considers the slow progress of the book. "I find the book
requires more care and thought than *The Scarlet Letter;* also
I have to wait oftener for a mood. *The Scarlet Letter* being all
in one tone, I had only to get my pitch, and could then go on
interminably. Many passages of this book ought to be finished with the minuteness of a Dutch picture, in order to give
them their proper effect. Sometimes, when tired of it, it
strikes me that the whole is an absurdity, from beginning to
end; but the fact is, in writing a romance, a man is always, or
ought to be, careering on the utmost verge of a precipitous
absurdity, and the skill lies in coming as close as possible,
without actually tumbling over. My prevailing idea is, that

the book ought to succeed better than *The Scarlet Letter*, though I have no idea that it will."

When the book was finished, Hawthorne stated again on several occasions his preference for this over his first romance; he thought it more characteristic of his mind, more natural for him to write. In later years he is said to have realized more fully the unique greatness of *The Scarlet Letter*, but his instinctive liking for the less somber story accords with what we read of his private life, and with the sketches in the *Twice Told Tales* which give a cheerful inkling of his nature. His wife recorded her delight as the story, in process of composition, was read to her. Her enthusiasm, not unnaturally, seems partial, yet her praise shows a discrimination of her husband's true gifts,—his ability to bring "up out of the muddied wells the pearl of price;" and she recognizes with satisfaction the book's increased cheerfulness over *The Scarlet Letter*.

Though less powerful and less unique than Hawthorne's masterpiece, *The House of the Seven Gables* can lay claim to being a truer picture of New England, and in every way a more lovable book. Its author thought it might suffer more severely from criticism because it was laid in less ancient times, and its defects as a portrait of life might therefore be easily noted by the average reader. But whatever the supposed date of the story, nothing that Hawthorne wrote belongs more completely in the past; age is its very element. Its truth also is without date, universal; the apparently special features in its realism are still traceable in New England to-day, and so near did the general theme of the romance come to a just portrait, that an irate gentleman named Pyncheon indorsed it by accusing Hawthorne of using his grandfather as the original of the villain in the story. The society described is strongly marked by tradition; the house itself is the very symbol of antiquity; the family live in the past, in inherited pride and inherited ambitions; the characters themselves are well on in years,—save Phœbe, whose youth seems a quaint exotic, a winter-flower. The passion of young hearts, which furnished the tragic problem and the atmosphere of *The Scarlet Letter*, is altogether lacking here; the warmth of Phœbe's nature and her love for Holgrave are solitary rays in the November sunset, no less chilly for their light.

As the earlier romance portrayed the effects of sin upon the sinners, so this story analyzes the effects of ancient wrong upon the last generation—sin working its will and receiving its reward, not at one moment, but in long process of time. The wrong that Judge Pyncheon has on his conscience, the injustice to Clifford, is not the book's subject, though it is the immediate concern of the plot; the Judge's sin was brought about by the ill-gotten estate that he coveted, and the ill-gotten estate had its ancestry in the original sin of the first Pyncheon—his legal murder of Maule, and the confiscation of Maule's property. The effects of this far-off crime are the romance's theme. Perhaps it is because the crime is so remote, that the story seems to move in a bloodless old age; the passion of that first ancestor is long-spent, and his blood after many generations is shown to us coursing feebly through an almost ghostly expiation. The familiar theme of the sins of the fathers, treated more dramatically in Ibsen's famous tragedy, is here studied in a quieter mood but with the same relentless grip on fate. In the actual limits of the story nobody does anything, nor shows initiative, if we except the vague and phantasmal flight of Hepzibah and Clifford. In the truest sense, all the characters suffer life, rather than live it; even Judge Pyncheon's hypocrisy makes the tacit plea for itself that the Judge is the involuntary reincarnation of the evil genius of his line.

Not only the evil but the good also in the Pyncheon family, their ideals and their pride even in adversity, are the gift of the past. The lost deed, which would have made them heirs of a princely estate in Maine, bestowed upon the family, from generation to generation, a sense of importance, causing "the poorest member of the race to feel as if he inherited a kind of nobility, and might yet come into the possession of princely wealth to support it." This pride of inheritance, where only pride is inherited, is common enough in New England, and in a measure was said to characterize the Hawthornes. In more conscious ways the author wrote his history into the book; it was his own ancestor John Hawthorne who hanged a witch and was cursed by the victim, and who thereafter lost the deed which would have given the family title to the town of Raymond, in Maine. And perhaps the trying acquaintance which Hawthorne had made with poverty during his married years had furnished him with the power to write as exquisitely as he does of Hepzibah's fine feelings, bruised by the rough necessities of life. In her the pride of family, based on an all but mythical claim, had evolved through time's magic into true delicacy and elevation of mind. Nothing in the book convinces more poignantly than the sight of the gaunt daughter of the Puritans setting the penny shop in order, in a heroic resolve, at whatever cost to her pride, to go into trade. When Hawthorne lets us see this unprepossessing gentlewoman agonizing over her first sale of a gingerbread doll, and refusing to take a child's money for it, he seems to plead for a kinder view of the New England temper, chill and angular as it sometimes appears, than he feels sure of finding in his readers; and on an earlier page he puts the plea into words. "What tragic dignity," he asks, "can be wrought into a scene like this! How can we elevate our history of retribution for the sin of long ago, when, as one of our most prominent figures, we are compelled to introduce—not a young and lovely woman, nor even the stately remains of beauty, storm-shattered by affliction—but a gaunt, sallow, rusty-jointed maiden, in a long-waisted silk gown, and with the strange horror of a turban on her head! Her visage is not even ugly. It is redeemed from insignificance only by the contraction of her eyebrows into a near-sighted scowl. And, finally, her great life-trial seems to be, that, after sixty years of idleness, she finds it convenient to earn comfortable bread by setting up a shop in a small way. Nevertheless, if we look through all the heroic fortunes of mankind, we shall find this same entanglement of something mean and trivial with whatever is noblest in joy or sorrow. . . . What is called poetic insight is the gift of discerning, in this sphere of strangely mingled elements, the beauty and the majesty which are compelled to assume a garb so sordid."

In this book, as in *The Scarlet Letter*, Hawthorne raises the problem of the punishment of sin, and solves it in much the same way; the course of retribution unfolds according to a higher will than man's, and time rather than the law pronounces sentence. In this respect the story has points of resemblance with Shakspere's *The Tempest*, and in the whole matter of poetic justice Hawthorne is as near as any other writer to the great poet. The wrong spends itself in time, or recoils upon the doer, and the victim has his compensation in such inward ways that the belated restoration of a stolen dukedom is irrelevant. So here, the murder of old Maule spends itself in one long curse upon the Pyncheon line, their ill-gotten wealth shrivels in the end to a worthless paper, and the last of Maule's descendants comes to his own, not by a restitution of his stolen rights, but through the natural force of his character. What an inherited grievance will do for character, molding it to a sensitive resistance to wrong in any form, is thus illustrated in Holgrave, who, without benefit of education, had been in turn a schoolmaster, a salesman, an editor, a peddler, a dentist, a sailor, a lecturer on mesmerism, and finally a daguerreotypist; but through these dangerously

varied employments his soul came unharmed, because it had
been true to one law of its own, not at all like the law of an
ordinary soul. Of ordinary convention, even of respecta-
bility in the narrow sense, the experience of himself and his
ancestors, from Maule down, had made him distrustful; the
last effect of the ancient wrong, and its reparation, was the
self-reliance which makes him the hero of the book. "The
true value of his character lay in that deep consciousness of
inward strength, which made all his past vicissitudes seem
merely like a change of garments; in that enthusiasm, so
quiet that he scarcely knew of its existence, but which gave
a warmth to everything that he laid his hand on; in that personal ambition, hidden—from his own as well as other eyes—
among his more generous impulses, but in which lurked a
certain efficacy, that might solidify him from a theorist into
the champion of some practical cause."

More than in *The Scarlet Letter*, the persons in this story
are strangely solitary figures, touched as it were by the very
quality of Hawthorne's own retiring nature, so that they meet
each other only at certain points, if they meet at all; never do
they mingle. The wonderful bond of loyalty between Hepzibah and Clifford leaves them entirely apart to the imagination, nor does the girlish Phœbe seem one with her much-
experienced, strange-thoughted lover. Uncle Venner lives in
his own world, which is somewhat hard to locate; his simple
mind furnishes the book with a sweet wisdom that no other
person in it is capable of, and his aloofness from human interests, save through unselfish contemplation of them, gives
him a kind of kinship with the legendary Alice Pyncheon
whose spirit haunts the house.

Much of the early method of the *Twice Told Tales* lives on
in this story. Hawthorne's proneness for the physical symbol
is in the repeated death-scenes of the doomed race, to whom
God gave blood to drink; it is found also in the influence of

the portrait of old Judge Pyncheon, which looks down upon the household with malign influence, and before which its tragedies are enacted. But the strongest resemblance to the early stories is in the musing, essay tone of the book; it seems to be, as one of Hawthorne's best critics has said, the climax of the every-day group of realistic, contemplative sketches, as *The Scarlet Letter* is the culmination of the finer tales. The atmosphere of the book, its quaintness and delicacy, is the product of the same fine observation, the same microscopic truth, that made the value of the essay-sketches in the first volume. To many readers this is the charm of the romance; without being greatly stirred by the shadowy story, they delight in the verity of the fragile characters, moving through the half-light of their uneventful world, which yet is convincingly portrayed.

The letter that James Russell Lowell wrote to Hawthorne on the appearance of the new book may well be taken as typical of its reception. "I thought I could not forgive you," he says, "if you wrote anything better than *The Scarlet Letter;* but I cannot help believing it a great triumph that you should have been able to deepen and widen the impression made by such a book as that. It seems to me that the 'House' is the most valuable contribution to New England history that has been made. It is with the highest art that you have typified (in the revived likeness of Judge Pyncheon to his ancestor the Colonel) that intimate relationship between the Present and the Past in the way of ancestry and descent, which historians so carefully overlook. Yesterday is commonly looked upon and written about as if of no kin to to-day, though the one is legitimate child of the other, and has its veins filled with the same blood. And the chapter about Alice and the Carpenter,—Salem, which would not even allow you so much as Scotland gave Burns, will build you a monument yet for having shown that she did not hang her witches for nothing."

In May, 1851, Hawthorne's second daughter, Rose, was born. Now that the book was out of the way, the happy life of his Lenox home filled his thoughts; for four months he did practically nothing but play with his children, making boats and kites for them, taking them fishing, and trying to teach them to swim. Of older folks, he saw most Herman Melville, and others sought him; but his interest was in the children, and it is not surprising that he next wrote for them. The *Wonder Book*, a collection of Greek stories retold for boys and girls, was written between the end of May and the first of July; before it was in the printer's hands, he says, Una and Julian "could repeat the greater part of it by heart, from hearing it read so often." The character of the volume was well described in a letter to the publisher in May: "I mean to write, within six weeks or two months next ensuing, a book of stories made up of classical myths. The subjects are: The Story of Midas, with his Golden Touch, Pandora's Box, The Adventure of Hercules in quest of the Golden Apples, Bellerophon and the Chimæra, Baucis and Philemon, Perseus and Medusa; these, I think, will be enough to make up a volume. As a framework, I shall have a young college student telling these stories to his cousins and brothers and sisters, during their vacations, sometimes at the fireside, sometimes in the woods and dells. Unless I greatly mistake, these old fictions will work up admirably for the purpose; and I shall aim at substituting a tone in some degree Gothic or romantic, or any such tone as may best please myself, instead of the classic coldness which is as repellant as the touch of marble."

Hawthorne succeeded in his purpose; he did substitute a "Gothic" tone, and he has been criticized for so doing. But whatever may be the feelings of a Greek scholar on his use of the myths, there are no two opinions as to the charm of the book for young people. Its effect upon his own children has been recorded, and thousands of others have also known it by heart; it is a classic of childhood's literature. The average reader neglects it in his estimate of Hawthorne's temper, or we should less often hear the romancer spoken of as darkly brooding, or as preoccupied with morbid thoughts; the happiness of his nature is here written unmistakably, as the energy and sanity of it is written in his note-books. Two years later Hawthorne wrote the *Tanglewood Tales*, a companion series, which he thus described to R. H. Stoddard: "I have finished the *Tanglewood Tales*, and they make a volume about the size of the *Wonder Book*, consisting of six myths,—the Minotaur, the Golden Fleece, the story of Proserpine, etc., etc., etc., done up in excellent style, purified from all moral stains, re-created as good as new, or better, and fully equal, in their own ways, to Mother Goose. I never did anything else so well as these old baby stories."

Hawthorne's next work was the compilation of his third volume of short stories, *The Snow Image and Other Twice Told Tales*, which was published in the beginning of 1852. The tales in this volume ranged in date from the beginning of his literary career to the period when he wrote *The Scarlet Letter;* it has been supposed that three of them, *The Snow Image*, *The Great Stone Face*, and *Ethan Brand*, were intended originally for publication with the romance. The volume not unnaturally makes a more miscellaneous impression than the first *Tales* or the *Mosses;* in general characteristics, however, it is thought of as their counterpart; Hawthorne had nothing further to say in the short story.

On the 21st of November, 1851, Hawthorne had moved from Lenox to West Newton, a suburb of Boston, where his sister-in-law, Mrs. Horace Mann, lived. The little red house had grown too small, and the successful author was looking for a permanent home for his family; the somewhat unattractive village he pitched upon served as a convenient point of departure for the search. His son suggests also that as

West Newton is near the scene of the Brook Farm experiment, and Hawthorne's mind was full of his next romance, based on that experience, he may have wished to refresh his memory of the locality; if there is any truth in the surmise, it would indicate a departure from Hawthorne's usual method of imaging his story.

The Blithedale Romance was published in 1852. It has attained much popularity, but is in all respects the feeblest of Hawthorne's writings. For the material of it he went to his Brook Farm days, intending to express his attitude toward the professional reformer, a type for which he felt much dislike. Practically everything in the novel is transferred, so far as outward incident is concerned, from his note-books of the community period; the life on the farm, with its initial snow-storm, the talk about mesmerism, the little seamstress from Boston who figures in the book as Priscilla—all are easily recognizable in their place. The finding of Zenobia's body is the description of an experience just before Hawthorne left Concord; on the night of July 9, 1843, as he tells in the journal, Ellery Channing took him to search for the body of a girl who had drowned herself in the river near by, and the incidents and personages portrayed in the note-book reappear in the romance almost unchanged. These are only the most obvious sources of the book in Hawthorne's life; other parallels can be found in great number.

One reason for the ease with which the sources can be identified, is that the raw material, so to speak, has been presented to us undeveloped and unfused. The most obvious fault of the romance is that it is unwrought; for once Hawthorne's art flagged. The plot is at best indefinite; what there is of it is all in the twenty-second chapter, where Fauntleroy's history is told, and the problem stated of his choice between recognizing and therefore shaming his older daughter, Zenobia, or keeping his other child, Priscilla, in obscure poverty.

Hollingsworth's relation with Zenobia and Priscilla, or Westervelt's with Zenobia, hardly rise to the importance of plot; they have no direction, and they no more than suggest a problem, and they are left unexplained and capricious. That such a story as is suggested in the history of Fauntleroy should go undeveloped, implies an unusual lack of energy in Hawthorne's imagination; the book is evidence of a weary mind grappling with a difficult idea in vain.

But the weakness of the romance is due probably to its subject. Hawthorne was at home only in the moral world, and only in problems of such gravity as to involve the salvation of a soul. Here there is no sin, no ancient wrong, nothing that connects itself with the idea of retribution; the evil studied is a mistaken goal of life, in Hollingsworth's zeal for reform, and the sad consequence of his errors is shown externally, in the breaking up of Blithedale and the suicide of Zenobia,— not in the effect upon his soul or hers. Hollingsworth's repentance is incredible, for he had not consciously done wrong; the change in attitude toward him is worthier of Dickens than Hawthorne. And the reader is surprised, but not convinced, at the statement that Coverdale loved Priscilla; having read the story, which owes what vitality it has to Zenobia, we know better.

Zenobia and Hollingsworth are the only two persons in the book that challenge attention. Not unnaturally, it was thought when the romance appeared that the heroine was Margaret Fuller, who had indeed been associated with the Brook Farm movement. Hawthorne denied that he had used her for a lay-figure, yet here too we may be permitted to distrust his knowledge of himself. Zenobia is a splendid creature of physique and impulse, a variant of Hester, or of Miriam in *The Marble Faun*. Her character, like theirs, begins in mystery; unlike theirs, it remains unexplained and undeveloped to the end. The suggestion of the theatrical in her suicide, the false pastoral vein she was assuming even in that moment of anguish, is in conflict with what else we know of her frank character; and admirable as she is to the imagination, she remains also unintelligible, though of her outward history we know more than of either Hester or Miriam, whom we learn to understand. Hollingsworth is evidently Hawthorne's conception of a professional reformer. That he should not feel with such a person, was inevitable. It is clear, however, that he does injustice to the type. Artistically, the character suffers as does Zenobia's, from incomplete development; we are not sure of his motives, and hardly follow him in his repentance. That Hawthorne suspected the indefinite drawing of this figure may be surmised from the judgment pronounced upon him—itself a confession of weakness from the viewpoint of art: "The moral which presents itself to my reflections, as drawn from Hollingsworth's character and errors, is simply this,—that, admitting what is called philanthropy, when adopted as a profession, to be often useful by its energetic impulse to society at large, it is perilous to the individual whose ruling passion, in one exclusive channel, it thus becomes. It ruins, or is fearfully apt to ruin, the heart, the rich juices of which God never meant should be pressed violently out, and distilled into alcoholic liquor by an unnatural process, but should render life sweet, bland, and gently beneficent, and insensibly influence other hearts and other lives to the same blessed end. I see in Hollingsworth an exemplification of the most awful truth in Bunyan's book of such, —from the very gate of Heaven there is a by-way to the pit!"

What popularity *The Blithedale Romance* keeps, is evidence largely of the hold of Hawthorne's other books upon the readers of each generation. It has been suggested that it attracts through the interest in the community experiment of which it mirrors the history. But to Young America Brook Farm is already something less than an idea; the reader who now comes fresh to the romance will probably find little in it beside the strange but glorious figure of Zenobia, and the pervading glamor of Hawthorne's fame.

IX

In June, 1852, the Hawthornes moved to the house in Concord which had been bought of Mr. Alcott, and which was to become familiar to literature as The Wayside, the author's permanent home. This house, with its twenty acres of land, is about two miles from the Old Manse, where Hawthorne's married life had begun. The early days in the new home were saddened by the death of his sister Louisa, in a steamboat disaster on the Hudson; with this large exception, life began anew with promise of quiet happiness, and Hawthorne could hardly have foretold how much wandering was still to be his. He was ready to rest; the last romance had indicated a wane of power, and he was clearly approaching the end—of his career, if not of his days. In this first summer in The Wayside he wrote a life of his old friend, Franklin Pierce, who was a candidate for the Presidency. The biography was used as campaign material, and Hawthorne was criticized for stooping to such work, but he considered it not an unworthy thing to use his genius in his friend's behalf. Upon his election Pierce, in turn, appointed Hawthorne to the Liverpool consulate; Hawthorne accepted the offer, as an opportunity for travel as well as service, and he arrived at his post in July, 1853.

His life abroad is written in his note-books. He continued in office until August 31, 1857, and for the next two years he traveled and resided in Italy; after a second brief stay in England, to complete *The Marble Faun*, he returned to Concord in June, 1860. All his important experiences are recorded in his journal,—the typical events and interests of official duty, the sight-seeing, especially the acquaintance he made with art and architecture, and the contact in general with a foreign life. Some passages in his account, such as the record of Miss Delia Bacon, which appears, condensed, in *Our Old Home*, in the *Recollections of a Gifted Woman*, have the acute and illuminating qualities of his best work; indeed the *Notes of Travel*, as the journal is now called, are in some respects the equivalent of a romance. Hawthorne came to the old countries with his nature made infinitely sensitive by practice of his art, and by the discipline of life. His travel and sight-seeing was to him preëminently a spiritual experience, in which his part was to submit his soul to the new influences, and watch the result. The notes become therefore a kind of lyrical romance, wherein the effect of living is contemplated in a characteristically passive way. The record of the consulate is comparatively uninteresting; it is in the same key of amused irony and final weariness as the briefer records of official life in Boston or Salem. Literary people, with the exception of the Brownings and some lesser folk, Hawthorne entirely failed to meet, though once he caught a glimpse of Tennyson at an art exhibition. He communed as much as possible with himself, and sought the less obvious but, for him, richer aspects of old world experience, when he sought it at all; if he visited an ancient church, it is said, he talked with the sexton rather than with the vicar. But it was himself he studied, rather than the place he visited. On a second visit to York he writes: "We went to the cathedral, and no sooner were we within it than we found how much our eyes had recently been educated, by our greater power of appreciating this magnificent interior; for it impressed us both with a joy that we never felt before. Julian felt it too, and insisted that the cathedral must have been altered and improved since we were last here. But it is only that we have seen much splendid architecture since then, and so have grown in some degree fitted to enjoy it."

It has been said that Hawthorne's remarks upon art and architecture do not show much insight. Without question he was an amateur in those fields, and his opinions frequently, if not always, disclose narrow judgment and perhaps misunderstanding of the form of expression. But if his remarks do not illuminate art, they do illuminate life; his wizard perceptions of values of character are written at their best in chance remarks upon what he sees in the galleries, or upon some fine ruin. When he reaches Rome he writes, "Whatever beauty there may be in a Roman ruin is the remnant of what was beautiful originally; whereas an English ruin is more beautiful often in its decay than even it was in its primal strength. If we ever build such noble structures as these Roman ones, we can have just as good ruins, after two thousand years, in the United States; but we never can have a Furness Abbey or a Kenilworth." Still more acute, perhaps because the subject is more directly human, is his comment upon the Madonnas of medieval art: "Seeing the many pictures of Holy Families, and the Virgin and Child, which have been painted for churches and convents, the idea occurs, that it was in this way that the poor monks and nuns gratified, as far as they could, their natural longing for earthly happiness. It was not Mary and her heavenly Child that they really beheld, or wished for; but an earthly mother rejoicing over her baby, and displaying it probably to the world as an object worthy to be admired by kings,—as Mary does in the Adoration of the Magi."

In spite of its length one other passage deserves quotation, for the fruitfulness of its suggestion; the ideas are not new, but they come with strong appeal through the medium of Hawthorne's deep nature: "I have a haunting doubt of the value of portrait-painting; that is to say, whether it gives you a genuine idea of the person purporting to be represented. I do not remember ever to have recognized a man by having previously seen his portrait. . . . It seems to be the aim of portrait-painters generally, especially of those who have been most famous, to make their pictures as beautiful and noble as can anywise consist with retaining the very slightest resemblance to the person sitting to them. They seldom attain even the grace and beauty which they aim at, but only hit some temporary or individual taste. Vandyke, however, achieved graces that rise above time and fashion, and so did Sir Peter Lely, in his female portraits; but the doubt is, whether the works of either are genuine history. . . . I observe, furthermore, that a full-length portrait has seldom face enough; not that it lacks its fair proportion by measurement, but the artist does not often find it possible to make the face so intellectually prominent as to subordinate the figure and drapery. Vandyke does this, however. In his pictures of Charles I, for instance, it is the melancholy grace of the visage that attracts the eye, and it passes to the rest of the composition only by an effort."

Without this extended experience of works of art, Hawthorne would hardly have written *The Marble Faun*. The four years in England were a sort of preparation for what he was to find in Italy. The journal records the stay in Paris and the trip through France; then came four months in Rome; and then Hawthorne leased the villa of Montaüto on the hill of Bellosguardo, near Florence. The old house, "big enough to quarter a regiment," and so mysterious in some of its parts that it seemed haunted, was fit scene for the writing of a romance. Here *The Marble Faun* was begun, and carried on with only such interruptions as came of visits to the Brownings, or to Powers, the sculptor, or to the galleries. The notebooks for this period are very full, and must have claimed much time.

At the end of the residence in Florence the Hawthornes returned to Rome, where Una fell ill of a fever, and all but died.

Somewhat unnerved by this experience, the family returned to England, through France, and at Whitby and Redcar and Leamington, successive stopping-places, the romance was continued, and finished on November 8, 1859. The following spring it was published.

If *The Marble Faun* be not Hawthorne's best story, as it certainly is not, it is most characteristic of his mind. Though laid in a foreign scene, and describing a foreign city and its art with a minuteness that renders it adaptable as a guide-book, it is peculiarly the product of that side of the Puritan nature which contemplates life's influence upon the soul. This is Hawthorne's distinct field, and the treatment of his theme is as remarkably his own. For subject there is a past crime or wrong, wherein Miriam is implicated; this secret is left unexplained, as Hester's first love for Dimmesdale is un-portrayed. There is an outward symbol, around which the story circles,—the statue of the Faun. There is a crime com-mitted within the limits of the story, and its results, in the souls of the guilty and innocent alike, are the central theme.

The effect of sin is the subject in all of Hawthorne's great stories; here sin is studied in its power to stain life, to rob it of innocence. Donatello and Hilda, in different ways—almost in different worlds—are ignorant of sin. In Donatello the impulsive crime develops his nature, so that, paradoxical as it seems, through it he becomes humanized, a living soul. Upon the innocent Hilda also the crime falls as a great ex-perience, if not an ennobling one. But the influence of the murder is shown most in the shadow it lays over the joy of youth. The fable of Donatello's ancestry serves to explain that marvelous understanding he has of birds and animals, through which he can inspire their confidence as though he were one of their kind; this is the innocence of his character as we first see it. Like Satyrane, in *The Faerie Queene*, whose ancestry is similar to his own, Donatello is very brother to all

harmless, soulless creatures. His crime comes home to him
when he calls to the wood creatures as of old, and they will
not approach his blood-stained hands. "They know it!" he
repeated, trembling. "They shun me! All nature shrinks
from me, and shudders at me! I live in the midst of a curse,
that hems me round with a circle of fire! No innocent thing
can come near me." In Hilda's character the effect of
the murder is more narrowly Puritanical, burdening her
conscience with sin not hers, destroying in part her delight in beauty, and substituting a deeper need of moral
truth.

Of the other two persons in the small group of the tragedy,
Kenyon is another version of Coverdale, in *The Blithedale
Romance*,—he is a shadow of Hawthorne himself, looking
upon life and studying it, but not greatly living it. Miriam is
a nobler Zenobia, or a less womanly Hester, as one chooses to
regard her. She rises above Zenobia through the superior
coherence of her nature, and she gains importance from her
secret past and her responsibility for the murder. That she
ever rises out of her misery, as Hester rose, is not stated, and
her fate is the more tragic, since her love is an evil gift for
Donatello, and she feels it to be so.

The sequel of the story is uncertain, as are the conditions
from which the plot rises; Donatello languishes in his prison,
and Miriam, no less unhappy, wanders at large. Kenyon and
Hilda are married, but they stand on the edge of the real
story, and only Hilda is involved in it. Thin and unreal as
the tale may seem, "artfully and airily removed from our
mundane sphere," as its author hoped, it has power to grip
imaginative readers with its central focus upon the soul,
fresh-stained with sin. Like all of Hawthorne's major work,
it has a sad outlook. The sin is not forgiven; only the innocent Hilda knows the power of absolution. The romance is
an old man's book, which views youth with affection and re-

gret, noting its swiftly earned experience and sorrow. "The world grows old, and growing old, grows sad."

X

In June, 1860, Hawthorne took up his life again at Concord, enlarged his house, renewed old friendships, and enjoyed the honor that comes at the end of a worthy career. His career was indeed at an end. He published in 1863 a portion of his notes on England in a volume called *Our Old Home*, and he contributed a not very happy article on the war, to the *Atlantic Monthly*, but his power was gone. Almost against his will he set to work at a new story; *The Dolliver Romance*, its final form, is only the fragment of an attempt. Although the theme had been in his mind for years, a sense of his incapacity to finish it held him back. His letters to his publisher, Field, show how dark the presentiment was. "There is something preternatural," he says, "in my reluctance to begin. I linger at the threshold, and have a perception of very disagreeable phantasms to be encountered if I enter. I wish God had given me the faculty of writing a sunshiny book." A little later he says, "I don't see much probability of my having the first chapter of the Romance ready so soon as you want it. There are two or three chapters ready to be written, but I am not yet robust enough to begin, and I feel as if I should never carry it through." Still later he puts his fears into stronger terms: "I hardly know what to say to the public about this abortive Romance, though I know pretty well what the case will be. I shall never finish it. . . . I cannot finish it unless a great change comes over me; and if I make too great an effort to do so, it will be my death."

Somehow it does not surprise us that Hawthorne had this eery foreknowledge of his end. His genius had dwelt so much among the shadows of life that the last great shadow found him ready and unafraid. He grew very quiet but very cheerful too, as though he wished to comfort the affectionate household for the grief soon to come. Once he was persuaded to visit Holmes, and his friend was frightened at his condition, so serious did it seem to the trained physician. Yet the disease was baffling; it appeared to be connected with the brain; it seemed at times to be connected more closely with the spirit, as though Hawthorne were tired of this world or had not the will to live.

At the end of March he was persuaded to undertake a Southern journey with his old friend and publisher, W. D. Ticknor, who wrote daily letters to Mrs. Hawthorne about the invalid's progress. But the journey came to a most tragic end in Philadelphia, where Ticknor suddenly died. Hawthorne summoned all his strength to perform the duties naturally devolving upon him, but when the funeral had been arranged for, and he returned to his home, he was clearly a dying man. The shock of this terrible experience had completely loosened his own hold on life.

As it was thought that nothing but change of scene could keep him alive, his old friend Pierce planned a trip with him into New Hampshire, which they undertook together in the beginning of May, 1864. When Hawthorne said farewell to his family he probably knew it was for the last time. On the eighteenth of May the travelers reached Plymouth, and stopped at the Pemigewasset House. The rest of the story is told in Pierce's letter to Field, written on the nineteenth: "He retired to rest soon after nine o'clock, and soon fell into a quiet slumber. In less than half an hour he changed his position, but continued to sleep. I left the door open between his bedroom and mine—our beds being opposite to each other—and was asleep myself before eleven o'clock. The light continued to burn in my room. At two o'clock I went to H——'s bedside; he was apparently in a sound sleep, and I did not place my hand upon him. At four o'clock I went into his room again, and, as his position was unchanged, I placed my hand upon him, and found that life was extinct. I sent, however, immediately for a physician, and sent for Judge Bell and Colonel Hibbard, who occupied rooms upon the same floor, and near me. He lies upon his side, his position so perfectly natural and easy, his eyes closed, that it is difficult to realize, while looking upon his noble face, that this is death. He must have passed from natural slumber to that from which there is no waking without the slightest movement."

He was buried at Concord, in Sleepy Hollow, on the twenty-fourth. At his grave stood practically all the men then living who were famous in American literature—Longfellow, Emerson, Lowell, and Holmes. The scene is immortalized in Longfellow's tender verses. The Rev. James Freeman Clarke, who had married Hawthorne twenty-two years before, now read the service over his grave, and among the flowers on his coffin lay a wreath of apple-blossoms from the Old Manse, and the manuscript of his unfinished romance.

In his special field Hawthorne has no rivals, nor even competitors; it is therefore hard to indicate his place in American literature. He is concerned chiefly with the inner life of the soul, and at his best he ranks high among all masters of spiritual tragedy. In so far as his preoccupation with spiritual things distinguishes him, he represents American Puritanism; he does not, however, represent it completely. He fails to portray its energy in action and its cheerfulness,—the elements of character that Mrs. Stowe delights in and illustrates. That Hawthorne did not himself lack these human qualities is proved by his journals and home records, which show him to have been true man, courageous and lovable, and lighted with the divine fire.

H B Stowe

HARRIET BEECHER STOWE

I

WHEN Mrs. Stowe as a child first heard the Declaration of Independence, the well-known phrases appealed to her, she says, as though they still were a call to arms in the cause of freedom. "The heroic element was strong in me, having come down by ordinary generation from a long line of Puritan ancestry, and just now it made me long to do something, I knew not what: to fight for my country, or to make some declaration on my own account."

The longing to do something, to make some declaration on their own account, was a familiar aspiration to the Beecher race. They had the capacity of devotion to a cause, and the two famous generations lived in years rich with opportunity for their gift. In them the passion for reform seemed a normal thing; it sprang from no ignorance, nor from a neurotic dissatisfaction with life, but from the human sympathies of great hearts in full-blooded bodies. Their lives were more than busy, and their accomplishment was immense, yet one is struck by the ease with which they worked; they were rapt or troubled by their visions, but the practical in their hands had a magic solution. Dreamers as they were, they were accustomed to success.

Some of this impression of facility, of toil lightly borne, is the effect of a strong vein of humor which made likeable the firm Puritanical purposes of most of the family,—a humor somewhat like Lincoln's, perhaps belonging by a mysterious compensation to many of the overworked spirits of those shadowed years. At least it is more a quality of modern America than of Puritanism; it makes the Beechers—those who had it—still seem of to-day, though their temper and some of their ideas have the stamp of an early time.

Devotion to a cause; immense—apparently facile—accomplishment; and humor;—it is easy to see these traits in Harriet Beecher Stowe. With but little amplification they would serve as a complete summary of her character, and as an adequate explanation of her career. She was altogether a Beecher, the most fortunate child of the gifted family, fortunate in her inheritance, in her opportune service, and in her reward.

Harriet Elizabeth Beecher was born June 14, 1811, at Litchfield, Connecticut. Her father was the Rev. Dr. Lyman Beecher, her mother his first wife, Roxana Foote. Of the five older children, Catherine, the eldest, had most influence on Harriet's character and career. The famous brother, Henry Ward, was born in 1813. Her mother died when Harriet was but four years old, yet her remarkable nature was treasured in almost precocious memories. One suspects that the sweetness in the children's character was the mother's gift, as one recalls the incident of the prize tulip bulbs which the children ate for onions, and their mother's gentle dealing with them. When she died, Henry was found digging impetuously in the garden, as he explained, "going to Heaven to find mamma." Mrs. Stowe herself records that what Augustine St. Clare says in *Uncle Tom's Cabin* of his mother's influence, applies absolutely to Roxana Foote and her children.

After her mother's death Harriet was taken to visit her grandmother at Nut Plains, near Guilford, Connecticut. The visit was remembered for the influence of her aunt Harriet Foote, a person of pronounced character, devoted to the teachings of the English Church and the Declaration of

Independence. Strength of character seems to have come to Mrs. Stowe from both sides of the family. She was made to stand up with her cousin Mary and the black servant girl and the bound boy, and recite the catechism; it struck her childish observation that the two servants stood behind her cousin and herself, because, as her aunt said, they should "order themselves lowly and reverently to all their betters." The other memory of this long winter visit was of her grandmother's familiarity with the Bible. Mrs. Foote's reading was of that sturdy old-fashioned kind that found pleasure in Dr. Johnson's works, next to religious books; and the child remembered the vividness with which the characters lived before her grandmother, as though they were personal acquaintances of hers.

These first years of Harriet's life reached their natural climax in her discovery of books. She early learned to read, and her curiosity was immense. Her father's library, forbiddingly theological, was romantic at least to the eye; she had that visual memory of books, of "their friendly, quiet faces," which marks the born reader. Her patriotic fervor was fed early by Cotton Mather's *Magnalia*—"stories that made me feel the very ground I trod on to be consecrated by some special dealing of God's Providence." And one day she found, at the bottom of a barrel of old sermons, a copy of the *Arabian Nights*, which opened to her once for all a world of pure imagination.

In 1817 Lyman Beecher married Miss Harriet Porter, of Portland, Maine. His family were fortunate in their stepmother. She was a conscientious woman, and reinforced the seriousness of purpose which already distinguished the Beecher tradition. Her first child, Frederick, born in 1818, died two years later. Isabella was born in 1822, and became Harriet's especial care; the thought that she was no longer the youngest girl in the family matured her, and from this time she seems to have shown the precocious side of her genius. Much of her rapid development was due to her teacher in English at the Litchfield Academy, John Brace, who had unusual success in teaching his pupils to write. His secret apparently was to give the children something to say, to inspire them with ideas and enlarge those they had. Under such constructive training it is little wonder that a child of real genius should advance rapidly, but the essay that Harriet wrote when twelve years old and read in public at the school exhibition, on the question "Can the Immortality of the Soul be proved by the light of Nature," is still an astonishing production. The Beecher facility marks the flowing style; the clearness and energy of the argument, and above all the strong oratorical element in the composition, are significant of one destined, like all her race, to plead a cause.

From 1824 to 1832 Harriet spent most of her time with her sister Catherine, who had established a school in Hartford. The years were outwardly quiet, but they saw Harriet through one of those religious crises that a sensitive nature in those days was likely to suffer. Her naturally bright nature was set, by the clumsy questions of a well-meaning pastor, to consider whether, if the universe were destroyed, she could be happy with God alone, and whether God was not justified in leaving her to be miserable in her sins. The result was intensified by her sensitive imagination, and these years were clouded for her, till with the wise help of her sister Catherine and her brother Edward, she assured herself in a sweeter theology.

In the meantime the family had left Litchfield. In 1826 Dr. Beecher had become pastor of the Hanover Street Church, in Boston. In 1832 he removed to Cincinnati, as President of the Lane Theological Seminary, and Harriet and Catherine joined the family there.

II

Lane Seminary was located at Walnut Hills, a pleasant spot well out of Cincinnati, and in seasons of rain and muddy roads, almost inaccessible; but the distance proved later an advantage, when it served as a defense against the riotous pro-slavery mobs in the city. The Seminary was poorly equipped in all but the men who conducted it; they carried into a rough country in wild days the best of Puritan tradition, in religion and democracy, and the Beecher capacity for success in practical ways seems to have been with the whole company.

It was at Walnut Hills that Harriet Beecher made the serious beginning of her writing, and the life itself there had the traits that were to color her genius. It was essentially a heroic life, a true missionary effort to forward righteousness; it was so far out of her youthful memories of New England as to have in it some strain of missionary exile, and to give a halo to the life left behind. Harriet's letters at first show the intellectual stimulus of the new experiences; she was busy in the school that Catherine and she were starting, and rough as the world about her seemed, it was at least novel. But there was little in the life to sustain such a nature when the novelty should cease, and the reaction came, apparently, in 1833.

It was in writing and in literary pursuits that she found her recreation. *The Western Monthly*, a local magazine, offered a prize of fifty dollars for the best short story. Harriet Beecher won it with the story *Uncle Lot*, later republished in the volume of New England sketches known as *The Mayflower*. Most of these pieces were written for the Semi-Colon Club, a literary society that took its name from their half-Columbus-like zest in the discovery of new worlds of pleasure. The whole volume represents a loving memory of New England scenes—idealized perhaps by exile, and a complete devotion to New England ideas,—both traits constant in her later work; and in detail the stories, though immature, are significant in many ways of the sort of genius that was to make her fame.

Uncle Lot is a realistic study of New England character, mingled with much religious idealism, almost propaganda. The combination of realism and idealism remains in all Mrs. Stowe's writing, but in this first story they are more noticeable because they seem incongruous; they do not blend in the slightest, and for the modern reader at least the religious strain is unconvincing. It is not difficult to see the origin of this double pattern in Mrs. Stowe's work. The idealizing tendency, usually religious, was her inheritance, and the product of her surroundings; it had its own appeal to the readers of the time. The realistic element springs from her proper genius, a peculiar ability to transfer life about her to paper, with the fidelity that comes from affection rather than from analytical study. What she herself would probably have thought most important in *Uncle Lot*, is the sudden conversion of the somewhat shallow and volatile James Benton to the Christian Ministry. But her genius is shown in the clever touches of New England peculiarity—the typical post-office; the fixed, conservative life of the village; the old people, who grow as old as they can, and then *last;* and the character of Uncle Lot himself, however crudely sketched—his rough rebellion against any apparent coöperation with God or man, and most of all, his great sorrow at his son's death. Immature as the story is, and alienating as its religiosity now seems, it interests by its truth, its fervor, and its dignity; the heroic flame already burns in it. Technically its cleverness is largely verbal; the structure is amateurish, but the language is deft and fluent.

The same criticism applies to all the pieces in the volume— for example, to the sketches called *The Sabbath*, a series of

pictures designed to show the bad results of departure from
the Puritan observance of the day.   Here again the least doc-
trinal section is the best—the picture of the grim discipline
of godliness that the children feared, dreading the Saturday
sunset, and finding their first theological hopelessness in the
promise that heaven would be an eternal Sabbath.   These
pictures show Mrs. Stowe's chief trait—that love of life, of all
living things, that made realism with her a thing of zest and
delight, and kept even her religious idealism human.   She
can portray the essential charm and value of Uncle Phineas'
rigid observance, but she sees with as keen eyes the uselessness of it for children, and she praises it on other grounds.
"The slave of worldliness, who is driven, by perplexing business or adventurous speculation, through the hours of a half-
kept Sabbath to the fatigues of another week, might envy the
unbroken quiet, the sunny tranquillity, which hallowed the
weekly rest of my uncle."   Puritanism fills the picture, but
it is a spirit that flames, a quiet that is rapture—not the still
mellow world of Hawthorne's art.

III

On January 6, 1836, Harriet Beecher married Professor
Calvin E. Stowe, her father's friend and colleague in Lane
Seminary.   The following summer he spent in Europe as
school commissioner of Ohio, while she paid a brief visit to
the East, that served to freshen her enthusiasm for the cause of
enlightenment and education.   On Professor Stowe's return
Lane Seminary rapidly became a center of the antislavery
movement in the West, and in spite of increasing household
cares, Mrs. Stowe had her part in every exciting event.   It
has remained a marvel that she could share the intellectual
life about her and continue her writing in the midst of homely
tasks that would have worn out many a stronger woman.   The
six children that were born to her in the next twelve years

made literary composition truly a matter of heroism. A friend describes a typical scene, in which Mrs. Stowe was persuaded to complete a story by dictation, with a baby on her lap, a great baking in process in the kitchen, a "new girl" to be looked after, and preparations for house-cleaning to be made.

"In ten minutes she was seated; a table with flour, rolling pin, ginger, and lard on one side, a dresser with eggs, pork, and beans and various cooking utensils on the other, near her an oven heating, and beside her a dark-skinned nymph, awaiting orders.

"'Here, Harriet,' said I, 'you can write on this atlas in your lap; no matter how the writing looks, I will copy it.'

"'Well, well,' she said, with a resigned sort of amused look. 'Mina, you may do what I tell you, while I write a few minutes, till it is time to mould up the bread. Where is the inkstand?'

"'Here it is, close by, on the top of the tea-kettle,' said I.

"At this, Mina giggled, and we both laughed to see her merriment at our literary proceedings. I began to overhaul the portfolio to find the right sheet.

"'Here it is,' said I. 'Here is Frederick sitting by Ellen,' glancing at her brilliant face, and saying something about "guardian angel," and all that—you remember?'

"'Yes, yes,' said she, falling into a muse, as she attempted to recover the thread of her story.

"'Ma'am, shall I put the pork on the top of the beans?' asked Mina.

"'Come, come,' said Harriet, laughing, 'You see how it is. Mina is a new hand and cannot do anything without me to direct her. We must give up the writing for to-day.'

"'No, no; let us have another trial. You can dictate as easily as you can write. Come, I can set the baby on this clothes-basket and give him some mischief or other to keep him quiet; you shall dictate and I will write. Now, this is the place where you left off; you were describing the scene between Ellen and her lover; the last sentence was, "Borne down by the tide of agony, she leaned her head on her hands, the tears streamed through her fingers, and her whole frame shook with convulsive sobs." What shall I write next?'

" 'Mina, pour a little milk into this pearlash,' said Harriet.

" 'Come,' said I, 'The tears streamed through her fingers, and her whole frame shook with convulsive sobs! What next?'

"Harriet paused and looked musingly out of the window, as she turned her mind to her story. 'You may write now,' said she, and she dictated as follows:

" 'Her lover wept with her, nor dared he again touch the point so sacredly guarded'—Mina, roll that crust a little thinner. 'He spoke in soothing tones'—Mina, poke the coals in the oven.

* * * * * * * *

" 'I know my duty to my children. I see the hour must come. You must take them, Henry; they are my last earthly comfort.'

" 'Ma'am, what shall I do with these egg-shells and all this truck here?' interrupted Mina.

" 'Put them in the pail by you,' answered Harriet.

" 'They are my last earthly comfort,' said I, 'What next?'

"She continued to dictate,—

" 'You must take them away. It may be—perhaps it *must* be—that I shall soon follow, but the breaking heart of a wife still pleads "a little longer, a little longer." '

" 'How much longer must the gingerbread stay in?' inquired Mina.

" 'Five minutes,' said Harriet.

" 'A little longer, a little longer' I repeated in a dolorous tone, and we burst into a laugh."

Yet in spite of these discouragements, it was during the early days of her busy married life that Mrs. Stowe saw her destiny as a literary woman unfold, and her family came to look upon her as their prophetess with the gift of written speech. In 1842 her husband wrote to her: "My dear, you must be a literary woman. It is so written in the book of fate. Make all your calculations accordingly. Get a good stock of health and brush up your mind. Drop the E. out of your name. It only encumbers it and interferes with the flow and euphony. Write yourself fully and always Harriet Beecher Stowe, which is a name euphonious, flowing, and full of meaning."

This gradual sense of her destiny as a literary woman was an important preparation for the writing of *Uncle Tom's Cabin;* Mrs. Stowe came to her great book with some consciousness of professional skill; its success was as little a matter of accident as such things can be. Indeed, it seems now as if Mrs. Stowe's life from the year 1833, before her marriage, was one rich preparation for her masterpiece. In that year she made a visit to Kentucky, in a slave-holding homestead that was the model of the Shelby's place in the novel. Her companion during the visit said afterward that Harriet apparently did not notice much that happened; she sat as though in thought most of the time. But many incidents found their place later in *Uncle Tom's Cabin*, incidents that she must have absorbed with that completeness with which a mind in a high state of emotion appropriates the most trivial circumstance.

This Southern visit gave Mrs. Stowe practically her only pleasant glimpse of slavery, and it proves her breadth of mind that she could make so much that is happy in her novel out of experience so scanty. Her chief knowledge of slavery was gained in the bitter struggle in the West, where the Southern colonists advanced their cause by riot and murder, and where the pitiful efforts of black fugitives to gain their freedom was a familiar occurrence before her very eyes. It was the hunted slave, or the family separated by legal sale, that took hold of Mrs. Stowe's imagination, and became the main theme of her book; this was what she knew most directly of the slave system. In the little school that she conducted for her own family, she included some colored children, who had no other opportunity for instruction. One day the mother of one of these brought the startling news that the child, never having been emancipated, was to be sold at auction to settle an estate. The money was quickly raised to redeem the child, but the incident left in Mrs. Stowe's memory one at least of the horrible realities of slavery. In 1839 she had for a servant a young colored girl, who had been brought by her mistress from Kentucky into Ohio, and left there. By the Ohio law she was free. It was learned, however, that the girl's former master was about to seize her and take her back into slavery. Professor Stowe and Henry Ward Beecher armed themselves one night and drove the girl to safety. The farmer with whom she was left, John Van Zandt, had been a slave-owner in Kentucky, but had freed his slaves and removed to Ohio, where he became the protector of such fugitives as this girl; he was the original of John Van Trompe in chapter IX of *Uncle Tom's Cabin*, and the sheltering of Eliza there described is of course founded on this real incident.

But Mrs. Stowe was to know slavery in more fatal aspects. A fierce war was waged by the pro-slavery mobs against open advocates of emancipation, and the few courageous editors who upheld the unpopular side were in danger of their lives. The printing shops were burned, the presses destroyed, and the type thrown into the river. In Kansas the free state settlers dredged for the type, as a matter of sentiment, and loaded them in their guns. It was during this dangerous period of the attacks on the newspapers that Lane Seminary, well known for its emancipation tendencies, was indebted for its safety, as Mrs. Stowe says, to its distance from the city, and to the depth and tenacity of Cincinnati mud. Many good friends of the Seminary fared badly. Dr. Gamaliel Bailey had his printing office destroyed, and was "induced" to leave that part of the country. Mr. J. G. Birney, his assistant, had been a property owner in Alabama, but had liberated his slaves and had joined Dr. Bailey in founding their antislavery journal, the *Philanthropist*. Mrs. Stowe's comment on the attacks on this paper shows her heroic vein, the fighting spirit in which she and her family faced this crisis,—" For my part I can easily see how such proceedings may make converts to abolitionism, for already my sympathies are strongly enlisted for Mr. Birney, and I hope he will stand his ground and assert his rights. The office is fireproof, and inclosed by high walls. I wish he would man it with armed men and see what can be done. If I were a man I would go, for one, and take good care of at least one window." But for the Beechers the climax of these newspaper attacks came with the murder of J. P. Lovejoy, the Illinois editor, who was besieged in his office by a Missouri mob and shot. Mrs. Stowe's brother, the Rev. Edward Beecher, was Lovejoy's intimate friend, and at first it was falsely reported that he also was killed. Hitherto the Beechers, though radically opposed to slavery, had felt much of the prevalent caution towards the out-and-out abolitionists; but this murder, so nearly concerning them, added flame to their ardor. Edward Beecher's wife, who urged Mrs. Stowe to use her pen against slavery, dated her own enthusiasm from this time; "I had been nourishing an antislavery spirit," she writes, "since Lovejoy was murdered for publishing in his paper articles against slavery and intemperance, when our home was in Illinois."

While these tragic experiences were preparing Mrs. Stowe for her great task, she had been training her literary gift not only by constant writing but by the best of reading. The novels of Walter Scott had come into the Beecher family in a somewhat dramatic manner, which Mrs. Stowe, a child at the time, never forgot. In 1822 at the death of Professor Alexander Metcalf Fisher, of Yale, who had been engaged to Catherine Beecher, his library came to her, and Dr. Lyman Beecher examined the books to see if they were "safe,"—for Professor Fisher was thought even by his betrothed to be theolog-

ically unsound.   Among the books was a set of Scott, and Dr.
Beecher seems to have begun with *Ivanhoe*, for he suddenly
appeared with it in his hand, saying, "I have always said
that my children should not read novels, but they must read
these."   The great romancer's stories of generous action
fitted well the peculiar genius of Mrs. Stowe; it would be interesting to know how deeply she was indebted to him for
the effectiveness of her scenes, the frequent realism of her
humor, the historical sentiment in such books as *The Minister's Wooing*.   In 1850, after the birth of her son Charles, she
read all of Scott's novels in order; a few months later she began *Uncle Tom's Cabin*.

In 1843 *The Mayflower*, the collection of Mrs. Stowe's early
sketches, had been published by the Harpers.   In September,
1849, Professor Stowe accepted a chair at Bowdoin College,
and his family removed to Brunswick in the next April, before
he himself was free to accompany them.   The responsibil-
ities and difficulties of moving into the new home fell on
Mrs. Stowe, and for a time she must have done little or no
writing.   But the winter of 1850 brought forth Henry Clay's
compromise, which Daniel Webster defended on March 7 in
the speech so disastrous to his reputation in New England.
The passage of the Fugitive Slave Act, by which citizens even
in free states were required to assist in the recovery of slave
"property," was the final wrong that kindled Mrs. Stowe's
indignation to a prophetic flame.   It was at this time that Mrs.
Edward Beecher wrote to her,—"Hattie, if I could use a pen
as you can, I would write something that would make this
whole nation feel what an accursed thing slavery is."   When
Mrs. Stowe came to these words in the letter, she rose to her
feet in sudden emotion and said,—"I will write something: I
will if I live."   This was in December.   In February, 1851,
during the Communion Service at the college church, Mrs.
Stowe experienced an inspiration not perhaps unlike the sud-

den visions of the old prophets; she saw the scene of Uncle Tom's death, and the reality of it moved her to tears. On her return to the house she wrote out the scene and read it to her family.

From this germ the story grew rapidly, though the first chapter was not completed for two months. The thoroughness with which Mrs. Stowe mastered available documents on the slavery question is shown in the *Key to Uncle Tom's Cabin*, published a year after the novel. But more than the gathering of documents went to the making of this book; the theme possessed the heart of the writer so thoroughly that, as she said, she could not control the story; it wrote itself. When the first instalment appeared in the *National Era*, June 5, 1851, Mrs. Stowe expected to write but a brief narrative, a few chapters. But the story unfolded itself, much as Scott's best stories took their destinies into their own hands, and the last instalment did not come until April 1, 1852. The *National Era* was a most proper medium for such a publication; its editor was that Dr. Bailey whom the Beechers had known in the stormy Ohio days, and who had been forced to leave Cincinnati because of his antislavery writings. For the story as a serial Mrs. Stowe received three hundred dollars. On the thirteenth of March, 1852, Professor Stowe arranged with John P. Jewett, a Boston publisher, for the appearance of the novel in book form, and it was published on the twentieth of that month, before its last serial instalment had appeared. On the first day three thousand copies were sold; a third edition was issued on the first of April; within the year over three hundred thousand copies had been sold in America; in England, where the book could not be protected by copyright, eighteen different publishing houses were busy supplying the demand during the first year. In Great Britain and the colonies the number of copies published was estimated at one and a half millions.

IV

The purpose of *Uncle Tom's Cabin* was to attack slavery, not to attack the South. Mrs. Stowe had the wisdom to see in the institution a national rather than a sectional wrong; much of the power of the book lay in this breadth of view. It is useless to deny that a story written under such circumstances and with such intentions is a "purpose" novel, but *Uncle Tom's Cabin* differs from others of the kind by so much restraint and so evident a desire for fairness, that it is almost tempting now to consider it a realistic study of life among the lowly, belonging in the broad humanitarian movement of the century. Remembering the violent aspects that the slavery cause had worn before Mrs. Stowe's eyes in Ohio, and considering the mass of unpleasant material she had in the documents published as the key to the novel, we must admire the gentleness with which the Southern slave-owner is pictured, and the skill with which the significant wrongs of slavery are distinguished and softened. Mrs. Stowe felt, she says, that to portray the institution as it existed would make the book too terrible to read; she therefore chose to represent only its brighter aspects. That she was in command of the worst facts of slavery is undeniable, yet the book makes its appeal through emotional suggestion, rather than by morbid exhibitions of horror; how much it gains by this reserve need not be pointed out. The same artistic impulse, or political wisdom, whichever it was, made the best characters—St. Clare, the Shelbys—Southerners, and the villain Legree, a Northerner. Perhaps the most surprising thing in the book, considering Mrs. Stowe's New England origin, is the fidelity with which she portrays in Miss Ophelia the New Englanders' lack of practical charity, which prevented them from understanding or caring for the negro in the concrete, although mentally they were devoted to the ideal of emancipation. If *Uncle Tom's*

Cabin helped to bring on the great war, at least it recorded the Northern inability to understand the negro, and the Southern appreciation of him, which seems to hold true to this day. Mrs. Stowe's own readiness to treat the enslaved race as equals was exceptional; in the veracious portrait of Miss Ophelia she sought to rouse the majority of Northerners, whose philanthropy for the negro, then as now, was at something more than arm's-length; the contrast to Miss Ophelia's failure to improve the negro "by dint of the utmost hammering and vehement effort" she intended to be Eva, who won the allegiance of the servants by love.

Among the Southerners themselves Mrs. Stowe makes a sharp distinction, all the sharper because in the simple art of the book there is place only for broad contrasts. St. Clare and his brother are the clearest illustrations, the one ideally democratic in spirit, though without energy to act, the other aristocratic and hard in temper, with the hasty pride of one who fits in blindly with his own days. It is significant that the evil in his brother's character was fostered, St. Clare thought, by the renegade Vermonter, Stubbs, who as his father's overseer had taught the family how to drive slaves. The contrast between the brothers is continued in their children. Eva, inheriting the best of her father's character and nothing of her mother's, is indeed a spoiled child, but uses her privileges in spontaneous acts of kindness. Henrique shows the worst effect of slave-owning on the character of children; naturally more generous than his father, he is fast becoming as irresponsible a despot in his small world, impatient and cruel with his servants, though charmingly chivalrous toward his girl cousin—the very paradox of the old Southern character. It is obvious that in Eva Mrs. Stowe was portraying an ideal character; yet she as well as Henrique suffers from the slave system. She is a spoiled child, as the best child would be with slaves to command, and her very goodness, as her worldly mother pointed out, made spoiled children of the slaves. Perhaps the essential wrong of the system is here more clear than Mrs. Stowe designed. The division of opinion between the St. Clare brothers is paralleled in other places,—in the two clergymen on the Mississippi boat, one of whom quotes "Cursed be Canaan" and the other the golden rule,—and in the second conversation on the boat, where the presence of the slaves furnishes a natural subject for discussion and opinion. But in these cases the difference of view is simply stated, not made the basis for character portraits.

The structure of the novel shows the same restraint and breadth that distinguish its general attitude. The plot is double, yet very simple. The two main horrors of slavery, the two common incidents in it that Mrs. Stowe rightly thought would appeal to the sympathy of the whole world, were the separation of slave families by sale, and the hunting of fugitive slaves. The first of these causes is really the heart of the book, for it is the sale of Eliza and her boy and the threatened sale of her husband that persuades them to run away; none of the chief characters in the story become fugitives simply for their freedom. But although the separation of the slave family is the initial subject, it was the fugitive slave that Mrs. Stowe had perhaps her most immediate sympathy for; if men could actually see their fellows, as she had seen them, in the desperate attempt to be free, their hearts would be touched. It is hardly too much to say that the purpose of the book is contained in this account of the antiabolitionist senator in chapter IX: "His idea of a fugitive was only an idea of the letters that spell the word,—or, at the most, the image of a little newspaper picture of a man with a stick and a bundle, with 'Ran away from the Subscriber' under it. The magic of the real presence of distress,—the imploring human eye, the frail, trembling human hand, the despairing appeal of helpless agony,—these he had never tried. He had never thought that a fugitive might be a help-less mother, a defenceless child,—like that one which was now wearing his lost boy's little well-known cap." The fortunes of Eliza and her husband are typical of the experience of those human beings who could not bear to lose their children through sale, and against whom the Fugitive Slave Act was passed. The majority of the slave population, who sub-mitted to their lot with characteristic patience, are repre-sented by Uncle Tom. The irony of the situation for the philanthropic master and mistress is that they are compelled to sell their slaves to a man they despise. What might be the fortune of any slave, no matter how faithful, under a system which regarded him simply as property, was told in Tom's life; his only alternative, flight, was represented in the story of Eliza and George Harris. The two stories are thus bound together logically, and artistically they have a kind of unity in the beginning, where Tom and Eliza are sold from the same place, and in the end, where Cassie, Tom's friend, turns out to be Eliza's mother, and it is George Selby who discovers the fact.

In this simple scheme Mrs. Stowe gives a picture of slavery as an institution, of the condition to which all who participate in it are reduced. When we consider the warmth of her sympathies, we wonder that she did such justice to the shortcomings of the negro race. To her mind slavery was responsible for practically everything except color that dis-tinguished the black man from the white, yet her accuracy of observation resulted in a portrait easily recognized as true, though it might be explained by other causes than slavery. It is significant that the slave who does not run away, but submits even to torture with a quixotic patience, is the full-blooded negro, Uncle Tom. It is he also who has most religion. He is so far an ideal of what the full-blooded negro might be, that even in the novel he is unique. Eliza and her

husband, Cassie and Madame de Thoux, all who show a
desire for independence and ability to get it, are more white
than black. Otherwise the slaves are degraded by their condition. St. Clare's servants are degraded by his mistaken
leniency, until even in the story they are insufferable. Legree's slaves are turned into beasts by the evil influence of
his own character, so that Sambo and Quimbo and Cassie,
in different ways, are hideous products of what must have
been no uncommon tyranny. In the heartlessness of Legree's
black slaves toward each other,—the mutual treachery of
Sambo and Quimbo, the satisfaction of the field hands when
Cassie was reduced to work among them, their delight at
the prospect of a slave hunt,—in these traits of the negro
character Mrs. Stowe was dealing with the volatile childishness of the race, for which slavery perhaps is not wholly
responsible. The truth of the portraiture is more convincing
at this point than the direct indictment of the institution.
Sam and Andy, on Mrs. Shelby's place, are quite as irresponsible as Sambo and Quimbo, though their childlike
natures have been shielded from evil; their behavior in the
pursuit of Eliza, though it is goodhearted and in the end
proves her salvation, is yet of a levity to shock even Mrs.
Shelby, who sympathized with their intentions. The total
impression that the black race leaves in the story is of a
simple childishness, with the handicaps and compensations
of such undevelopment; and the artistic defect of the book
is that when Mrs. Stowe attributes all of that undevelopment to slavery she must leave her story and argue, and the
argument does not convince. This weakness is worst felt
in the last pages, where George Harris contemplates the
future of "his race"; the reader knows that Uncle Tom, not
he, is the representative of the negro, and as the story shows,
their two careers would be far apart, in either slavery or
freedom. It was this weakness in the story that Dickens

criticized. "If I might suggest a fault in what has so charmed me," he wrote, "it would be that you go too far and seek to prove too much. The wrongs and atrocities of slavery are, God knows, case enough. I doubt there being any warrant for making out the African race to be a great race or for supposing the future destinies of the world to lie in that direction."

The irresponsibility of the negro character is portrayed especially in Topsy, the whimsical problem who "just growed." Perhaps no person in the book is more often referred to. The contrast between the child and Miss Ophelia is one of the best in the story, as it is not only striking in it-self but typical of the paralyzing astonishment that over-takes the Anglo-Saxon nature on its first experience of negro ways. Topsy gains a certain interest from the large amount of attention showered upon her by Eva and Miss Ophelia; there is little in her nature but perversity, and the depth of her affection for Eva does not convince the reader as readily as it does Mrs. Stowe that she ever became a useful member of society.

The problem of slavery was too real a thing, and had come too near Mrs. Stowe's notice, for her to treat it other-wise than realistically. But the poetical, idealizing strain in her genius, fostered by reading Scott, showed itself in those parts of the story where she was drawing least on actual experience. Cassie is of the race of Scott's wildly romantic heroines—Flora McIvor and Norma; the mystery of her past, her almost superhuman power, her astonishing influence over Legree, the strain of insanity or fanaticism in her, are molded from Scott's material by weaker hands. The one negro trait she seems to possess is a love of masquerading and show; she makes the most of the garret mystery before she runs away—or rather, walks off—for she is perfectly free to go and come at all times, and apparently could have escaped when she would.

But in spite of the childishness of her devices—the bottle inserted through the board to provide ghostly shrieks for Legree's benefit, and the white sheet for midnight apparitions,—she is a striking figure, and represents the demonic strain in the African, to which Mrs. Stowe recurred in *Dred*. It is to the romantic quality of her imagination also that we owe the two most stirring scenes in the book, Eliza's escape over the ice, and the defeat of the pursuers among the rocks, when Tom Loker was shot. Both incidents were founded on actual occurrences; they are told, not only with a sympathy that makes them seem perfectly real, but with an emotional elevation which gives them the quality of romance.

Far more important than the indication of the negro taste for the supernatural, the mysterious, is the varied portrayal of the black man's capacity for religion. *Uncle Tom's Cabin* is more than anything else a religious book. It was the author's great pride that her story had been the means of saving many souls. The religion of Eva may be rather lightly dismissed by the modern reader; the death scene, like the death of little Nell, made its own appeal to an earlier taste, which now seems mawkish; and we object to the killing off of Eva just for the religious effect, since there is no stronger reason why she should die. But the religion of Uncle Tom is convincing throughout. It deepens as he suffers, and it gives the book its point as a rebuke to the Christianity that held men as other than immortal souls. Uncle Tom's death, like Eva's, is necessary for the effect; without his torments as proof of his faith he might have been somewhat of a bore; even as it is, he is perhaps too perfect, too infallible,—a kind of negro Natty Bumpo, who has got religion; but Mrs. Stowe knew only too well that the horror of his fate was based on fact, not on literary effect, and she convinces us of the genuineness of his religion. She is careful to distinguish between the emotional, imaginative religion of the true negro, and the comparatively cold faith, even skepticism, of those of mixed blood; and perhaps the most solemn religious appeal is made through the character of a white man, where St. Clare is conscience-stricken by the description of the last judgment.

Breadth of view and charity in the treatment of an unsettled problem; truth in the portraiture of negro character, with its faults as well as virtues; a sense of actuality in the general representation of slavery; and a strong and genuine religious feeling,—these are the qualities that make *Uncle Tom's Cabin* a great book. Its lack of literary subtlety has been to its advantage; its simple structure is not too simple for its direct message. To show American slavery as it was, Mrs. Stowe said, was her purpose; but translated into specific terms of her deep human interest, that meant to show the slave as he was,—in the tragedy of his divided family, in the tragedy of his efforts for freedom, in the tragedy of his patience. The picture she drew, whatever may be its literary faults, has been generally accepted by mankind, and no other portrait of the same subject is likely to take its place.

V

Uncle Tom's Cabin was received with fairness by many Southerners, but it could not be expected that those who earnestly championed slavery would approve of it. As the influence of the book gathered and made itself felt, a counter attack formed rapidly. It was said that Mrs. Stowe had misrepresented the facts, wilfully or otherwise; that slavery as she pictured it did not exist; that the slaves were in fact contented with their lot. At least one novel was written to show another side of the question—*Aunt Phillis' Cabin, or Southern Life as It Is;* but even in the South such books had little success. Of two columns of this story printed in the *Southern Press*, a clergyman of South Carolina wrote, "The editor might have saved himself being writ down as an ass by the public if he had withheld his nonsense. If the two columns are a fair specimen of Mrs. Eastman's book, I pity her attempt and her name as an author." But serious literary defenses of slavery would not have been unreasonable, nor would they have troubled Mrs. Stowe. The personal attacks upon her character, however, were of a nature quite unworthy of the chivalrous South; evidently the Legrees were getting into print. From an Alabama paper came this not exceptionally harsh criticism: "The plan for assaulting the best institutions in the world may be made just as rational as it is by the wicked (perhaps unconsciously so) authoress of this book. The woman who wrote it must be either a very bad or a very fanatical person. For her own domestic peace we trust no enemy will ever penetrate into her household to pervert the scenes he may find there with as little logic or kindness as she has used in her *Uncle Tom's Cabin.*"

Mrs. Stowe had too much confidence in her cause to be seriously annoyed at such vague and futile assaults, but she felt it due to herself to publish the documents and experiences upon which she had based her picture of slavery. The *Key to Uncle Tom's Cabin,* 1853, was not, perhaps, stronger than the novel, as Mrs. Stowe expected it to be; but it presented a mass of material which could not be explained away, and which must have had its effect on the popular mind. Its only literary interest is the proof it gives of Mrs. Stowe's skilful or fortunate restraint in selecting incidents for the novel. She is rightly credited with little literary fineness, and a general indifference to literary structure; but in her one great novel her instinctive choice of what would be immediately and permanently effective, considering all she might have written and the emotional excitement in which she wrote, is entirely remarkable.

Meanwhile she was finding practical opportunity for work against slavery that would have confirmed her in her impressions of the evil, if she had needed any reassurance. In 1852, in the Spring, she visited her brother, Henry Ward Beecher, in Brooklyn, and there interested herself in the Edmonsons, a slave family that the great preacher had once before served well. In 1848, Emily and Mary Edmonson attempted to escape from slavery, were arrested, and were sold for the New Orleans market. Their father, a free man, came North to raise the amount asked for them, $2,250. Henry Ward Beecher found the old man on his door-step, took him to Plymouth Church, and by the eloquence of his appeal raised the entire sum that evening.

Now two other members of the Edmonson family were to be sold, and the mother, a slave woman, came North in the desperate hope of imitating her husband's success. At Mr. Beecher's home she found Mrs. Stowe, who was so deeply touched by the age and the devout character of the slave mother that she undertook to raise the price of the children, or pay it herself. She then started a subscription, which Jenny Lind and her husband headed, and as the amount to be raised this time was only twelve hundred dollars, she accomplished her purpose in three or four weeks.

During this visit of Mrs. Stowe's her husband was called to a professorship in the Theological Seminary at Andover, and she took charge of one more removal and setting up of the home. The life at Andover was to prove altogether to her taste—in a New England community of the best traditions, with the adequate comforts her literary success had made possible, and with the society of cultured men and women; it was a marked change from the unlovely Ohio days,—Mrs. Stowe, true Puritan, even doubted if it was right for her to enjoy such happiness: "I am almost afraid to accept it," she wrote, "and should not, did I not see the hand that gives it all, and know that it is both firm and true." But it may be questioned now whether the residence at Andover was of ad-

vantage to Mrs. Stowe's writing. She had been bred among
theologians, and was most at home in the religious atmosphere. In a novel of a great cause, a plea for humanity, the
religious strain went naturally with the sublime subject; but
there was danger that in less lofty writing it might become a
mannerism. Whether or not Mrs. Stowe became too habitually the preacher, the religionist, in her later work, is probably a matter of taste; her religion was too fervid and sincere
to degenerate into mannerism. But it was unfortunate at
least that at the moment of her great success, when she was
open to more influences than at any time before in her somewhat provincial life, she should have returned to what seems
to have been an almost exclusively theological atmosphere.
A little more experience of the world might have saved her
later from the well-intended but too credulous defense of
Lady Byron. With all respect for the seminary community,
one feels a certain sinking of the heart on reading this description of the secular amusements of the gifted author of
the most popular book in America,—"Last evening a number of us climbed Prospect Hill, and had a most charming
walk. Since I came here we have taken up hymn-singing to
quite an extent, and while we were all up on the hill we sang
'When I can read my title clear.' It went finely."

In April, 1853, Mrs. Stowe sailed for England with her
husband and her brother Charles. She had been invited to
make the voyage by the Antislavery Society of Glasgow, and
many similar organizations invited her to meet with them;
she was treated as the authorized ambassador of the cause,
and few Americans have had such a reception in the old
country. Her letters give vivid descriptions of the entire trip;
their tone is one of absolute happiness and enjoyment, and
one wonders if she ever again experienced such light-hearted
pleasure. Nothing but her own nature, simple and true,
could have taken her unspoiled through such an ordeal of

flattery and homage. When she landed at Liverpool she was met by a great crowd, that stood silent, apparently because it was Sunday, while she passed through. In the hospitable English home near Liverpool, where she was entertained for a few days, she met the foremost people of the city, and had her taste of real lionizing. Her own account of her entrance into Scotland is full of homely thrills, for to her as to so many travelers, the country of romance and canniness made its peculiarly direct appeal. When she neared the border she and her companions sang almost hysterically the Scotch airs they knew, since they would "never come into Scotland for the *first* time again." They recognized famous parts of the landscape, and fell to recalling Scott's novels, that had filled the land for them with memories. But at one small station where the train stopped in the dark, Mrs. Stowe had the greeting that perhaps touched her most; a crowd of simple folk were waiting to speak to her, for love of her book, and finding out her carriage, they reached through the window to shake her hand and to say "Ye 're welcome to Scotland." "I shall never forget the thrill of those words," she writes, "nor the 'Gude night.'"

Her Scotch experiences were all much alike; in Glasgow, Edinburgh, Aberdeen, and Dundee she was charmingly entertained by her admirers, and in each place the public seemed determined to make her at home in their city, as Scotchmen know how to do. They were at the train to greet her when she came, and to wish her God-speed when she went; and they had enormous gatherings in her honor. A national penny offering, amounting to a thousand pounds, was collected and presented to her at Edinburgh, to be used in America for the slaves; the contributors were people of all classes who had read and loved *Uncle Tom's Cabin*. Mrs. Stowe's picture was on exhibition in all the shops, and she was delighted when one small boy in Edinburgh, trying to distinguish her in the crowd, suddenly called to a comrade, "Heck, that's her; see the *courls!*" She remembered also the gigantic Scotch farmer, one of the Duke of Argyll's men, who asked to be presented to her, because he had read her book and would walk six miles to see her any day. But for all the brightness of these days, it was not in her serious nature to miss the moral of it; she left Scotland realizing the enormous influence a work of fiction might exert, and determined to use that power conscientiously in the cause of humanity.

From Scotland she went to London. Her reception in England was as cordial as in the north country, but it was from the men of letters and the aristocracy, rather than from the public. She met Dickens, Gladstone, Macaulay, Kingsley, and Hallam, to name but a few, and in an unlucky hour she met Lady Byron, who won her heart by a few remarks "on the present religious aspect of England,—remarks of such quality as one seldom hears." She visited Kossuth, on the outskirts of London, and came away happy with his parting benediction. At Stafford House the Duchess of Sutherland invited a remarkable group of the most brilliant people in English society to meet Mrs. Stowe, and at the close of the evening presented her with a gold bracelet, shaped like the slave's shackle, with the dates of the abolition of the slave-trade and slavery in England, and the words "We trust it is a memorial of a chain that is soon to be broken."

These honors, like the Scotch tributes, left Mrs. Stowe as modest about her achievements as she was when a child in Litchfield. She hardly dwells longer on them in her letters than on the humors of her experience,—her repeating Gray's *Elegy* in a churchyard near Windsor for the poet's sake, and finding later that it was the wrong churchyard; and especially her ordering a dress from a dressmaker, innocently believing that in London the dressmaker was a trusted member of society, as in a Maine village,—only to learn from an uproar in the public press that she had patronized a manager of sweatshops. After three months of uneventful sight-seeing on the Continent, she returned to America in September. Her record of the trip was published in *Sunny Memories*, 1854, a collection of letters written during the journey or just after; the title is true to the spirit in which she had made her first acquaintance with foreign lands.

On her return to America Mrs. Stowe naturally occupied a conspicuous position in the growing crusade against slavery; the public recognition abroad of her services added even to the prestige of her book at home. She found innumerable opportunities awaiting her, and into all she threw herself with characteristic enthusiasm, finding good use for the money intrusted to her for the benefit of the slaves, and writing whenever a word from her could bear fruit. Of this minor writing the most important was an eloquent appeal to the women of America to use their influence on the side of freedom in the coming national crisis. The main argument was based on the degrading effect of slavery upon the white family. Though the appeal was necessarily brief, it indicated the slightly different ground from which she was planning the next attack on slavery. This was her novel *Dred*, which appeared in the spring of 1856. Though it is now a forgotten book, at least in comparison with its great predecessor, it had almost as great a success at first; Queen Victoria was not alone in preferring it to *Uncle Tom's Cabin*.

VI

In the earlier novel Mrs. Stowe had given a general picture of slavery, from the standpoint of the slave. In *Dred* she undertook to show the pernicious effect of the system upon the white man,—upon the aristocratic owner and the poor white squatter alike. In *Uncle Tom's Cabin* the strongest appeal had been made, perhaps unintentionally, through those characters who were more white than black, yet suffered the full misery of slavery along with the less ambitious and less sensitive negro. It is this cruel mixing of the races, which left the inhuman fathers the right to sell their children or keep them in slavery, that forms the degradation of the aristocratic white family in *Dred*. Mina Gordon, the heroine, and her brother Tom, had the same father as Harry, their slave overseer; they are ignorant of the relation, but he is not; and when Tom attempts to sell into slavery the widow of his Ohio cousin, Harry knows it is his own sister who is in danger. Tom Gordon exhibits the depraved effects of slavery upon an undisciplined nature, installed by the system in a position of absolute power over his fellow-creatures; he is the darker version of Henrique St. Clare in the earlier novel, the boy of spirit turning tyrant by mere force of opportunity. The tragedy is more horrible in *Dred* since Tom is lord over his own flesh and blood; there is nothing, perhaps, in *Uncle Tom's Cabin* so powerful as the moment when Tom Gordon sees Harry's wife and tells her husband he intends to appropriate her. In the first half of the novel the development of this theme is as terrible as the old Websterian tragedy.

But *Dred* is in many ways a disappointing book, and in nothing more than the ease with which its many problems are solved. Harry manages to save his wife, with no greater suffering than the sense of injustice. Mrs. Stowe had told once for all the experiences of a runaway slave; she apparently did not care to repeat the portrait; her interest in Harry and his wife was confined to their relations with his white brother. For the reader, however, the easy solution vitiates the original force of the problem. The same criticism applies to the entire story. We are first introduced to Miss Gordon at the critical moment in her butterfly career, when she has engaged herself to three lovers at once, and has returned from a fashionable boarding-school in the North to take charge of her

Southern estate, of which she understands nothing. No wonder that her brother Harry feels somber misgivings for himself and the rest of the "property." But the reader promptly finds that any worry at this point is unnecessary; Mina suddenly becomes a sensible, tender-hearted woman, dismisses the two lovers she does not wish to marry, and engages herself publicly to Clayton, a high-minded idealist. Under his guidance she begins to care for her estate with such wisdom and philanthropy as must surely make her an unwelcome member of her community; but that problem is disposed of by her sudden death. On his own plantation Clayton continues his humane program for raising the negro race, till he is in serious danger of his life; that problem is avoided in the story by his leaving the state. So the personage from whom the book chances to take its name, is also, in the artistic sense, a disappointment; the problem of Dred's mystical character, and the suggestive possibilities in his power to protect and lead even the well educated of his race, are alike disposed of when he is killed by the slave-hunters. The fact is, Mrs. Stowe had material enough for several plots, all too large and suggestive to be treated in her flowing, discursive manner; the complexity of the material is as much a misfortune in *Dred* as the simplicity of theme was the salvation of *Uncle Tom's Cabin*. Only one thread of the rich tangle is really traced throughout its length; Tiff gains something from the fact that his career is shown whole and consistent.

It will not be difficult to see that *Dred* has no very obvious unity; Mrs. Stowe seems to have had some doubt as to the proper name of the story, and certainly the inspired negro is its hero only incidentally. Perhaps it would be overrash to suggest any person in it as hero or heroine. It is this grave failure in plot that has doubtless caused *Dred* to be generally forgotten. But the first popularity of the book was due to something more than the glamour of its predecessor; in detached situations and in the characters it is more convincing, more subtle, and more human than *Uncle Tom's Cabin*. The great religious fervor that seemed to purge the first story of all but its crude, sinewy virtues, was on the whole absent in *Dred;* Mrs. Stowe approached the second book, not simply as a reformer, but as a world-famous author, and both the merits and faults can perhaps be traced to this reëstablishment of her normal art. The antislavery documents on which the first book had been based, were now better fused in her mind, so that the characters and scenes blend into a more consistent world, yet that world seems further removed from actual experience. Nothing new could be said on the main problem of slavery after *Uncle Tom's Cabin; Dred* simply repeats the first indictment with more skill in some ways, with less in others. It would not be far out of the way to see in Mina Gordon a new version of Eva—the spoiled child with a loving heart, pathetically isolated in her social world by her wish to be of service to her people. The resemblance is strongest in the melodramatic death that takes both characters out of the stories; aside from that, Mina is more human and more interesting than Eva, yet it is obvious that the young woman's perfectly normal wish to be useful in the world, cannot compete in immediate effect nor in fame with the precocious spirituality of the child. The fine character of St. Clare is suggested in many persons in the second story; the best of his nature is in Clayton, whose capacity for action wins respect that could not be given the paralyzed will of Eva's father. Yet the very difference destroys in Clayton the romantic vein that made St. Clare attractive. There is no one in *Dred* so degraded as Legree; Tom Gordon is the nearest approach to him, yet the reader feels in a subtle way, as Mrs. Stowe intended, that Gordon is the victim of a system. The original license in his father's nature is in him the cause of drunkenness and reckless evil doing, but he seems less calculating in his wickedness than Legree, and to that extent less of a fiend.

In the person of Dred himself Mrs. Stowe develops the African turn for mystery and supernaturalism which she had indicated in Cassey. Like Cassey, too, Dred faintly suggests the ultra-romantic figure in a Scott novel, standing somewhat outside the plot, yet creating the special interest of the story. The first appearances of Dred are remarkably effective, and the scene at the camp-meeting where he utters his prophecy from the darkness is one of the best things in Mrs. Stowe's work. Yet here again the fine opportunity comes to little; with all his foresight and his Hebraic eloquence and his uncanny inspiration, Dred meets a very human fate, and we feel cheated in the former rumors of his invulnerability. It is typical of the whole book that his home in the swamp, so minutely described, is not used as a vital element in the situation. And in a deep sense Dred's prestige is taken from him at a critical moment when Milly, the religious heroine of the story, successfully answers his call to arms with the simple doctrines of Christian charity.

The case is strong against the artistic construction of *Dred*. In structure it is amorphous, and few of the characters do anything. Yet those readers who preferred it to *Uncle Tom's Cabin* could easily have defended their opinion on the ground that the pictures, taken separately, seem truer to the imagination, and in one character, Tiff, Mrs. Stowe had idealized the negro even more convincingly than in Uncle Tom himself. In the first novel, where her interest primarily was in the black man, she made out a better case for the mulatto and the quadroon; in *Dred*, intending to picture more particularly the experiences of the mixed races, the incidental portrait of the black man is best. Evidently there was some paralysis of her genius at the points where she followed a conscious purpose. Tiff, the loyal servant of the woman who had made an imprudent marriage with a most convincing specimen of "white trash," is brought into the story to show the immense superiority of the black man over the worst of the sovereign race. But the attention soon fixes upon his pride in his mistress' family, and his ambition to bring up the impoverished children in the traditions of their blood. It would be impossible to find a more beautiful picture of slavery at its best; if this had been the whole story, neither this book nor *Uncle Tom's Cabin* would have been written; that Mrs. Stowe could do the institution such justice is another proof of her unusual fairness.

Tiff is entirely lacking in Uncle Tom's heroic qualities and he is not well trained nor experienced in religion; Milly, the servant of Mina's aunt, takes Uncle Tom's place in the latter respect. But Tiff's deficiencies really make him attractive, since they leave him with a single mastering passion, loyalty to the family. His uncouth efforts to train the children in polite ways, his advice as to the correct use of the English language, and his unerring instinct for a descendant of a genuine "first family," are not less pathetic for being often ridiculous. And in Mrs. Stowe's favorite field of religion Tiff is the occasion of what seems a more effective appeal than the scenes between Eva and Tom, when he asks Mina to read the Bible to him, and the thoughtless girl realizes that she also is hearing it for the first time.

The material of *Dred*, it will have been seen, is simply that of *Uncle Tom's Cabin* in another form. The neglect of the book to-day can be explained by its obvious deficiencies in form,—deficiencies that with the one great exception marred all Mrs. Stowe's work. But the characters are in the main suggestive and true, and there are strong themes and situations everywhere in the story, too many for the author to develop, and too many to mention here. They show sometimes an unexpected dramatic instinct, as in the appeal of Clayton's case,

where his victorious decision for the wronged slave is re-
versed, as a matter of conscience, by the judge, his own father;
and sometimes they show a delightful subtlety of attack, not
to be found in *Uncle Tom*, as where Milly, after years of sad
experience, is made to remark quite naïvely that "white
chilen, when they 'haves themselves, is just as good as black,
and I loves 'em just as well."

VII

In August, 1856, Mrs. Stowe visited England for the second
time, accompanied by her husband, her son Henry, her sister
Mary and her two eldest daughters. The leisurely journey
that she made in England, France, and Italy was of course
quieter and more private than her first triumphant progress,
but the prestige of *Uncle Tom's Cabin* was still strong and
Dred was in great demand; the letters home show that Mrs.
Stowe's welcome among the best minds was not less sincere
and warm. If there were no public testimonials to her service as emancipator, there were more private testimonials
to her success as an author; letters from Harriet Martineau
and others in praise of *Dred* especially pleased her. Many considered the novel her best work, though Prescott protested
gently against the "premature smothering" of the heroine.
But the record of this trip, like that of the third visit to Europe,
in 1859, suggests in many ways that the heroic period in Mrs.
Stowe's career was passing. Her nature is still enthusiastic
and cheery, her comments on life and thought have still her
characteristic zest, but on the one great theme she has had
her say, and it is easy to see now that so far as her art is concerned she is already living in the past. Unsustained by the
fire of a just cause, her genius flags somewhat; the note
of weariness shows first perhaps in her inadequate portrait of Charles Kingsley, whom she visited, and later in
her gossip about spiritualism, toward which she exhibited

the same simple credulity as she was to show toward Lady Byron.

Professor Stowe was obliged to return to America in September, and a month later his son Henry followed, to enter Dartmouth College. Mrs. Stowe's return in June was saddened by the tragic death of this boy, drowned in the Connecticut at Hanover. Something of the stern theology her childhood had known now returned to add to Mrs. Stowe's sorrow; loving and good as this son had been, she felt dark questionings as to his spiritual state. The record is in a letter to her sister Catherine,—a significant fact, since Catherine had suffered even greater agony of mind years before, when on the drowning of her lover, Professor Fisher, she could allow herself no faith in his salvation. So when *The Minister's Wooing* began to appear in December, 1858, in the *Atlantic Monthly*, it is not surprising that Mrs. Stowe made the new story turn upon the supposed shipwreck of an unconverted son. Much in the novel that must have seemed of first importance to the author, was the record of her own experience, or the experience of her sister Catherine. But as often happens, the general reader will disagree with the author, and find the power of the book in other places.

So good a critic as Lowell thought *The Minister's Wooing* the most characteristic of Mrs. Stowe's works,—that on which her fame would rest. He based his opinion on the fact that it dealt with New England life, which the author knew more intimately perhaps than any other writer, and it had—so he thought—no immediate moral purpose to dry-rot its fame. If his prophecy has not come true, perhaps the explanation lies in Ruskin's complaint that Mrs. Stowe was "too disdainful of what ordinary readers seek in a novel, under the name of 'interest'—that gradually developing wonder, expectation, and curiosity." It is true that the novel does not grip the reader as it should, considering the fine elements in it; the sad conditions of its composition explain much of its low vitality, which was to characterize almost everything that Mrs. Stowe wrote from that time. But the other fact remains that she here had a special purpose in view, a religious moral to teach; it was her great artistic misfortune, as Lowell feared, to be the preacher still. Criticism seems ruthless which condemns the theological comfortings the book was intended to convey to parents of boys who had died before they joined the church; but the fact remains that the most respectful reader is now reconciled to skipping that part of the story.

Much more convincing to the modern mind is the beautiful story of the Minister's sacrifice. In Dr. Hopkins Mrs. Stowe drew the portrait of one of those large minds and simple hearts which New England theology bred, and with which she had had an almost unique acquaintance. Artistically there is no false note in the portrait, though Ruskin somewhat irritably objected to the extreme simplicity that was blind to Mary's love for her lost sweetheart, James Marvyn. But the simplicity is made credible in the story by the devotion of Mrs. Scudder and the other faithful sisters of the congregation, who so tempered this practical world for the comfort of their idealizing pastor, that he never stopped to question where his new shirts and fresh-curled wigs came from; and Mrs. Scudder with the same loving calculation set aside her daughter as his wife before he or she realized the disposition of their fate, which all three considered the will of a kindly Providence. The minister's sacrifice is all the more affecting when he learns that he is unconsciously forcing a child's heart; the touch of indignation and the sudden gathering of his dignity at the news finely humanize his too unworldly character; the reader, mindful of the abundant preachment of the book, is inclined to think with the grateful James Marvyn that this one act of the Doctor's is worth many sermons.

Like *Dred*, the novel is weak on the formal side. It falls
into two parts, separate both in plot and in treatment. The
New England life described in the first chapters is the work
of that loving realism which distinguished Mrs. Stowe's early
sketches. It was a life she knew well, both in circumstance
and in character, through experience or immediate family
tradition. Her manner in portraying it is subdued almost to a
fault, but in its quiet tone the picture is minute, full of humor,
and rich in its illumination of the early New England mind.
In this general setting lies the main story of the minister and
his betrothed, and it is the best part of the book. In the story
of Aaron Burr and Virginie de Frontignac, however, Mrs.
Stowe essays the historical romance. The two figures are far
too brilliantly colored to subdue themselves to the environment or the manner of the main story, and they play no essential part in the plot. Their presence, though an artistic
fault, could be more easily overlooked if they were not so
beautifully drawn and so intrinsically interesting. When
they appear they bring a subtle promise that something is to
happen, and though they leave the stage simply, with the
promise unfulfilled, the imagination is unfortunately attracted
to follow them rather than Mary or James or Dr. Hopkins.
It is somewhat remarkable, in view of her ancestry and training, that Mrs. Stowe should have pictured the French woman
with such delicacy and sympathy; her character is true to
her nation, and is one more witness to the author's largeness
of heart, which had made *Uncle Tom's Cabin* a popular novel
in Paris.

The problem of the negro is referred to in the novel, though
the remoteness of the time makes any large treatment of emancipation unfitting. Mrs. Stowe cleverly makes the doctrine
of freedom one of Dr. Hopkins' utopian theories, so that
whatever discussion there is seems in keeping with his brave,
unpractical nature; nothing could be more delightful in its

way than his devout counsel to Simeon Brown, his worldly, slave-dealing friend, to win the favor of God by setting free all his property. Equally effective in other directions is the scene in which Zebedee Marvyn sets free Candace and her husband Cato. Candace is one of Mrs. Stowe's best negro characters, loyal, childlike and humorous; she is also interesting as a Northern slave, in an economic world far different from the plantation states. Though her position in the home seems more obviously menial than that of Aunt Chloe, for example, Candace is a Southern negro in her capacity for feudal allegiance; she seems out of place, an impossible product of her environment, as we feel in her delightful wrestlings with the Calvinistic Catechism.

Where Mrs. Stowe is not moved to directness by the earnestness of her cause, she is nearer eighteenth-century models of novel writing than she is to either Scott or Cooper. It would be fairer to say that she follows the essayists, for a chronological reading of her works induces the opinion that she is more interested in ideas than in stories, and this expository interest grows upon her. Without the Addisonian art or lightness of touch, her genius unfolded itself in comments upon the story, rather than through its development. It was this tendency in the earlier chapters of *The Minister's Wooing* that Lowell protested against, as a tendency to preach; it places the story among those leisurely books that are little likely to be cheaply popular, and which need to be of first excellence to be really good at all. In his own development of the Addisonian manner Irving had raised this style of writing to a perfection Mrs. Stowe could not equal, and on the larger scale of the novel Thackeray seems to have monopolized the mastery of the sentimental comment and the confidential aside. But Mrs. Stowe lacked only the art and the training to excel in her own way; she had naturally the poetical temperament that broods and reflects upon life, and stores it

up in wise images. At her best she enriches her story with
this philosophical harvest of experience, in a manner not too
discursive to help the story on; and if she is at her best but
seldom, it is well to remember such fine examples of it as the
description of the minister's impractical idealism,—a passage
that Lowell marked with exceptional praise:

"There is a ladder in heaven, whose base God has placed in
human affections, tender instincts, symbolic feelings, sacra-
ments of love, through which the soul rises higher and higher,
refining as she goes, till she outgrows the human, and changes,
as she rises, into the image of the divine. At the very top of
this ladder, at the threshold of paradise, blazes dazzling and
crystalline that celestial grade where the soul knows itself no
more, having learned through a long experience of devotion,
how blest it is to lose herself in that eternal Love and Beauty
of which all earthly fairness and grandeur are but the dim
type, the distant shadow. This highest step, this saintly elevation, which but few select best spirits ever on earth attain, to
raise the soul to which the Eternal Father organized every
relation of human existence and strung every chord of human
love, for which this world is one long discipline, for which
the soul's human education is constantly varied, for which it
is now torn by sorrow, now flooded by joy, to which all its
multiplied powers tend with upward hands of dumb and ignorant aspiration,—this Ultima Thule of virtue had been
seized by our sage as the *all* of religion. He knocked out
every round of the ladder but the highest, and then pointing
to its hopeless splendor, said to the world, 'Go up thither and
be saved!'"

Lowell's prophecy that *The Minister's Wooing* would lead
Mrs. Stowe's other work by virtue of its record of New England life, does not seem likely to come true, so far as its fame
is concerned, but when all account is taken of the faults and
merits of the story, our opinion comes back to his point that
Mrs. Stowe could portray the old Puritan mind with peculiar
authority. The persons in this book explain much that

puzzles one in the popular idea of the early New Englander. There is the sternness, the thrift, the practical sense, even the slyness, of the traditional Yankee, and there is of course such a capacity for deep religious feeling as would be hard to match outside the Puritan character. But just as vitally there is a tradition of culture and art, of the lighter graces of life, and more unexpected under a system of rigid religious dogma, a great spiritual curiosity, a yearning for the unseen beauty and truth that the world may contain. It is this side of the New England character that was to produce Emerson and Hawthorne and Lowell, and Mrs. Stowe herself. It is shown in the story as something not quite understood by the persons themselves; Mary inherits it from her dead father, and is troubled at her own generous impulses, thinking them often motions of sin; and her lover, James Marvyn, inherits it from his mother, and determines to see the world, to the scandal of a family where the other sons, in Stevenson's phrase, were "sedentary folk and known in the land." This large curiosity imprisoned in a narrow fate is specifically ascribed to Marvyn's mother. Not only are such baffled desires the very tragedy of a limited country horizon, but as Mrs. Stowe describes them they seem the romance and the power of New England character:

"What might be that marvelous music of the *Miserere*, of which she read, that it convulsed crowds and drew groans and tears from the most obdurate? What might be those wondrous pictures of Raphael and Leonardo da Vinci? What could it be to see the Apollo, the Venus? What was the charm that enchanted the old marbles,—charm untold and inconceivable to one who had never seen even the slightest approach to a work of art? Then those glaciers of Switzerland, that grand, unapproachable mixture of beauty and sublimity in her mountains!—what would it be to one who could see it? Then what were all those harmonies of which she read,—masses, fugues, symphonies? Oh, could she once hear the *Miserere* of Mozart, just to know what music was like! And the cathedrals, what were they? How wonderful they must be, with their forests of arches, many-colored as autumn-woods with painted glass, and the chants and anthems rolling down their long aisles! On all these things she pondered quietly, as she sat often on Sundays in the old staring, rattle-windowed meeting-house, and looked at the uncouth old pulpit, and heard the choir faw-sol-laing or sing fuguing hymns; but of all this she said nothing."

VIII

The Pearl of Orr's Island, published serially in the *New York Independent* in 1862, was planned as early as 1852, when the Stowes first went to Andover. It was written in 1858, simultaneously with *The Minister's Wooing*, when Mrs. Stowe was saddened by the death of her son. It is not surprising that the tone of the story is solemn, nor that the horrors of drowning enter the plot, as they had the plot of *The Minister's Wooing*. If that novel is a realistic study of old New England life, the *Pearl of Orr's Island* is a poetical dream of it,—one almost suspects, an attempt to preserve it in the Theocritean manner. The gentle Whittier preferred it to Mrs. Stowe's other works; he called it "the most charming New England idyl ever written." It is rich externally in language, in poetical imagery and even,—what is rare with its author,—in felicities of style and cadence. It leaves the reader with many striking pictures, such as the finding of Moses with his surroundings, the two children floating out to sea on their first perilous voyage. But what enriches the book most is the sense of deep and broad experience of life that belongs to practically all the characters; simple as their fortunes are, they have lived much. In no other book has Mrs. Stowe given so consistent an impression of experience.

But it is easy to explain the slight fame of the book, in spite of its real excellences. Its sentimentality is excessive; Mara's death, for example, is as wilful murder as ever author committed on a defenseless girl, though in view of Mrs. Stowe's summary way with her other delicate heroines, the reader might have guessed there was no hope for her from the first. Another phase of the sentimentality, unimportant in itself but carried to an astounding degree, is the propensity of the characters, especially in the beginning of the book, to sing hymns. The names of the tunes are recorded. When Zephaniah sets sail in his boat for the meeting-house on the mainland, he raises his Sunday-morning psalm. When Mrs. Pennel and Miss Ruey are together the night of the storm, Miss Ruey sings a hymn to her companion, though the tune is difficult and her voice inadequate through age; she remarks with a fitness Mrs. Stowe would never have been intentionally guilty of, "I remember singin' that ar to Mary Jane Wilson the night she died."

As an idyl of New England life the story suffers, in that much of its best quality would be true of life on any other shore. It is not localized as successfully as *The Minister's Wooing*, or later, *Poganuc People*. Miss Roxy, Miss Ruey, Mrs. Kittridge, and the Pennels seem to belong to New England society, but Mara and Moses, Mr. Sewell the minister, Sally Kittridge, and above all her delightful story-telling father, are characters so general in their qualities that they might be met in any quiet community, in any age. The two most admirable people are Captain Kittridge and his daughter; and Sally's fidelity to Mara when Moses asks for her love, is not typical of New England life in an exclusive or distinguishing way, any more than is her father's love of children and his ability to tell them fairy stories. This sense of the unauthenticity of the book as a document of New England life, together with the languid movement of the plot, perhaps accounts for the general oblivion that has overtaken what is in many ways an unusual book.

Before the publication of *The Pearl of Orr's Island* Mrs. Stowe's interests had been completely engrossed by the Civil War. Her son Frederick enlisted in the First Massachusetts Volunteers. She bore the parting from him with the heroism to be expected of her character; everything she wrote of him suggests a kind of Spartan joy in his devotion to the cause her genius had served. When his regiment left Boston for the front she was in Brooklyn, but succeeded in meeting him at the depot in Jersey City. Somewhat over a year later she was in Washington at a Thanksgiving dinner for the fugitive slaves. Her son, now a lieutenant, was stationed near by, and she procured his absence from the regiment for forty-eight hours. The following July he was seriously wounded at Gettysburg. He was then a captain, and his character and ability might have carried him far. But the fragment of shell had injured his brain permanently. It was for his sake that Mrs. Stowe bought a Florida plantation after the war, but his health did not mend. Some years later he sailed for California, hoping for the benefit of a long voyage; he reached his destination, but nothing more was ever heard of him.

The war brought a less personal but still bitter tragedy to Mrs. Stowe in the attitude of the English toward the North. It was naturally incomprehensible to her that the country which had idolized her for the attack on slavery should side with the slave states when the attack became actual. The genuineness of the well-remembered welcome and praise so few years before could not but seem insincere now. She comforted herself in the loyalty of a few powerful friends, such as the Duchess of Sutherland, who kept their faith in the cause of freedom. Her own impetuous Beecher blood is evident in her criticisms of the Northerners in prosecuting the war. She had tried to get her son transferred from the infantry to the cavalry, because the cavalry saw more active service; and in the same spirit she would have had slavery abolished sooner than it was, and she blamed Lincoln for being too slow. Her childhood aspiration to make some declaration on her own account was still her guiding impulse, and she required the same immediateness of the nation's leaders.

One telling opportunity of speaking out for the cause presented itself. In the height of the popularity of *Uncle Tom's Cabin* more than half a million women in Great Britain had signed an address to the women of the United States, and had forwarded it to Mrs. Stowe. This remarkable document, representing every class of society in England, had pleaded for the abolition of slavery. In January, 1863, Mrs. Stowe published in the *Atlantic Monthly* a singularly adroit reply. After acknowledging the pleas contained in the address, she recounted the tremendous events which through the intervening eight years had agonized the country in war, and had finally led to the emancipation of the slaves. Then with the greatest dignity and restraint she made the charge against England which of course was the purpose of the reply. She reminded her readers that after all the English pleas for the slave, England had morally supported the South, and the North had made the fight with every discouragement from overseas. The vigorous scorn that had flashed in many a page of *Uncle Tom's Cabin*, spoke again:

"Step after step has been taken for liberty; chain after chain has fallen, till the march of our armies is choked and clogged by the glad flocking of emancipated slaves; the day of final emancipation is set; the border states begin to move in voluntary consent; universal freedom for all dawns like the sun in the distant horizon, and still no voice from England. No voice? Yes, we have heard on the high seas the voice of a war-steamer, built for a man-stealing Confederacy, with English gold, in an English dockyard, going out of an English harbor, manned by English sailors, with the full knowledge of English government officers, in defiance of the Queen's proclamation of neutrality! So far has English sympathy overflowed. We have heard of other steamers, iron-clad, designed to furnish to a slavery-defending Confederacy their only lack,—a navy for the high seas. We have heard that the British Evangelical Alliance refuses to express sympathy with the liberating party, when requested to do so by the French Evangelical Alliance. We find in English religious newspapers all those sad degrees in the down-sliding scale of defending and apologizing for slaveholders and slaveholding, with which we have so many years contended in our own country. We find the President's Proclamation of Emancipation spoken of in those papers only as an incitement to servile insurrection."

This reply of Mrs. Stowe's had considerable influence in changing the trend of English public opinion. It is worthy of remembrance as her last direct plea for the slaves, the cause of freedom out of which her fame arose.

IX

In this same year, 1863, Professor Stowe resigned his position at Andover, and the family returned to Hartford, where Mrs. Stowe built a home on a spot that had been a favorite with her in girlhood. In the next ten years the growing industries of the city crowded the Stowes from the neighborhood, and they removed in 1873 to what remained their permanent Hartford home. At the close of the war Mrs. Stowe also bought a home in Florida, largely, as we have seen, for the sake of her son Frederick, but partly in order to do something in a private way for the upbuilding of the South. Here, at Mandarin, on the St. John's River, she spent her winters, working among the colored people and winning the affection of all her neighbors. Her philanthropy was as closely as ever identified with religious work, but by this time she had joined the Episcopal Church, to which her daughters already belonged, and she interested herself in a plan of the Bishop of Florida's for establishing a line of churches along the river.

This change of her church was a matter for much autobiographical reference in her later writing. Her poetical nature had been attracted by the beauty of the English ritual as much as anything; theologically, however, the whole Beecher family had moved steadily away from the stern Calvinism of two generations back, and Mrs. Stowe's liking for the English Church was simply a result of that broadening liberality reinforced, perhaps, by the far-off traditions of her mother's family. The matter is of importance only because it loomed large in her own mind and in her later writing; the casual reader will not appreciate it, any more than he will guess that *The Minister's Wooing* was attacked as unorthodox.

The novels that Mrs. Stowe wrote, in steady succession, to the end of her life are in general of a mild sort of excellence; they would hardly have made her fame unsupported by her earlier success, but they deserve more praise and remembrance than they usually receive. *Agnes of Sorrento*, 1863, was begun as a short sketch in Florence, during the winter of 1859–1860. Mrs. Stowe's genius was not strongly in the direction of romances, and this novel is hardly to be considered seriously in judging her abilities. Of a much finer quality is *Old Town Folks*, 1869, and *Old Town Fireside Stories*, 1871, in which she wrote up the stories and reminiscences of her husband, who had an original humor, and evidently could piece out boyhood memories with mature imagination. The characters and incidents are all founded on actual life; the much admired portrait of Sam Lawson simply preserved in Mrs. Stowe's best art a personage her husband often described. Professor Stowe himself, whose delicate physique and mental activity had made him subject all his life to such psychological experiences as highly imaginative natures sometimes know, appears in both books as the "visionary boy."

The autobiographical element increases in these later stories; Mrs. Stowe turned back to memories of an earlier

New England, or to mental experiences of her own, and one who is interested in her personality will find in these pages an attraction they might not otherwise possess. Her son and biographer thought that *Old Town Folks* was the last of her works that would survive the generation for which they were written, and the opinion is probably correct; its value is as an authentic picture of long-departed life in New England, just as the charming *Poganuc People*, 1878, is a sentimental picture, broadly idealized, of the author's own girlhood. But even these last books have a brightness of tone and frequently a charming humor that makes one regret their rapid fall and oblivion. *My Wife and I*, 1872, and *We and Our Neighbors*, 1875, forming one continuous story of life in New York, have much of this general charm, as well as some most attractive characters like Jim Fellows. The second book is further interesting for the evident influence of Holmes' *Elsie Venner*, in the doctrine illustrated by Dr. Campbell and the Rev. Mr. St. John, that the saving of souls may often be a physiological problem. But Mrs. Stowe knew little specifically of life out of New England, and the ways of high society were not her proper subject. There is little hope that these two novels will ever be referred to as recognizable portraits even of an old-fashioned New York.

Among much less important writing the biographer of Mrs. Stowe must notice her unfortunate defense of Lady Byron, which brought cruel criticism upon her at the time, and which can be excused now only because of the loyal friendship which prompted it. Lady Byron's character had appealed forcibly to all the pity and romance in Mrs. Stowe's nature. Now after her death when the *Recollections* of the Countess Guiccioli were achieving popularity, Mrs. Stowe felt it but plain justice to her friend to publish Lady Byron's privately communicated version of her trouble with the poet. This version, appearing in the *Atlantic Monthly*, September, 1869, under the title *The True Story of Lady Byron's Life,* astonished the reading world on both sides of the ocean. In the discussion that followed Mrs. Stowe thought it necessary to put the facts, as she believed them, before the English public in a small volume, *The History of the Byron Controversy.* Lady Byron's charges against her husband were so gross, and Mrs. Stowe was so entirely without evidence to prove them, that her impulsive championship left her in a position of embarrassment; her admirers must always feel with George Eliot, who wrote to Mrs. Stowe her wish that the subject had never been stirred up.

In 1872 Mrs. Stowe accepted an engagement to give readings from her works throughout the New England states. The following year she repeated this successful venture in the West, but both absences from her husband had been rendered anxious by his gradually failing health. From that time her life was quiet, with such writing to occupy her as she chose to do. The last honor she received was a reception which Houghton, Mifflin & Co., her publishers, gave her in Newtonville. A poem from Whittier was read, and Dr. Holmes spoke, and read a poem of his own; speeches and letters brought the guest the assurance of the love and admiration that rewarded her useful life. Her brief reply was devoted with characteristic zeal to portraying the improvement of the negro's condition in the South, and to hopeful praise of his character.

She died on July 1, 1896, and was buried at Andover by the side of her husband, who had died ten years before.

X

It is Mrs. Stowe's fate to be remembered among American novelists for a single great book. It seems hardly just that her records of earlier New England, made with such loving realism as she was capable of, should be dwarfed into neglect by her one colossal success. There will still be thoughtful readers to cherish them for their truth and humor. But it must be confessed that even these few will cherish Mrs. Stowe's general novels only in a qualified sort of devotion, after all; for those whose wide reading gives them the finer taste to appreciate the pure gold in *The Minister's Wooing* or *Old Town Folks* or *Poganuc People*, are the very spirits to whom Mrs. Stowe's shortcomings as an artist will seem most grievous. In spite of themselves, they will not keep quite out of mind Lowell's wicked description of the "water gruel of fiction, thinned with sentiment and thickened with morality." It is best to agree with the public judgment, which lets Mrs. Stowe's fame rest safely on the inspired book in which the best of her mind and heart won the world. Her history is complete, with little poetical exaggeration, in the verse of one of those she served,

> " At a stroke she gave
> A race to freedom and herself to fame."

BRET HARTE

I

THE American frontier, which Cooper immortalized in the beginning of its western course, had its last and perhaps most unique record in the writings of Bret Harte. His fame is identical with the nation's memory of early California. Whether the picture he drew was accurate, or colored by a sentimental temperament, must remain a conjecture; for he has taught his admirers to see the rough mining life through his eyes, and his critics, when they would controvert him, are embarrassed by the lack of other accounts than his. So quickly did the fabulous progress of the coast overlay with convention—comparatively speaking—the rude society he knew, that in *The Luck of Roaring Camp* he already viewed the miners through an idealizing haze of romance; and a brief period later, when Eastern repute had adopted him, the life he wrote about had become a thing of memory, and no later first-hand portrait of it could fairly be compared with his.

One reason why Bret Harte's fame rests in California is that he was strangely incapable of drawing any other life. He was in no sense a literary artist, though his friends have made the claim for him. It might be doubted whether he had even ordinary talents for writing. Certainly the glimpse we have of him in his editorial days, writing and rewriting a simple note to ask a man to dine with him, suggests not scrupulous artistry, but some meagerness of training or inspiration. Only when he wrote of California was he possessed of the magic of genius. His temper was one with the recklessness and romance of the new country; he had the advantage also of approaching it from the East, so that it took hold of him with the surprise and fascination that his stirring portraits of it had for Eastern readers. In default of better evidence, one can well believe his California stories to be accurate, since only these, of all he wrote, are convincing, and their power is in the subject, not in the writer's skill.

But if he is the last term in that frontier progression which began with Cooper, Bret Harte is also a culminating figure in one development of American humor—a development with which, it is needless to say, Cooper had nothing to do. The South during the second quarter of the century supplied the material for much humor of the newspaper kind, and out of the mass of ephemeral sketches dealing with border or provincial life came half a dozen books, still worth reading, which prepared the way for the tales of the mining camps. About 1840 appeared Augustus Baldwin Longstreet's *Georgia Scenes*, which seems to have had the good fortune of influencing a scene in Mr. Thomas Hardy's *The Trumpet Major*. In 1840 appeared a similar book of broad humor, *Major Jones's Courtship*, by another Georgian, William Tappan Thompson. In 1846 and 1853, respectively, appeared Johnson Jones Hooper's *Adventures of Captain Simon Suggs*, and Joseph Glover Baldwin's *Flush Times of Alabama and Mississippi*. These two books portrayed the unsettled life of those days in Alabama and Mississippi, and one thinks of them as finding their way up the great river for the inspiration of Mark Twain, whose early humor was in much the same strain as theirs. From Massachusetts also Captain George Horatio Derby—"John Phœnix"—had been exploring the West and making known to the East the humor of the Californian coast in the sketches later collected as *Phœnixiana*, 1855. Bret Harte is not a lonely figure in our literature, save as his genius obscures these lesser men; nor is Dickens the only source of his literary tradition.

II

Bret Harte was born on August 25, 1839, in Albany, New York. He was named Francis Bret, but shortened the name when he began to write. His father was a teacher of Greek at the Albany College, a small seminary; his mother, whose name was Truesdale, apparently contributed to his character the restless, unliterary part of it, if we may judge from the story that she accompanied him to California. His ancestry was of English, German, and Hebrew sources; his father was a Roman Catholic, his mother a Protestant. If his heredity and early environment served him at all, they must have prepared him for the heterogeneous elements of California life.

He was a delicate child, and his mother seems to have sheltered him from the father's admirable purpose to give him an education. He was allowed to run pretty wild, most of the time out-of-doors, where he learned to know the little city, and according to his own later account, became acquainted with its honorable history, and idealized its traffic, the number of ships in its river and canals, and the quantity of timber, wheat, barley, wool, and tobacco in their cargoes. In his leisure he also found out books; he read *Dombey & Son* as it first appeared, in his seventh year, and from that moment Dickens was his master. Smollett, Fielding, Goldsmith, Cervantes, and the other great story-tellers that would be found in his father's library, he read and re-read, and when he was eleven he wrote a poem, *Autumn Musings*, cynical and worn in tone, and sent it to the New York *Sunday Atlas*, which published it. His family showed unusual sense in resisting the usual parental impulse to praise; in fact, they pointed out that the poem was very poor indeed, and Bret Harte remembered his discouragement so keenly that he afterward wondered that he ever wrote verse again. It would have been a blessing quite unmixed if he could have enjoyed such effective discouragement at the other end of his life.

The years of his boyhood in Albany he idealized, in talk long afterwards with his friends; and he told of his disappointment on revisiting childhood scenes. But it may be doubted if the idealization were not the product of a Dickens-like sentimentality, acquired with literary consciousness, rather than the true result of memory; one may well feel that Bret Harte never wholly lived any part of his life except those years in California on which his genius throve; of his boyhood nothing survives in his writing, and he never made his own the experiences that lay open to him in the East or in Europe.

The circumstances that led Bret Harte to California are not quite clear. He was seventeen years old when he sought his fortune there, in 1856, and the simplest reason for his going is that he was lured by the promise of gold in the new country. But it appears that his mother accompanied him—his father was already dead—and what record we have of his occupations in the Pacific state suggests that he had no very definite purpose at all. We wonder why a delicate youth should have undertaken the long journey and the uncertain, adventurous life, and we wonder why his mother should have undertaken it also. Whatever was the motive, Bret Harte immediately found himself in a region of frontier confusion, every separate whirlpool of which aroused some vital response in his nature. His very lack of purpose completed his education by withholding him from almost no acquaintance with this rough but fascinating chaos, and the panorama of those days was stamped in his heart as was the London of his boyhood on the heart of Charles Dickens. The Spaniard, the Greaser, the Chinaman; the gambling house, the warehouse where the trunks of forgotten "forty-niners" were stored, and were finally sold at auction; the scenes of sudden death, mingled with glimpses of humor and chivalry in the actors of the tragedy—all that went to make up the stock material of his stories, Bret Harte learned for himself at first hand. He tried mining, and then became a messenger of the Adams Express Company; he seems to have prospered financially as little in one position as the other, but the stage-coach days gave him a knowledge of the road and its dangers which he later drew upon in the tales. From the perils of the stage-coach he went to the supposedly quiet position of drug clerk. But a mistake in a prescription, according to his own account, proved nearly fatal to the patient, and Bret Harte, having somehow learned to set type, became a printer on a local newspaper. A brief taste of this career satisfied him, and he became a school teacher. But as the bulk of the expense of the school, he tells us, "was borne by a few families in its vicinity, when two of them,—representing perhaps a dozen children or pupils—one morning announced their intention of moving to a more prosperous and newer district, the school was incontinently closed."

Bret Harte had some experience also as an Indian fighter,—and beyond that his western adventures had no more to offer in the way of material for future writing. The best record of these adventures is in the use he made of them, in the stories of his first fortunate period; and a general picture of the scene and its manners is in the lecture now prefixed to the *Tales of the Argonauts*. What this varied life gave to Bret Harte needs no further elucidation, but it is evident that he brought to the opportunity a certain adaptable genius, the power to enjoy its myriad shapes, which he says was the secret of life in Argonaut days.

Out of the haphazard career which he first knew in California, Bret Harte stepped, by a stroke of good fortune, into a somewhat permanent position, from which he could cultivate his genius with considerable freedom of mind. He had indeed begun his writing while in the composing-room of *The Golden Era*, whose editor, Joe Lawrence, had probably encouraged him to contribute at the usual rate of a dollar a column. In this paper *Mliss* appeared, and the young author began to sign his name to his articles with some consciousness of a literary personality. But he was not established in the community until he occupied a minor position in the General Surveyor's office in San Francisco, a post which he held when he met his future wife, Miss Anna Griswold. With characteristic optimism he undertook the responsibility of maintaining a home on what must have been meager resources; he was married August 11, 1862, by the Methodist minister at San Rafael.

This optimistic step was justified, shortly after, by Bret Harte's appointment as secretary to the Superintendent of the Mint. In his account of *Bohemian Days in San Francisco* he tells us that on his arrival he first lived with "a distant relation—a second or third cousin," who kept "a rather expensive half-club, half-restaurant in the lower part of the building." Nearby stood the United States Branch Mint, "and its tall factory-like chimneys," he says, "overshadowed my cousin's roof. Some scandal had arisen from an illegal leakage of gold in the manipulation of that metal during the various processes of smelting and refining. One of the excuses offered was the volatilization of the precious metal and its escape through the draft of the tall chimneys. All San Francisco laughed at this explanation until it learned that a corroboration of the theory had been established by an assay of the dust and grime on the roofs in the vicinity of the Mint. These had yielded distinct traces of gold. San Francisco stopped laughing, and that portion of it which had roofs in the neighborhood at once began prospecting. Claims were staked out on these airy placers, and my cousin's roof, being the very next one to the chimney, and presumably 'in the lead,' was disposed of to a speculative company for a considerable sum. I remember my cousin telling me the story—for the occurrence was quite recent—and taking me with him to the roof to explain it, but I am afraid I was more attracted by the mystery of the closely guarded building, and the strangely tinted smoke which arose from this temple where money was actually being 'made,' than by anything else. Nor did I dream as I stood there—a very lanky, open-mouthed youth—that only three or four years later I should be the secretary of its superintendent. In my more adventurous ambition I am afraid I would have accepted the suggestion half-heartedly. Merely to have helped to stamp the gold which other people had found was by no means a part of my youthful dreams."

The Superintendent of the Mint must have been somewhat lenient with his secretary, or Bret Harte must have shown a conscientious interest in official duties which deserted him later in life, for his connection with the Mint seems to have been altogether happy. His work left him leisure to write and to make friends; to his office at the Mint a literary acquaintance, George Barnes, brought Samuel Clemens, one memorable day, when the great humorist told to his small but delighted audience the story of *The Jumping Frog of Calaveras*. It was from his office in the Mint that Bret Harte began to publish his burlesques, the *Condensed Novels*, in *The Golden Era*, and continued them in *The Californian*. And while occupying this position he met Mrs. Fremont, wife of the Pathfinder, and through her, Thomas Starr King, the preacher, after whom his second son was named, and for whom he felt perhaps the greatest admiration he paid to any man in the West. Among his other friends were Charles Henry Webb, who owned and edited *The Californian*, founded in 1864, and Charles Warren Stoddard, the author of *South Sea Idyls*.

In 1865 appeared Bret Harte's first original volume, a book of poems entitled *The Lost Galleon*. It must have been before this date that he edited the collection of western verse which has its immortality in his own account of it, *My First Book*. Humorous in intention as his record obviously is, it gives a vivid cartoon of literary endeavor and literary criticism at that time and place. A bookseller engaged the young unsuspecting writer to compile a single volume of representative Californian verse, such as had appeared in the periodicals and newspapers of the coast. The bookseller was unwise enough to announce his purpose to the general public, and the editor was deluged with unsolicited material, even manuscript contributions, until the volume, though carefully winnowed, was three times its desired size. "There was clearly nothing to do," Bret Harte goes on, "but to make a more rigid selection—a difficult performance when the material was uniformly on a certain dead level, which it is not necessary to define here. Among the rejections were, of course, the usual plagiarisms from well-known authors imposed upon an inexperienced country press; several admirable pieces detected as acrostics of patent medicines, and certain veiled libels and indecencies such as mark the 'first' publications on blank walls and fences of the average youth." When the reduction was finally made, and the book published, it sold with a strange rapidity, apparently to all those gentlemen who thought their verses should be found in it. A storm of criticism arose from the papers whose pet writer had been omitted, and Bret Harte gives several examples of what he calls the "direct style of the Californian 'sixties,'" of which the following is usually considered the most characteristic:

"The hogwash and 'purp' stuff ladled out from the slop-bucket of Messrs. ———— & Co., of 'Frisco, by some lop-eared Eastern apprentice, and called 'A compilation of Californian Verse,' might be passed over, so far as criticism goes.

A club in the hands of any able-bodied citizen of Red Dog, and a steamboat ticket to the Bay, cheerfully contributed from this office, would be all-sufficient. But when an imported greenhorn dares to call his flapdoodle mixture 'Californian,' it is an insult to the state that has produced the gifted 'Yellow Hammer,' whose lofty flights have from time to time dazzled our readers in the columns of the 'Jay Hawk.' That this complacent editorial jackass, browsing among the dock and thistles which he had served up in this volume, should make no allusion to California's greatest bard, is rather a confession of his idiocy than a slur upon the genius of our esteemed contributor."

The amusing account Bret Harte gives of the care with which he edited this volume, would probably stand as a description of all his literary work at this time. He was a conscientious craftsman, as all his friends of those days bear witness. One gets the impression that this carefulness was due to thinness of inspiration, more than to fastidious taste, yet the evidence shows that he was hard to satisfy in his own work. However rough had been his western experiences, as a writer he was a child of luxury from the first; he could not get on, says one comrade, unless the writing materials, the light and heat, and even the adjustment of the furniture of the writing room were as he desired. In personal appearance also he showed nothing of the frontiersman. Joaquin Miller gives the portrait of him in those days: "I found a spare, slim young man, in a chip hat and a summer dress of the neatest and nattiest cut, who took me cordially into his confidence at once. I liked his low voice, his quiet, earnest, and unaffected manner from the first. He had neat editorial rooms, where he made me welcome, although he was then engaged as Secretary in the Mint. . . . I think he was the cleanest man I ever met. He was always as clean, modest, and graceful of speech as a girl."

III

His life in a unique frontier had not stunted Bret Harte's interest in the older world; his early prose bore witness to the influence of Charles Dickens, and his first volume contained sincere patriotic lyrics inspired by the war. But neither literary tradition nor public affairs on a large scale counted permanently with him. He had one message and no other to leave us, and the fortuitous discovery of that message, as desirable and unexpected as an argonaut mine, now brought him into sudden fame.

In 1868 Anton Roman, a San Franciscan bookseller and publisher, founded a new magazine, *The Overland Monthly*, and upon the advice of Stoddard, Noah Brooks and others, invited Bret Harte to edit it. The venture seemed at first somewhat precarious, but the young editor was finally installed, and contributed to the first number, in July, a laudatory poem to San Francisco. As the magazine advertised itself as "devoted to the development of the country," the energetic lines may be suspected of the official laureate note. It had indeed been Bret Harte's intention to write a short story for the magazine's first appearance, but he could not complete it in time, and it was not till the August number that he printed his famous *Luck of Roaring Camp*, the history of which he makes almost as entertaining as an imagined tale.

That this story was written with the deliberate intention to exploit a local and peculiar type of life, is the author's unmistakable claim. It is not necessarily uncharitable to suppose that since the claim was made long after the author had won world-wide recognition, perhaps he read back into his half-forgotten intentions something of his fortunate achievement. But what is more interesting and quite beyond question, is the fact that this first great picture of Bret Harte's country was rejected by that country, and accepted as true, with much reluctance, only after the East had greeted the writer as a master. To be rejected by the people he describes is, however, the common fate of the novelist of a section.

The trouble with the story began, Bret Harte says, before it was printed.

"He had not yet received the proof sheets when he was suddenly summoned to the office of the publisher, whom he found standing the picture of dismay and anxiety with the proof before him. The indignation and stupefaction of the author can well be understood when he was told that the printer, instead of returning the proofs to him, submitted them to the publisher, with the emphatic declaration that the matter thereof was so indecent, irreligious, and improper that his proof-reader—a young lady—had with difficulty been induced to continue its perusal, and that he, as a friend of the publisher and a well-wisher of the magazine, was impelled to present to him personally this shameless evidence of the manner in which the editor was imperilling the future of that enterprise. It should be premised that the critic was a man of character and standing, the head of a large printing establishment, a church member, and, the author thinks, a deacon. In which circumstances the publisher frankly admitted to the author that, while he could not agree with all of the printer's criticisms, he thought the story open to grave objections, and its publication of doubtful expediency."

The offended author read over his story in its new printed dress, and was so convinced of its quality that he declined to change it. But no one could be found who thought as well of it as he did, and it was finally suggested that as his editorial insight must have been prejudiced in his own interest as an author, it would be becoming for him to withdraw the story.

"This last suggestion had the effect of ending all further discussion, for he at once informed the publisher that the question of the propriety of the story was no longer at issue; the only question was of his capacity to exercise the proper editorial judgment; and that unless he was permitted to test that capacity by the publication of the story, and abide squarely by the result, he must resign his editorial position. The publisher, possibly struck with the author's confidence, possibly from kindliness of disposition to a younger man, yielded, and *The Luck of Roaring Camp* was published in the current number of the magazine for which it was written, as it was written, without emendation, omission, alteration, or apology. A not inconsiderable part of the grotesqueness of the situation was the feeling, which the author retained throughout the whole affair, of the perfect sincerity, good faith, and seriousness of his friend's—the printer's—objection, and for many days thereafter he was haunted by a consideration of the suffering of this conscientious man, obliged to assist materially in disseminating the dangerous and subversive doctrines contained in this baleful fiction. What solemn protests must have been laid with the ink on the rollers and impressed upon those wicked sheets! What pious warnings must have been secretly folded and stitched in that number of *The Overland Monthly!* Across the chasm of years and distance the author stretches forth the hand of sympathy and forgiveness, not forgetting the gentle proof-reader, that chaste and unknown nymph, whose mantling cheeks and downcast eyes gave the first indications of warning.

"But the troubles of the *Luck* were far from ended. It had secured an entrance into the world, but, like its own hero, it was born with an evil reputation, and to a community that had yet to learn to love it. The secular press, with one or two exceptions, received it coolly, and referred to its 'singularity;' the religious press frantically excommunicated it, and anathematized it as the offspring of evil; the high promise of *The Overland Monthly* was said to have been ruined by its birth; Christians were cautioned against pollution by its contact; practical business men were gravely urged to condemn and frown upon this picture of Californian society that was not conducive to Eastern immigration; its hapless author was held up to obloquy as a man who had abused a sacred trust. . . . But, fortunately, the young *Overland Monthly* had in its first number secured a hearing and position throughout the American Union, and the author waited the larger verdict.

The publisher, albeit his worst fears were confirmed, was not a man to weakly regret a position he had once taken, and waited also. The return mail from the East brought a letter addressed to the 'Editor of *The Overland Monthly*,' enclosing a letter from Fields, Osgood & Co., the publishers of *The Atlantic Monthly*, addressed to the—to them—unknown 'Author of *The Luck of Roaring Camp*.' This the author opened, and found to be a request, upon the most flattering terms, for a story for the *Atlantic* similar to the *Luck*. The same mail brought newspapers and reviews welcoming the little foundling of Californian literature with an enthusiasm that half frightened its author; but with the placing of that letter in the hands of the publisher, who chanced to be standing by his side, and who during those dark days had, without the author's faith, sustained the author's position, he felt that his compensation was full and complete."

The Californian audience that at first rejected *The Luck of Roaring Camp* was of course not the same community that figured in its pages. There seems to have been a wide difference in this as in other respects between the typical mining camp and the enterprising city community, which aspired to the sound prosperity and the conventional good name of the East. To this all but Puritan audience Bret Harte had addressed *Mliss* and his other early work, and it was not entirely strange that they should have been reluctant to see the new story go out as descriptive of them. Their taste in literature was made more cautious by frontier jealousy for their rising city; they read Eastern magazines of the better class, and even foreign papers of acknowledged quality were not uncommon. Bret Harte later found more difficulty, he says, in procuring a copy of *Punch* in an English Provincial town, than in the prosperous mining centers of the West. That there was in California this conventional, conservative society must be remembered when the truth of Bret Harte's pictures is weighed; this normal part of the community, which his best work neglects, never cared to acknowledge that he had accurately portrayed California, and their objection seems perfectly reasonable, in the sense that he portrayed only the section of the life that interested him. In another sense, however, his genius did create a complete record of the Coast, for in such annotations as the preface from which we quoted, he left perhaps the most vivid glimpses we have of the transplanted Puritan; the scrupulous printer has no other immortality than by way of foot-note to the masterpiece he would have suppressed.

The success of the story led the author to contribute to his magazine *The Outcasts of Poker Flat, Tennessee's Partner*, and other tales, which within a year reappeared in a volume entitled *The Luck of Roaring Camp and other Sketches*. Meanwhile as editor he displayed both energy and ability in encouraging his writers and building up the *Monthly*; Stoddard and Joaquin Miller testified to the inspiring help they had from one who might easily have been preoccupied with his own success. Along with this literary work Bret Harte was trying to continue his duties in the Mint—with what profit to the Government it is impossible now to tell. The appearance in the magazine of *The Heathen Chinee*, in 1870, brought his fame to such a sudden height that the Eastern world of letters persuaded him to return to it. He was never proud of the extravagant verses that took the English-speaking world by storm; Ah Sin, Truthful James and Bill Nye were the easiest names with which to bore him at a dinner party; his interest in the poem lay in his own humorous audacity in modeling its versification upon the antiphonal dirge at the end of Swinburne's *Atalanta in Calydon*. Yet this poem brought to him an invitation that was almost a command to return to his own part of the country, and accordingly, early in 1871, he left California for New York.

His progress across the continent was the great triumph of

his life. Looking back now, we find it difficult to understand such a furor of welcome as awaited him in city after city. He was hailed as a new prophet in American letters with far more acclaim than any of the older prophets had enjoyed—partly because of the strangeness of the world he portrayed, and partly, perhaps, because of a fascination in himself which could have no other record than the enthusiastic memory of his friends. At first he lived up to the high expectations, especially on the personal side; he made an unusually interesting lion, so striking in appearance was he, with so much vague romance for a halo. What sort of fascination he exerted upon the Eastern mind may be illustrated from Fanny Kemble's impression of him at a slightly later date:

"He reminded me of our old pirate and bandit friend, Trelawney, in his appearance, though the latter was an almost orientally dark-complexioned man, and Mr. Bret Harte was comparatively fair. They were both tall, well-made men of fine figure; both, too, were handsome, with a peculiar expression of face, which suggested small success to any one who might engage in personal conflict with them.

"He told us of one of his striking experiences, and his telling of it made it singularly impressive. He had arrived at night at a solitary house of call on his way, absolutely isolated and far distant from any other dwelling—a sort of rough, roadside tavern, known and resorted to by the wanderers of that region. Here he was to pass the night. The master of the house, to whom he was known, answered his question as to whether any one else was there by giving the name of a notorious desperado, who had committed some recent outrage, and in search of whom the wild justices—the lynchers of the wilderness—were scouring the district. This *guest*, the landlord said, was hiding in the house, and was to leave it (if he was still alive) the next day. Bret Harte, accustomed to rough company, went quietly to bed and to sleep, but was aroused in the middle of the night by the arrival of a party of horsemen, who called up the master of the house and inquired if the man they were in pursuit of was with him. Upon receiving his repeated positive assurance that he was not, they remounted their horses and resumed their search.

"At break of day Bret Harte took his departure, finding that for the first part of his journey he was to have the hiding hero of the night (thief or murderer, probably) for his companion, to whom, on his departure, the master of the house gave the most reiterated, precise, and minute directions as to the *only* road by which it would be possible that he could escape his pursuers, Bret Harte meanwhile listening to these directions as if they were addressed to himself. They rode silently for a short time and then the fugitive began to talk— not about his escape, nor about the danger of the past night, nor about the crime he had committed, but about *Dickens' last story*, in which he expressed such an eager and enthusiastic interest, that he would have passed the turning of the road by which he was to have made his escape if Bret Harte had not pointed it out to him, saying, 'That is your way.' "

The national attention to Bret Harte was noticed abroad, and was practically his introduction to foreign readers. One English paper devoted much space to his triumphal progress across the Continent, half in derision of America's enthusiasm, and half in appreciation of his true genius. It was once asked, the paper said, Who reads an American book?

"The question is now repeated only as a note of triumph. But since Sydney Smith's phrase has become its own refutation, there have not been those wanting who, in the spirit of it, have asserted that America has not known its great writers until they had been recognized by the Old World, and the earliest fame of Irving, Emerson, and Hawthorne, has been claimed as European. Whatever may be said on this very doubtful theory, certain it is that in the present instance America has got far ahead of us, for we fear that not a few of the most intelligent English readers will be found asking, Who is Mr. Bret Harte?—and what has he said or done?

"We answer, he is a young author who has succeeded in making all America burst into inextinguishable laughter. He has done this not by ingenuity of misspelling, nor by grotesqueness of literary grimace, but by a series of really humorous works, capped by a local satire that has raised the cachinnations into a hearty roar that can only be described as national. Though Mr. Harte's universal popularity is in his own country recent, and has not found us on this side of the water sufficiently released from the heaviness of the tragedy at our doors to swell it, yet there are some in this country, as in America, whose divining rods search out genius as far as California, and distinguish it from the base ores, as the miners, with whom Mr. Harte is so familiar, their nuggets of gold. There have been readers here also of the excellent *Overland Monthly*, whose appearance in California was one sign of the disappearance of chaos and of the beginning of a higher social stratification. They have marked in that periodical the exquisite sketches of life, portraits of character, curious stories—now replete with drollery, now deepening with pathetic touches—which already announced that a mind of singular power and originality had begun its task in that far-off country."

Other countries were as cordial as England. The new stories promptly appeared in French, and were favorably criticized in the *Revue des Deux Mondes*, and in Germany Ferdinand Freiligrath made an admirable translation of the best tales, to which he prefixed a charming introduction. With this generous greeting from the high places of his profession, Bret Harte must have felt that his destiny was irresistible; he must have dreamt, one would think, of some undivined ore of inspiration to be struck in the East, to match his phenomenal fortune in the West. If we allow ourselves the privilege of that speculation which the true historian deplores, and wonder what would have been Bret Harte's fate if in his hour of prosperity he had remained on the Coast, we can see now at least an equal chance of happiness for him; we may even be tempted to think that his final choice of the East was a mistake. His was not a nature to bear prosperity when it became luxury, and California challenged his genius rather than encouraged it; the unsettled, precarious land still kept a bracing tone of danger which he needed. Had he stayed in San Francisco, it seems that a busy and honored career would have unfolded for him. Before he decided upon the change, he had been appointed Professor of Literature in the University of California, and had he entered upon his duties, the teaching blood of his inheritance might have asserted itself, and in any case his place in the community would have been increasingly dignified and permanent. But he put his literary fate boldly to the venture, and came East, and, as his kindest critics must think, he never again justified the high hope of his countrymen in his genius.

IV

New York was Bret Harte's new home, though he had engagements to write for magazines in other places. His work was in demand, but chiefly that part of his work which dealt with California. The public was not yet sated with his Western World; if he drew few pictures, and none important, of any other life, his excuse can easily be found in the pressure upon him to repeat his successes. His golden fortune followed him, too, in the form of innumerable opportunities. *Two Men of Sandy Bar*, an arrangement from other stories, was put together for Stuart Robson; the one long novel in his works, *Gabriel Conroy*, was written; and one notable variation from the frontier themes was made in *Thankful Blossom*, written in the old Washington house at Morristown. But in some fatal way the luck had changed, and it was not long before the heralded genius had proved a disappointment to all but a few loyal friends.

The simplest explanation of what happened is to say that Bret Harte's head was turned by his sudden success. In the East as in California he was the same gentle, fascinating spirit, winning easily the good will of all who met him, and leaving them with a sense of his genius. But he had become indolent and to a certain extent irresponsible. Not all of his contracts were fulfilled, and what he did write was not of a kind to advance his reputation. At the same time he got into the habit of living at expensive places in the summers—Newport and Lenox for example,—and very shortly he was living beyond his means, with no reasonable prospect of getting on his feet again. His fame had not yet made him rich and he lacked the discretion to wait quietly till his ship should come in. Moreover, he had a childlike ignorance of finance, excusable in a poet, but not likely to render him popular with his creditors. It was easy for cheap scandal-mongers to circulate false reports of his business methods, some of which amused him, but none of them could do him other than harm. He was particularly amused, as his biographer tells us, by the legend "that while he lived at Morristown he retained the postage stamps sent to him for his autographs, and these applications were so numerous that with them he paid his butcher's bill; but that the slander had been denied *on the authority of the butcher!*"

Partly to offset the increased expenditure of Eastern life, partly no doubt to satisfy the popular wish to see and hear him, Bret Harte began to lecture on his California memories. Several of the experiences we have quoted were first given to the public in this oral form, and the belauded young author seems at first to have been successful, financially and otherwise. Boston accepted him in a most thoroughgoing way, to judge by an enthusiastic letter of James T. Fields'. Artists and clergymen—"chaps with brains," were in his audience and they had not heard so good a lecture for many a year. But other places were less appreciative, and in Canada especially Harte was thoroughly discouraged. His letters to his wife in the early spring of 1873 show his distaste for lecturing as an occupation; they also show that his manager was incapable, and that much of the ill success of the lecturing doubtless was to be laid at that door. But it may well be questioned by those of us who never saw Bret Harte whether he had the qualities of a lecturer for the generation that knew Phillips and Curtis and remembered Emerson. The lyceum tradition was still high; the people who went to lectures did so with a serious purpose; at least they expected the lecturer to stand for a serious purpose, as to their minds Mrs. Stowe did when she gave her readings. Whatever Bret Harte's personal charm, he stood for no cause, and his measure of success on the platform seems to have been but a fad. In the Autumn of 1873 he had to report some adverse along with kindly comment, in a letter from St. Louis: "I certainly never expected to be mainly criticized for being *what I am not*, a handsome fop; but this assertion is at the bottom of all the criticism. They may be right—I dare say they are—in insisting that I am no orator, have no special faculty for speaking, no fire, no dramatic earnestness or expression, but when they intimate that I am running on my good looks—save the mark! I confess I get hopelessly furious. You will be amused to hear that my gold 'studs' have again become 'diamonds,' my worn-out shirts 'faultless linen,' my haggard face that of a 'Spanish-looking exquisite,' my habitual quiet and 'used up' way, 'gentle and eloquent languor.' But you will be a little astonished to know that the hall I spoke in was worse than Springfield, and *notoriously* so—that the people seemed genuinely pleased, that the lecture inaugurated the 'Star' course very handsomely, and that it was the first of the first series of lectures ever delivered in St. Louis."

Later his letters home speak more openly of his cares, and he tells his wife of his growing financial difficulties. He was well paid for his work, and he had the seeming advantage of beginning his Eastern career with great prestige; but that favorable breeze of fame was probably his undoing. His obligations to his friends could hardly have been greater than

Hawthorne's, but the author of *The Scarlet Letter* escaped criticism by the very apparent seriousness of his life, and by his honorable discharge of his debts. Bret Harte invited comment of the undesirable kind by assuming that he could not miss success. His friends claim that he finally paid his debts; so John Hay assured Joaquin Miller. "Hay assured me that he did not owe one dollar in New York; that he was a man of singularly strict sense of honor in money matters; that he had once offered to assist him when ill in Washington, but that Bret Harte had seemed so hurt at the idea that he was sorry he had tried to help him."

"I may mention," Joaquin Miller continues, "that after I had the letter from Hay I advertised here in St. Louis for any and all bills against Bret Harte, promising to pay in full without regard to the statute of limitations. Only one man, a printer, put in any sort of a claim, and this one man's own statement was to the effect that Bret Harte paid most of the bill, claiming that was all he had agreed to pay."

It is Bret Harte's misfortune that the circumstances of this period of his life, whatever they were, have passed into an unpleasant tradition. He is still thought of as improvident and to a certain extent indolent. This last impression of him has its real ground, however, in his record abroad. In 1878 he accepted a government post, as Hawthorne had done, and leaving his family at Sea Cliff, he sailed for England, and thence journeyed to Crefeld, Prussia, where he was to be Consul. He never returned to America; so far as American literature is concerned, his departure was the end of his career.

V

Hawthorne became in time weary of all official duties, but Bret Harte was weary of his when he began. He felt his appointment as a kind of exile, and the necessity of leaving his family behind made the beginning of his work as inauspi-

cious as possible. His first letter to his wife from Crefeld,
July 17, 1878, sets the tone of too many of his days abroad.

"I left London Friday morning and reached Paris the same
night, intending to come here the next day, but I found myself so worn out that I lingered at Paris until last night—three
days. . . . I have audaciously travelled alone nearly four
hundred miles, through an utterly foreign country, on one or
two little French and German phrases, and a very small stock
of assurance, and have delivered my letters to my predecessor, and shall take possession of the Consulate to-morrow.
Mr. ———, the present incumbent, appears to me—I do not
know how far I shall alter my impression hereafter—as a very
narrow, mean, ill-bred, and not over-bright Puritanical German. It was my intention to appoint him my Vice-Consul—
an act of courtesy suggested both by my own sense of right and
Mr. Lenard's advice, but he does not seem to deserve it, and
has even received my suggestion of it with the suspicion of a
mean nature. But at present I fear I may have to do it, for
I know no one else here—I am to all appearance utterly
friendless; I have not received the first act of kindness or
courtesy from any one, and I suppose this man sees it. I
shall go to Bavaria to-morrow to see the Consul there, who
held this place as one of his dependencies, and under whose
direction ——— was, and try to make matters straight.
"It's been up-hill work ever since I left New York, but I
shall try to see it through, please God! I don't allow myself
to think over it at all, or I should go crazy. I shut my eyes to
it, and in doing so perhaps I shut out what is often so pleasant
to a traveller's first impression, but thus far London has only
seemed to me a sluggish nightmare through which I have
waked, and Paris a confused sort of hysterical experience. I
had hoped for a little kindness and rest here. Perhaps it may
come. To-day I found here (forwarded from London) a kind
little response to my card from Froude, who invites me to
come to his country-place—an old seaport village in Devon-
shire. If everything had gone well here—if I can make it go
well here—I shall go back to London and Paris for a vacation
of a few weeks, and see Froude at least.
"At least, Nan, be sure I've written now the worst; I think

things must be better soon. I shall, please God, make some friends in good time, and will try and be patient. But I shall not think of sending for you until I see clearly that I can stay myself. If the worst comes to the worst I shall try to stand it for a year, and save enough to come home and begin again there. But I could not stand it to see you break your heart here through disappointment, as I mayhap may do."

In a few days Harte took a more cheerful view of his prospects, especially after he had seen his own works in translation displayed for sale in a shop-window—a pleasant omen that his genius, if not himself, had found welcome. But this first letter is perhaps significant in its hopelessness, its lack of energy, its implied assumption that the world owed Bret Harte a living, and the little German town in particular owed him personal friendship,—and that within twenty-four hours of his arrival. As a matter of fact, hospitable friendship came his way just after the despondent letter was written. But he had already been made welcome to England, on that brief passage which he refers to as "a sluggish nightmare," and with all allowance for his discouraged state of mind, one is puzzled by his querulousness, and his readiness to arrange at once for a "vacation of a few weeks."

Whatever impression the Old World made on him, the record of his English days is pleasantly set down by his friends. Joaquin Miller was at hand to greet him on that first visit, when "on his way to the Consulate at Crefeld, up the Rhine, a piteously small place for such a large man. He had a French dictionary in one pocket, he told me, half laughing, and a German dictionary in the other. London wanted to see him, of course, and although 'the season' was over, all the literary men and women gathered about, and were simply charmed by his warm-hearted and perfect ways. 'George Eliot' asked after John Hay, and told Bret Harte that one of his poems was the finest thing in our language.

"He could not rest until he stood by the grave of Dickens. But I drove him here and I drove him there to see the living. The dead would keep. But at last, one twilight, I led him by the hand to where some plain letters, in a broad, flat stone, just below the bust of Thackeray, read 'Charles Dickens.' "

Joaquin Miller may well have been prejudiced in favor of his old friend in a strange land. But the English themselves accepted his works and himself with a generosity not usually accorded to American writers, so that Harte had small reason to think or speak slightingly of his stay among them. Of course the depression natural in that first letter home must not be taken too seriously. It is, however, all the more interesting in view of the fact that the English gave him as kind a greeting as he ever had from his own people, and to this day their memories of him are pleasanter on the whole than his countrymen's. The point is worth illustrating at some length, as an instance perhaps of the Puritan bias in American popular criticism, which rejects Poe and in a measure Bret Harte for faults of character, though their work is too high in quality to escape even Puritan praise. The English attitude toward both men has been more generous, or the ocean interval has given them a truer perspective. Justin McCarthy, in his *Reminiscences*, describes Bret Harte as he knew him, and the whole passage deserves quotation.

"I had never heard of the author who has since become so famous, when I read one day his marvellous little poem, 'Jim.' As well as I remember, the poem was not even signed with his name, or if it was, the name did not convey to my mind any manner of idea. But when I read the little poem— that wonderfully dramatic story inspired by all the soul of feeling, full of humor, of fire, of pathos—I felt certain that a new poetic force had arisen in the English language. I met Bret Harte in San Francisco, and I met him afterward in New York. He was then a very young man—it was years ago, 'I must not say how many, but a great many,' to alter slightly a

line in Edgar Allan Poe's poem. When I went back to resume
my life in England, I found that the literary world had already discovered Bret Harte, and that he was welcomed into
a secure fame. I well remember that my old friend Tom
Hood, who is long since dead, wrote to tell me that he was
preparing an article on the new American poet, and to ask me
whether I knew if Bret Harte was really the young poet's
name, or was only what French people never do call a 'nom
de plume.'

"Since that time Mr. Bret Harte has established himself in
this island, first (as American Consul) in Glasgow, and afterwards in London, where he has now (1899) been settled for
many years. No one is made more cordially welcome in literary society, and, indeed, in society of any kind which he
chooses to favor with his presence. I have met him at all
sorts of gatherings—Bohemian and Belgravian—and no one
can meet him without being the happier for the meeting. He is
one of the few Americans who have no especial gift of speech-
making, and he is not a great talker—at all events, he certainly makes no effort to shine in conversation, although it is
not possible to converse with him for many minutes without
discovering, if one did not know it before, that he is conversing with a man of original mind, of that keenest observation
which is keen because it is poetic, and of a humor still as
fresh as it was when it first created for European readers the
life of the canvas town and of Poker Flat. There is one house
in London which, somehow, I especially associate with recollections of Bret Harte. Of course he is to be met with in
numbers of London houses; but at this particular house of
which I am now thinking, one had a chance of meeting him
in a small congenial company, and of talking with him and
of hearing him talk. I am speaking of the house which has
for its gifted and charming hostess my friend Mrs. Henniker,
the accomplished sister of Lord Crewe, and daughter of
Monckton Milnes, the poet, scholar, and politician, afterwards Lord Houghton. . . . Mrs. Henniker's is just the
house where one who knows his way about London would
naturally expect to meet Bret Harte; and I have been happy
enough to get the chance every now and then of meeting him
there. The 'snowfall of time' has been showing itself very

much on Bret Harte's head of late; but it is a premature snow-fall; for he was a handsome young fellow when I first saw him in California, and I know the number of years since that time far too exactly to allow me to believe that Bret Harte has yet grown old."

So much for Harte's fame in England. He became known there not only through his visits, "vacations of a few weeks," to Froude and others, but through the public lecturing he shortly undertook in 1879. *The Argonauts of '49* was the lecture offered, and the English hailed it with their traditional appreciation of the unusual in American writing. In the universal applause Harte might well have thought his invasion of England as fortunate as Artemus Ward's. Financially, however, the tour was not successful, and he returned to Crefeld in low spirits, having cleared, as he wrote his wife, only two hundred dollars. A second tour, better managed, brought him more money, and perhaps more enjoyment. It seems to have been harder each time to return to Crefeld, where there was little to interest him. His friends at home and abroad probably used their influence; in 1880 he was removed from Germany to the Consulate of Glasgow—a change immediately productive of greater cheerfulness when his inquisitive Scotch landlady looked over his luggage and sternly asked where was his Bible.

His incumbency of this office was notable for the increased amount of writing he did in it, beginning with the story *Found at Blazing Star*. So busy was he with his friendships, his "vacations of a few weeks," and his literary work, that as one of his best friends said, the only place he was sure not to be found in was the Glasgow Consulate. It has been said that the large number of stories from his pen which appeared in American magazines at this time gave his government the impression that he was neglecting his duties. Doubtless the government had better evidence than that, and in

1885 he was removed. For the rest of his life he lived in London.

His English friends, besides Froude and William Black, the novelist, were many. The letters which have been published show Bret Harte at his best, and give at least an indication of the personal charm which, for those who knew him, seems to have made up for substantial achievement. He wrote much and planned much more; he especially desired to make a place for himself in the drama, in both serious plays and comic operas; one libretto he submitted to his friend Sir Arthur Sullivan. But the play he had written for Stuart Robson, *Two Men of Sandy Bar*, had been a failure, the comic operas never reached the stage, and none of the plays he himself wrote had any success. To this day, however, his stories furnish more skilful dramatists with plots.

In 1902 it was evident to his friends that Bret Harte's health was failing. For several summers he had enjoyed the Surrey landscape and air, and he now visited Camberley, at the home of his friend, Madame Van de Velde, in the hope of recuperating. His condition did not improve, nor did it grow alarming, until May 5, 1902. On that day he suffered two severe attacks of hemorrhage, and toward evening he died. He was buried in Frimley churchyard, in the presence of his family and a few friends.

IV

Bret Harte's prose work naturally divides into three chronological groups—the stories written in California, those written in New York, and those written abroad. Of the first group, however, there is a great difference between Harte's earliest works and the stories that began with the *Luck of Roaring Camp;* and in the second and first group there is, in the opinion of most critics, a wide gulf between the pieces that follow his true Californian inspiration and those that try to break new ground. So, in spite of the chronology, the lover of Bret Harte's prose thinks of the California tales as the distinctive part, preceded by some experimental sketches, and followed—even sometimes interrupted—by unfortunate excursions into regions not subject to his genius.

The preliminary sketches, which are now entirely negligible except for purposes of criticism, are obviously and confessedly in the manner of Dickens. The great story-teller was Harte's master from the first. Though their gifts were essentially different, it is easy to see their points of contact, and something of the Dickens strain was in the younger man's work to the last. His verses on the death of his master, *Dickens in Camp*, show what he thought he admired in the Englishman's genius; it is little Nell that he praises, wandering and lost on English meadows—the sentimental Dickens. Such admiration is probably typical of young people, and the fact that Harte kept it till 1870 proves the claim of eternal youth that his friends made for him. But sentimentality was not the strength of Dickens, nor of Bret Harte. Humor of a greater variety, a faculty for minute observation and realism, and a sense of what Stevenson called the poetry of circumstance—these are the common bonds between the two writers.

Great as are Bret Harte's gifts as a humorist, perhaps his twofold vein of romance and realism is his distinction. He had an extraordinary power of observation and a perfect memory; sentences spoken long before came to his lips with the very intonation of the first utterance; his command of detail amounted to mimicry. Here he resembled Dickens, and like him also he impressed people, for this reason, as being by natural endowment an actor. It is thus that Watts-Dunton remembered him.

"Bret Harte," he says, "had read somewhere about the London music-halls, and proposed that we should all three take a drive round the town and see something of them.

At that time these places took a very different position in public estimation from what they appear to be doing now. People then considered them to be very cockney, very vulgar, and very inane, as, indeed, they were, and were shy about going to them. I hope they have improved now, for they seem to have become quite fashionable. Our first visit was to the Holborn Music Hall, and there we heard one or two songs that gave the audience immense delight—some comic, some more comic from being sentimental—maudlin. And we saw one or two shapeless women in tights. Then we went to the Oxford, and saw something on exactly the same lines. In fact, the performers seemed to be the same as those we had just been seeing. Then we went to other places of the same kind, and Bret Harte agreed with me as to the distressing emptiness of what my fellow-countrymen and women seemed to be finding so amusing. At that time, indeed, the almost only interesting entertainment outside the opera and the theaters was that at Evan's supper-rooms, where, under the auspices of the famous Paddy Green, one could enjoy a Welsh rarebit while listening to the 'Chough and Crow' and 'The Men of Harlech,' given admirably by choir-boys. Years passed before I saw Bret Harte again. I met him at a little breakfast party, and he amused those who sat near him by giving an account of what he had seen at the music-halls—an account so graphic that I think a fine actor was lost in him. He not only vivified every incident, but gave verbal descriptions of every performer in a peculiarly quiet way that added immensely to the humor of it. His style of acting would have been that of Jefferson of 'Rip Van Winkle' fame. This proved to me what a genius he had for accurate observation, and also what a remarkable memory for the details of a scene."

It is easy to recognize this gift in individual stories; in a more general way Watts-Dunton's anecdote explains Bret Harte's literary method,—explains how he could write with such fresh, convincing power of his California experiences years after they occurred. But with such a talent he might have been expected to observe closely in other regions of life, and store up new experiences with the same relish. His failure to do so leads us to consider the other side of his genius, his sense of romance, the poetry of incident. In his delightful essay Stevenson reminds us that certain places and scenes inevitably suggest certain incidents as the proper drama for the setting. Who of us has not felt the tragic romance of the scene in *Bleak House*, or the comedy of scene in *Pickwick Papers?* The dark alleys, gloomy woods, and midnight hours that Dickens so gloriously refurbishes out of the honored storehouse of melodrama, and fits them out with their appropriate incidents; the innumerable quaint English inns, whose cozy fires suggest toasted cheese and the kettle on the hob, and pleasant midnight conviviality, and whose unaccountable twisted hallways suggest late adventures on the journey bedward—out of such scenes how naturally and convincingly come the great humorist's stories! And Bret Harte, after several false starts, developed one certain literary instinct; he learned what sort of incident went inevitably with the new Argonautic scenes, and every reader knows at heart that his instinct was true. It has been said in his favor justly, that he had to find a new kind of character and incident to fit an entirely new scene, and that therefore he could have no help from earlier writers. In this respect he is more original than Dickens, whose scenes and accompanying incidents were far from new in the English novel. But Bret Harte never learned to find the true incident for any other scene. He mastered the single formula and used it perfectly. One is inclined to wish he had been content with it. It was Harte's originality and his realism that impressed Dickens; as Forster tells in his *Life*, he found in *The Luck of Roaring Camp* and *The Outcasts of Poker Flat* "such subtle strokes of character as he had not anywhere else in late years discovered; the manner resembling himself, but the matter fresh to a degree that surprised him; the painting in all respects masterly, and the wild rude thing painted a quite wonderful reality."

An important resemblance between Dickens and Bret Harte has been found in their optimism, their humanitarian hope and belief in the best of life. It is a fair question whether a trait so broadly characteristic of their times can be limited to a mere resemblance between two men. And in their humanitarianism there is one marked divergence. Dickens puts himself into the position of his characters, taking upon him for the moment their fortunes and personalities, and making the reader follow him. Bret Harte feels no such Virgilian sympathy; he interests the reader in the characters, but as a dramatist, not as an advocate. The sorrow of life in the California world is great. Death in many forms, accidents and bereavements, make up the greater part of Harte's pictures. But he cares little for the sorrow in itself; he is not disturbed by it, as Dickens is; rather he accepts it with a kind of satisfaction, as Homer did, as the authentic mark of all human experience. The effect in his work is far from severe or unfeeling, and in the end he enlists the sympathy of many people whom Dickens could never reach. But you cannot imagine Bret Harte attempting to better the social conditions of the gold camps. His appreciation of them for the purposes of art is too great for him to desire a reform that would destroy their quality.

In his earliest work we can see Bret Harte feeling his way toward realism, toward the romance of scene and incident, and toward his humanitarian point of view. *Mliss* is a fair example of that earlier style. It has a romantic heroine, with a disreputable father; there is an abandoned mine that later turns out to be rich; there are villains and hairbreadth escapes. Little, however, is made of the scene itself, or of the characters peculiar to it. The inspiration of the story is literary. That a child of uncertain parents should be left an orphan and turn out to be an heiress, is no new thing in fiction.

The influence of Dickens is most clear in the short sketch

called *High-Water Mark*. The scene that suggests the tale
is tragic, and is described at length, Dickens-fashion, to prepare the reader's curiosity. Under the stilted, imitated rhetoric it is not difficult to recognize Harte's faculty of close observation, but he had not yet found his idiom.

"The vocal expression of the Dedlow Marsh was also melancholy and depressing. The sepulchral boom of the bittern,
the shriek of the curlew, the scream of passing brant, the
wrangling of quarrelsome teal, the sharp querulous protest of
the startled crane, and syllabled complaint of the 'Kildeer'
plover were beyond the power of written expression. Nor was
the aspect of these mournful fowls at all cheerful and inspiring. Certainly not the blue heron, standing midleg deep in
the water, obviously catching cold in a reckless disregard of
wet feet and consequences; nor the mournful curlew, the de-
jected plover, or the low-spirited snipe, who saw fit to join him
in his suicidal contemplation; nor the impassive kingfisher—
an ornithological Marius—reviewing the desolate expanse;
nor the black raven that went to and fro over the face of the
marsh continually, but evidently couldn't make up his mind
whether the waters had subsided, and felt low-spirited in the
reflection that after all this trouble he wouldn't be able to give
a definite answer. On the contrary, it was evident at a glance
that the dreary expanse of Dedlow Marsh told unpleasantly
on the birds, and that the season of migration was looked forward to with a feeling of relief and satisfaction by the full-
grown, and of extravagant anticipation by the callow brood.
But if Dedlow Marsh was cheerless at the slack of the low tide,
you should have seen it when the tide was strong and full.
When the damp air blew chilly over the cold glittering expanse, and came to the faces of those who looked seaward like
another tide; when a steel-like glint marked the low hollows
and the sinuous line of slough; when the great shell-incrusted
trunks of fallen trees arose again, and went forth on their
dreary purposeless wanderings, drifting hither and thither, but
getting no farther toward any goal at the falling tide or the
day's decline than the cursed Hebrew in the legend; when the
glossy ducks swung silently, making neither ripple nor furrow

on the shimmering surface; when the fog came in with the tide and shut out the blue above, even as the green below had been obliterated; when boatmen, lost in that fog, paddling about in a hopeless way, started at what seemed the brushing of mermen's fingers on the boat's keel, or shrank from the tufts of grass spreading around like the floating hair of a corpse, and knew by these signs that they were lost upon Dedlow Marsh, and must make a night of it, and a gloomy one at that,—then you might know something of Dedlow Marsh at high water."

With such a beginning as this—a scene calling surely for tragic circumstance, some permanent horror, Bret Harte tells a mild story of a woman washed away with her infant child in a high flood, and safely stranded at low tide on Dedlow Marsh, where Indians find her and restore her to her husband. The scene was well set, but it goes unused; Harte had not yet learned to find the proper incidents for a romantic situation. In the conclusion he is conscious himself that the horror of the Marsh has not been caught in the story, and his last words are meant for additional assurance that in spite of the tale, the Marsh really is grewsome: "Not much, perhaps, considering the malevolent capacity of the Dedlow Marsh. But you must tramp over it at low water, or paddle over it at high tide, or get lost upon it once or twice in the fog, as I have, to understand properly Mary's adventure, or to appreciate duly the blessings of living beyond high-water mark."

VII

In *The Luck of Roaring Camp* Bret Harte came to his own simply because he discovered the true possibilities of romantic incident in the Western life he knew. From that time he wasted no thought on the outward machinery of plot—the forgotten mines that suddenly prove rich, the floods and explosions that alter the fate of the mining camps; these incidents indeed occur, but in their place and in true proportion.

They no longer provide the central material for the plot. Bret Harte had discovered that the romance of the coast was not in outward things, but in the curious mixture of characters and races, brought together for the moment into the sudden whirlpool of the mining towns, and immortalized in his pages before they had fused, or any of their peculiarities were dimmed. The *Luck* begins, not in description, but in the simple statement of the incident which makes the romance of the story—the birth of a child in the rude camp where was no other woman to attend "Cherokee Sal." All the poetry of incident that Stevenson loved is for this story contained in three sentences—enough to give the character of the camp, and the mother, and the startling incongruity of the event: "It was, perhaps, part of the expiation of her sin that, at a moment when she most lacked her sex's intuitive tenderness and care, she met only the half-contemptuous faces of her masculine associates. Yet a few of the spectators were, I think, touched by her sufferings. Sandy Tipton thought it was 'rough on Sal,' and, in the contemplation of her condition, for a moment rose superior to the fact that he had an ace and two bowers in his sleeve."

Out of this brief statement of the situation grows every element in the story; there is no such waste of romantic opportunity as in *High-Water Mark*. The absence of female nurses in the camp leads naturally to the installation of "Jimmy," the ass, and "Stumpy," in the maternal offices,—one of the broadest effects of humor in the story; "'Me and that ass,' he would say, 'has been father and mother to him!'" The character of the men in Roaring Camp is plainly enough indicated by the extra cards up Sandy Tipton's sleeve; and the regeneration of the camp through the mere presence of the child is forecast in that first unusual sympathy for its mother.

The end of the story, the destruction of the camp by the mountain torrent, has been charged with sentimentalism, and its artistic truth questioned because it is accidental. Accident certainly plays a large part in the solving of Bret Harte's plots,—as in *The Outcasts of Poker Flat*, and *In the Carquinez Woods;* and the use he makes of such melodramatic devices is sentimental. So Dickens solves many a story by accident. But Bret Harte's world is one in which the unexpected catastrophe is the usual thing; in the mining camp accident is normal. The fires, explosions, floods and all other forms of sudden peril are implicit in the wild gamble of the Argonauts' life, and we can accept it, not as a method of escape for the embarrassed author, but as experience truly portrayed. And the reserve of Bret Harte's manner when he records such misfortunes—his impassive acceptance of the given fact in his own fiction, is in the very manner of the seasoned gambler, who takes his luck as it comes; and the reader in time learns to accept the change of fortune in these stories with much the same philosophy as Mr. John Oakhurst, in *The Outcasts of Poker Flat*, to whom "life was at best an uncertain game, and he recognized the usual percentage in favor of the dealer."

Perhaps it is because Bret Harte creates so successfully this atmosphere of normal chance, that he can give us, with little change in the facts, stories that actually happened. *Tennessee's Partner* is such a transcription from life. It has the imaginative power of a fresh creation; it seems typical of the life of the men, in incident and character, and the hero himself is one of the most original in our literature. It was this story that Clara Morris used to think of when she wanted to shed tears in the play, and many readers have found it the most touching of Bret Harte's tales. The worthless Tennessee is not without virtues; at least he is reckless and has a sense of humor, and he acquires some merit vicariously from the devotion of his partner. The latter has no sense of humor—an unusual lack in Bret Harte's miners; his forgiving faithfulness is in constant danger of becoming maudlin, but it is saved to our respect by the unsoftened contrast of the Partner's good intentions and his outward circumstances and manners—the donkey cart, the grave-digging, the funeral speech.

The keynote of the Argonaut life was incongruity. In that one quality lay its fitness for literary use. Unlike the other great frontiers recorded in books, the mining country represented no progress of ideas, no clash of civilizations; it was the scene of a crusade without a cross, as Bret Harte says, an exodus without a prophet. It produced no heroic material such as Cooper's frontier yielded him; the clash of Chinaman and miner, fatally undignified, could not be idealized to anything like the literary proportions of the struggle between Indian and settler. It produced no fund of mystery, as the Indian or African frontier has done in later years; the interests and the fortunes of the forty-niners were hopelessly frank. But it produced, as its very essence, unlimited incongruity, from which the romance of incident arose on one hand, and the humor of character on the other. For a background there was the Spanish country, with Spanish names and enough Spanish traditions to endow it with some natural breath of old-world poetry. Upon this aristocratic priming the gold boom laid humanity in all its colors, insanely mixed. The scholar, the criminal, the poet, the Mexican, the New Englander, the Virginian, were as brothers in the camps, and individually none of them was without paradox. "The greatest scamp had a Raphael face, with a profusion of blonde hair; Oakhurst, a gambler, had the melancholy air and intellectual abstraction of a Hamlet; the coolest and most courageous man was scarcely over five feet in height, with a soft voice and an embarrassed, timid manner. The term 'roughs' applied to them was a distinction rather than a definition. Perhaps in the minor details of fingers, toes, ears, etc., the camp may have been deficient, but these slight omissions did not detract from their aggregate force. The strongest man had but three fingers on his right hand; the best shot had but one eye."

It is part of the same incongruity that the wild justice of the Argonaut country was administered with surprising dignity, and in the worst camps standards of honor and morality at times ran high. Never had optimistic romancer more effective opportunity to idealize his subject than Bret Harte; he saw daily instances of generosity on the part of reckless men which would grace the Christian character anywhere, and he teaches his reader to expect sudden discoveries of the god in the brute, as the ancient Greek could dream of coming upon a spirit of loveliness in brook and tree. Yet the converse was also true, and serves to keep the picture in balance; the Argonaut was capable, in his human moments, of markedly downward paradoxes; a gambler contributing to a new Methodist church did so because the gambling-houses were monotonously numerous, "and it 's variety that 's wanted for a big town."

In one respect only is Bret Harte liable to the charge of idealizing his characters; he gives them credit for personal beauty, in phrase too sweeping for even the admiring reader to credit. "They were singularly handsome, to a man," he says. "Not solely in the muscular development and antique grace acquired through open-air exercise and unrestrained freedom of limb, but often in color, expression, and even softness of outline. They were mainly young men, whose beards were virgin, soft, silken, and curling. They had not always time to cut their hair, and this often swept their shoulders with the lovelocks of Charles II. There were faces that made one think of Delaroche's Saviour." Some exaggeration of affectionate memory should surely be allowed for this description, written in after years for an English lecture, for it is not surprising that the race of adventurers whose varied ante-

cedents and unfailing adaptability won Bret Harte's devotion, as they have won the love of young natures since, should
wear such features in the hero-worshiping eyes of youth.

The stories in which Bret Harte's genius for the effective
scene and the romantic contrast is exhibited, are too numerous to mention; these already noted are fair examples in his
most typical field. But outside the specific studies of the mining camp, his genius works effectively upon the fringe of the
western society,—he draws masterly portraits of that vaga-
bond race who follow the frontier for no reputable reason other
than personal freedom. *Salomy Jane's Kiss* brings together
three striking characters of this sort—old Madison Clay,
violent and lawless, but with a passionate code of personal
honor; John Dart, the horse-thief, inspired to better things
by the love of Madison's daughter, and Salome Jane herself,
indolent and proud, but capable of untold depths of passion.
The scenes through which the brief plot advances are pitched
in one high key of romance,—as when the posse stop to let the
older horse-thief say farewell to his wife, and Salome surprises
John Dart, doomed and handsome, with the kiss she would
have bestowed only on a man about to be hanged; or when
Dart makes his desperate escape; or when Salome, in a conversation full of surprises, learns from her father that the man
she kissed is at large; or when she meets Dart in the woods,
and after the murder, flees with him. Incidents and scene
here are both highly melodramatic, but the true romance is in
the characters, to meet any one of whom is adventure in itself.

VIII

A genius founded upon the possibilities of contrast in life
must inevitably be humorous, and Bret Harte's reputation is
largely that of a humorist. It has been claimed for him by an
admiring English critic that his chief good fortune is to be un-
American in his humor,—and as the critic could not justly

discover a resemblance to the humor of any other nation, he concludes that in this respect Bret Harte is original and individual. Doubtless he is so, but he is one with his countrymen in this important respect, that his humor grows out of an exceeding optimism. The contrast that with him is cardinal in human nature is the surprising presence of good qualities in the low and the outcast. The potential goodness of Roaring Camp or of Tennessee's Partner would do for one extreme of this humor; at the other we have the delight of discovering wisdom in Yuba Bill or Salome Jane. When Clay asks his daughter what she will say to her angry and rejected suitor when he hears that she kissed a condemned man, she answers, that she will promise to kiss the unsuccessful lover when *he* is on his way to be hanged; the humor of the reply is less in what is said than in the surprise that the languid Salome Jane should say it. To the Englishman for whom Mark Twain in his most reckless moments and Artemus Ward are the typical American humorists, the analytical, keen, restrained sort of wit in which Bret Harte excels must seem unnational. But it must be remembered that practically all the elements in his stories, even the wit, are transcripts from life; he has given illustrations at some length of the commonness of what seems in his pages unique. It is not in his stories that we read of the teamster who, when rebuked for swearing at his cattle, replied in astonishment, "Why, Miss, you don't call that swearing, do you? Why, you ought to hear Bill Jones exhort the impenitent mule!"

To exaggerate, to overstate, is, in English thought, the method of American humor. To understate, however, to surprise by the inadequacy of the rhetoric, is as common to certain types of the Yankee mind—and surely as common in Bret Harte's pages—as in the cockney jokes in *Punch*. If Harte and the Connecticut Yankees are not learning their style of humor from the great English comic weekly, as the lat-

ter probably are not, then these Western stories may be taken
as the documents for a hitherto unexpressed type of American
humor—a universal type, because rising from human nature.
Bret Harte's humor, far from retarding the development of
his stories, gives them often their speed, as the same quality
in the best of Mark Twain's humor—say, *The Man That
Corrupted Hadleyburg*, gives speed to his stories, by contrast-
ing the situations and the characters without further analysis.
What could be more concise, saying much in little, than the
opening of *Mr. Thompson's Prodigal?*

"We all knew that Mr. Thompson was looking for his son,
and a pretty bad one at that.   That he was coming to California for this sole object was no secret to his fellow-passengers;
and the physical peculiarities as well as the moral weaknesses
of the missing prodigal were made equally plain to us through
the frank volubility of the parent.   'You was speaking of a
young man which was hung at Red Dog for sluice-robbing,'
said Mr. Thompson to a steerage passenger one day; 'be you
aware of the color of his eyes?'   'Black,' responded the passenger.   'Ah!' said Mr. Thompson, referring to some mental
memoranda, 'Charles's eyes was blue.' "

In one respect not often noticed Bret Harte's humor is
bound up with the best of his genius.   He had a gift for
parody which involved technical skill and appreciation of the
very highest order.   Perhaps only Calverley and Swinburne
in the nineteenth century were better parodists of this kind.
Harte seemed able to take on the very nature of the man he
was imitating, no matter to what purpose he was putting the
assumed gift.   As has been said, he particularly enjoyed his
own wonderfully accurate use of Swinburne's measure in *The
Heathen Chinee*.   Only an artist as clever as himself could
realize all the pleasure he had in writing the *Condensed
Novels*, those extraordinary parodies of many authors, done
with unfaltering skill at various periods of his life.   The best

known of these humorous and subtle criticisms on his brethren
in the craft is the following scene in Cooper's style:

"Genevra had not proceeded many miles before a weariness seized upon her fragile limbs, and she would fain seat
herself upon the trunk of a prostrate pine, which she previously dusted with her handkerchief. The sun was just sinking below the horizon, and the scene was one of gorgeous and
sylvan beauty. 'How beautiful is nature!' murmured the
innocent girl, as, reclining gracefully against the foot of the
tree, she gathered up her skirts and tied a handkerchief
around her throat. But a low growl interrupted her meditation. Starting to her feet, her eyes met a sight which froze her
blood with terror.

"The only outlet to the forest was the narrow path, barely
wide enough for a single person, hemmed in by trees and
rocks, which she had just traversed. Down this path, in
Indian file, came a monstrous grizzly, closely followed by a
California lion, a wild cat, and a buffalo, the rear being
brought up by a wild Spanish bull. The mouths of the three
first animals were distended with frightful significance, the
horns of the last were lowered as ominously. As Genevra was
preparing to faint, she heard a low voice behind her.

" 'Eternally dog-gone my skin if this ain't the puttiest
chance yet!'

"At the same moment, a long, shining barrel dropped
lightly from behind her, and rested over her shoulder.

"Genevra shuddered.

" 'Dern ye—don't move!'

"Genevra became motionless.

"The crack of a rifle rang through the woods. Three
frightful yells were heard, and two sullen roars. Five animals
bounded into the air and five lifeless bodies lay upon the
plain. The well-aimed bullet had done its work. Entering
the open throat of the grizzly it had traversed his body only to
enter the throat of the California lion, and in the like manner
the catamount, until it passed through into the respective
foreheads of the bull and the buffalo, and finally fell flattened
from the rocky hillside.

"Genevra turned quickly. 'My preserver!' she shrieked,

and fell into the arms of Natty Bumpo, the celebrated Pike
Ranger of Donner Lake."

Bret Harte's humor is remembered especially in connection
with two of his characters—Colonel Culpepper Starbottle and
Yuba Bill. The Colonel's name suggests the Dickens influence, and it is not difficult to detect the vein of Dickens-
like exaggeration in the character. Colonel Starbottle is
noted for his eloquence, of the florid kind, his readiness to
fight duels, and his susceptibility to the fair sex—traits that
lend themselves rather easily to the purposes of exaggerated
humor. But Harte portrays the not too admirable Colonel
with such completeness that he is felt to be a type, not a carica-
ture. He is unusual among Bret Harte's other creations for
the preponderance of the realism of his appearance over the
optimism; for once, the author lets us suspect or see plainly
more weakness in human nature than even the humor of the
story can quite compensate for. And Colonel Starbottle was
apparently among Bret Harte's few imagined characters.
From Virginia he once wrote to his wife a letter that indicates
the sort of American Colonel Newcome he intended Colonel
Starbottle to be:

"Imagine my sitting down to dinner with a gentleman in the
dress of the early century—ruffles, even *bag-wig* complete—
a gentleman who has visited these springs for the last forty
years! Who remembers 'Madison, Sir,' and 'Mousie, Sir,'
and asked me what I thought of the poems of Matthew Prior!
I have seen people that I believed never existed off the stage—
gouty old uncles in white flannel; stiff old dowagers who per-
sonify the centennial. And all this undiscovered country
within four hundred miles of New York. I never had such
a chance in my life, and I look back upon poor Colonel Starbottle as an utter failure. If I could dress Robson and get
him to speak as I heard the real Virginia Colonel Starbottle
speak yesterday, I could make him famous."

Perhaps it should be added that the modern Virginian is tempted to think this portrait as fanciful and untrue to facts as was Colonel Starbottle himself.

Yuba Bill, the stage-driver, is a finer creation, more original and more human. He, too, seems to owe something to Dickens, and the resemblance is not simply that like Tony Weller he drove a coach. He indulges habitually in the kind of sarcasm that marks the speech of the Wellers, father and son. When the Hon. Judge Beeswinger, Member of Assembly, asked Yuba Bill if there were any political news, the reply was in the Weller manner,—" 'Not much,' said Bill, with deliberate gravity. 'The President o' the United States hazn't bin hisself sens you refoosed that seat in the Cabinet. The ginral feelin' in perlitical circles is one o' regret!'" But Yuba Bill is otherwise far different from any type that Dickens knew. He gains from that romantic contrast of scene and incident, of which Bret Harte was master. Driving the crazy coach through all manner of dangers, over all sorts of country, with the greatest variety of passenger, in the happiest atmosphere of adventure, Yuba Bill is a quiet man, never loquacious, as were the Wellers; depending upon the keen analyzing power of his sarcasm for his command of men; and yet essentially chivalrous and very brave. The silence in his nature, and the heroic services to the community which make up the usual course of his duties, invest him with a certain grandeur that suggests Leatherstocking. The two men would have understood each other, and one wishes they might have met.

IX

Bret Harte is to be considered a novelist only by courtesy; he was a writer of short stories. His one long novel, *Gabriel Conroy*, and his shorter ones, such as *Maruja*, are not among his successes. The difficulty seems to have been that the length of a novel drew Bret Harte away from that contrast of scene and incident upon which his genius worked. In the novels he has his hands full managing the plot, and both characters and scene escape from his control. In *Gabriel Conroy* the outward incidents, such as the rescue of Madame Devarges and the discovery of silver in the mine, determined the story; the persons in the plot are of slight interest.

It is somewhat odd that Bret Harte should not have written a great novel of character, for he had the ability to revive his characters, John Hamlin, Oakhurst, Colonel Starbottle, in many different tales; one wonders why he could not have carried them with equal effect through numerous episodes. The solution probably is that he wrote well only about this one section of life—the section he best knew; and he knew it only in fragments. To write of more than one detached fragment meant to compose, and to compose meant a literary effort, apart from life, unsuited to Harte's genius. The panorama of incidents in which he set his gallery of portraits, gives him the effect of a novelist; he has in the mass of his Western stories a volume and unity of effect such as neither Poe nor Hawthorne attained in short stories. If his genius had taken such a direction, the material he had in hand deserved the larger form, not of the novel, but the epic.

What service he performed for the world as well as for his country's literature, is admirably stated in Mr. Chesterton's words: "He discovered the intense sensibility of the primitive man. To him we owe the realization of the fact that while modern barbarians of genius like Mr. Henley, and in his weaker moments Mr. Rudyard Kipling, delight in describing the coarseness and crude cynicism and fierce humor of the unlettered classes, the unlettered classes are in reality highly sentimental and religious, and not in the least like the creations of Mr. Henley and Mr. Kipling. Bret Harte tells the truth about the wildest, the grossest, the most rapacious of all the districts of the earth—the truth that, while it is very rare indeed in the world to find a thoroughly good man, it is rarer still, rare to the point of monstrosity, to find a man who does not either desire to be one, or imagine that he is one already."

INDEX

INDEX